SCALES OF JUSTICE

SCALES OF JUSTICE

FENTON BRESLER

Weidenfeld and Nicolson
London

Copyright © *The Sunday Express* 1973

All rights reserved. No part of this publication may be reproduced, stored in a retrieval system, or transmitted, in any form or by any means, electronic, mechanical, photocopying recording or otherwise, without the prior permission of the copyright owner.

ISBN 0 297 76529 9

Printed in Great Britain by
Willmer Brothers Limited, Birkenhead

Contents

	List of Illustrations	vii
	Introduction	xi
1	George Henry Storrs – The Mystery Murder	1
2	Frank Smith – Accidental Killer or Murderer?	10
3	Alfred Moore – Did an Innocent Man Hang?	19
4	Edward Black – Condemned Before his Trial	28
5	Devlin and Burns – The Strange Alibi	39
6	John Williams – Conviction by a Trick	48
7	Probert and Parker – Hanged for £6	60
8	David Greenwood – Convicted by a Button	69
9	John Alexander Dickman – A 'Triumph' of Circumstantial Evidence	80
10	Herbert John Bennett – Defender's Error	92
11	Charlotte Bryant – A Mistake over Arsenic	102
12	Steinie Morrison – A Grievous Blunder	111
13	Scottie Mason – The Lucky Thunderstorm	120
14	Professor Joad – All Because of a Train Ticket	129
15	Sir Leo Money – Influence and the Law	139
16	Ivor Novello – The Tragedy of a Rolls	151
17	Mrs Cornwallis-West – An Ageing Beauty	162
18	Edward Slovik – Shot for Cowardice	173
19	Victors' Court Martial – The Sequel to the 'Great Escape'	184
20	Comrie Camp – The War Criminals who Escaped the Headlines	195

Illustrations

Between pages 112 and 113

The author visits the site of Eddie Slovik's execution in Sainte Marie-aux-Mines, France (*photograph by courtesy of the author*)
Alfred Burns (*photograph by courtesy of London Express*)
Police Constable Jagger (*London Express*)
Edward Devlin (*London Express*)
Sir Edward Marshall Hall, KC (*photograph by courtesy of the Press Association*)
The Bryants' house (*London Express*)
Alexander 'Scottie' Mason (*photograph by courtesy of Associated Newspapers*)
Ivor Novello in *The Dancing Years* (*photograph by courtesy of the Radio Times Hulton Picture Library*)
The Brains Trust in 1941 (*Radio Times Hulton Picture Library*)
Alfred Moore (*London Express*)
'Patsy' Cornwallis-West (*Radio Times Hulton Picture Library*)

Acknowledgments

All the articles in this book have been published at various times in the *Sunday Express*. The author and publishers would like to thank the *Sunday Express* for permission to publish them in book form.

Introduction

I have collected together this selection from articles of mine in the *Sunday Express* firstly because, over the years, many readers have been kind enough to ask me to do so; and secondly because I wanted to try and convey in book form something of the excitement that I have experienced in undertaking this kind of literary detective-work.

Perhaps the word 'excitement' sounds excessive. But I use it advisedly. Take, for example, the case of Herbert John Bennett told in Chapter 10. Bennett was hanged for the murder of his wife Mary Jane as long ago as January 1901. How could I possibly hope to find something new to write about the case? I have always made it a rule never to write about a story from the past where it would merely be what cynical Fleet Street journalists call 'a clippings job': going to the extensive library of past newspaper clippings that every large newspaper runs and telling the story merely from them.

Of course, you have to use clippings. Contemporaneous newspaper reports must inevitably provide the basic framework of any recounting of a past event. But if you tell your story merely from clippings, it cannot help being stale. The faded newsprint somehow contaminates the freshness of your typewriter ribbon.

So how on earth was I going to take on the Bennett Trial? I had thought for many years that Sir Edward Marshall Hall, KC, his leading council, had made a grievous error of judgment in his conduct of Bennett's defence. But that much had already appeared in Marshall Hall's first-class biography by Edward Marjoribanks way back in 1930. If I was to write about the case for a leading national Sunday newspaper, I must do better than merely regurgitate old material.

The essential in this kind of exercise is to visit all the major scenes of the story. It is amazing how in a local public house or at the local library or even – as once happened to me – merely by asking someone in the street, you can find a link with a case many years back in time.

And so it worked out with the Bennett Case. I was able to talk with an old lady, then in her early eighties, who was in the same house on that September night over seventy years ago when twenty-three-year-old Mary Jane Bennett went out to her death. Suddenly one was no longer dealing with an old, half-forgotten case remembered only by a few specialized collectors of legal biographies. One was dealing with a real event: something that happened in the life of the sharp-eyed old lady to whom I was talking and which had left so profound an impression upon her that she still remembered it in considerable detail.

Sometimes I think I am perhaps a little too enthusiastic in my determination to make these forays into the past as genuine and 'fresh' as I possibly can. For example, in the case of David Greenwood, told in Chapter 8, I begin my account: 'The ground was soft and muddy beneath my feet as I approached the spot, half-hidden by trees . . . where over fifty years ago an atttractive young girl had been brutally murdered.' In fact, when I had driven out to Eltham Common in south-east London to visit the scene of the crime it was an absolutely awful late winter day in 1970. It had been raining hard and there was still a depressing drizzle. I could see the spot where Nellie Trew had been killed from my parked car. I observed from there that the ground was soft and muddy. I did not have to get out of the car for that. But I wanted to begin the article by saying that the ground was soft and muddy *'beneath my feet'*: it gave it more immediacy. So I solemnly got out of my car, left its warm and snug protection and walked, probably looking rather like an amiable idiot, through the mud in the drizzle.

I don't want to over-estimate the importance of this selection of cases, even though they range over a fairly wide field and through seven decades. I claim for them no great criminological value. I hope they tell their stories in a readable and entertaining way. Sometimes, they highlight worthwhile and praiseworthy features of our legal system: sometimes, they seek to expose its stupidities and its failures. In particular, I personally am convinced that Edward Black (Chapter 4) and John Alexander Dickman (Chapter 9) should never have been hanged: the evidence simply was not there to justify the ultimate penalty.

But one thing I do claim for this selection. That it is as honest and objective as I could make it. Nothing is slanted to prove a point. There are no 'angles'. What you will read did really happen. The questions that I pose in the narrative are geared to only one aim: trying to get at the truth. That mystery in the search for which so many judges – and juries – have floundered.

SCALES OF JUSTICE

1   *George Henry Storrs*
The Mystery Murder

Over sixty years ago there was an imposing mile-long coach road leading to a large Victorian mansion. Now the winding track which climbs the Cheshire hillside above the towns of Dukinfield and Stalybridge is rutted and overgrown. On one side of the hill a modern housing estate straggles upwards, but at the summit all is remote and bleak. The once well-tended gardens have reverted to nature, and all that remains of the mansion are a few clumps of mouldering bricks.

'The house became derelict after the murder. The family moved out. Eventually, it was pulled down,' I was told.

For this is all that remains of Gorse Hall, the scene of one of the strangest, most mysterious murders in the history of British crime.

The story begins on the night of 10 September 1909. It was 9.30. George Henry Storrs, owner of Gorse Hall, and his wife Mary were alone in the dining-room. Suddenly, a voice called out from the other side of the window: 'Hold up your hands or I'll shoot!'

A shot was fired. There was the sound of breaking glass. Storrs – a brave, strongly built man aged forty-nine – jumped to the window and wrenched aside the blind.

Facing him through a hole in the shattered glass was a revolver.

For a moment, intruder and owner confronted each other silently. Then: 'I'm going out after him!' Storrs told his wife. 'No, Harry, don't! Please!' cried Mrs Storrs. She ran forward to restrain him.

But it was not necessary. By then the man had gone – as strangely as he had come. Man and wife were left alone staring out into the dark September night.

Who was the intruder? What was his motive? There were only two possible explanations: an attempt at armed burglary, which seemed unlikely as the man did not continue, or else an attempt to settle some private grudge, with the man losing his nerve.

Storrs was certainly the sort of man who might have enemies. He was a tough, successful business man, a real-life 'Crowther of Bankdam' – millowner, building contractor, and industrialist. A sort of Joe Champion of television's *Champion House* – more than sixty years back. Such a man might easily have been involved in bitter disputes over business matters, but it seemed unlikely there could be any other reason for enmity against him. His name was utterly free of any breath of scandal. He was one of the wealthiest, most powerful, most respected men in the area.

Perhaps that was why the police, when told of the incident, made great efforts to give him adequate protection. Thereafter, every night there was at least one policeman on guard at Gorse Hall.

Every night, that is, until the night of 1 November, nearly two months later. By that time the immediate shock of the incident had worn off.

This particular night was polling night in the local municipal elections. Every available policeman was needed for extra duties. So Mr Storrs agreed to a police request that for that one night the special guard should be removed.

And at shortly after nine o'clock once again an intruder crept through darkened grounds towards the isolated house.

Mary Evans, the cook, was busy preparing supper in the kitchen when suddenly she turned round. Standing behind her was a man with a gun. 'Don't say a word – or I'll shoot!' he said.

But she screamed and ran into the dining-room. There, parlourmaid Ellen Cooper was laying the supper-table, Mary Storrs was sewing, Marion Lindley, the Storrs' niece, was writing and Storrs himself was playing patience.

'Oh, sir, there's a man in the house!' cried Mary Evans.

Storrs again proved he was no coward. He went to the door and stepped out into the hall. The three women heard a strange man's voice say, 'Now I've got you!'

There was the sound of a struggle. The women ran into the hall – where Storrs was grappling with the intruder. Storrs seemed more than a match for him: taller, bigger, more powerful. Mrs Storrs easily managed to grab the gun from him and hurried upstairs to ring the alarm-bell, which had been installed since the earlier incident. The others ran out of the front door for help.

Alone, the two men fought: grimly and at length. Finally, the intruder drew a knife. Fifteen times he plunged it into Storrs's back, chest, and side. Yet still the burly, muscular mill-owner hung on.

He even managed to overcome his slighter, smaller assailant. With failing strength, he dragged him into the scullery and slammed the bolt on him. Then he slumped to the kitchen floor, dying. And there he was found by Marion Lindley, when she returned a few minutes later with some men she had found outside the house.

There was no sign of the intruder. He had smashed the scullery window, clambered out, and escaped.

'Who was the man?' asked PC Buckley. 'I don't know, I don't know,' spluttered the fast-sinking Mr Storrs.

Some of those present were later to say in court that they got the impression he did know, but did not want to answer. Soon he was beyond answering anything. At ten minutes to ten he died.

An old lady at Dukinfield can still remember that night: 'I was about ten or eleven at the time. We were playing up in the fields next to the house. We got back at about half-past nine. And, oh! the commotion! "Don't you know Mr Storrs has been murdered?" they told us.'

It was indeed a tremendous shock for the community. 'One of the most cruel, dastardly, and cold-blooded crimes ever perpetrated in this district,' said one local newspaper. 'The performer of the ghastly crime has the curse of Cain upon his head,' trumpeted another.

The police were almost chaotic in their attempts to find the culprit. By the evening of the following day it was already rumoured in the Press that they 'had a clue and were hoping to make an important arrest'.

In fact, they made two arrests: one in each of two nearby villages. But, shamefacedly, the police had to release both men within a few hours. Both had cast-iron proof of their innocence.

The inquest, in Gorse Hall's own dining-room, was formally opened on 3 November. It was almost immediately adjourned 'to give the persons in the house time to get over the terror and excitement the murder has caused and enable them to make clear statements of the occurrence,' explained the coroner.

Two days later the police issued a detailed description of the wanted man who, after all, had been seen by no fewer than four eye-witnesses at very close range. This is what it said:

About 25 to 27 years of age, 5 ft. 6in. to 5 ft. 8 in. in height, thin features, very fair to pale complexion, slight moustache, very light. He is supposed to be dressed in a brownish mixture cap, and dark tweed suit. He has the appearance of a working man.

The police also provided a spur to recognition: a £100 reward. But for nearly two weeks, despite the Storrs family increasing the reward to £500, nothing happened. The inquest continued its sluggish course. Gossip and tittle-tattle abounded. The local children sang a sad little song:

The moon shines tonight on Gorse Hall window where Storrs was murdered November 1st
And now he lies in the cemetery sleeping...

But there were no 'hard' developments. Police ardour seemed to have petered out.

Then suddenly on 12 November a printed notice was issued from the superintendent's office at Dukinfield. It was circulated to all police stations in the area. There is a copy of it, carefully preserved under glass, at Stalybridge public library. It named a man the police wished to see. He was Cornelius Howard, a reservist in the Royal Field Artillery. It described him as being about thirty-one years old, of slender build, pale complexion, clean shaven or with a light moustache.

Who was Cornelius Howard? What was his connection with the case? The notice gave no clue.

It did not reveal that Howard was the murdered man's estranged cousin. That they had not spoken for eleven years. That Mrs Storrs, married for eighteen years, had never even met him. That although Storrs had been wealthy, prosperous, and successful, Howard had been a comparative failure, drifting from his father's pork pie business into the Army and then into a succession of different jobs.

The implication was obvious: some private family grudge or feud erupting into revenge – and murder.

At 5.00 am on Wednesday, 17 November 1909, Cornelius Howard was arrested. Surprised by a keen-eyed policeman in the yard of the Co-operative Stores at Oldham. He gave a false name: John Ward. He was clean shaven.

At Oldham police station he admitted his true identity – and that he knew the police wanted to question him. He was searched. And a pair of socks saturated with blood was found in his pockets, together with a small knife which looked recently sharpened.

His clothes were bloodstained, his trousers cut and his legs bruised. Everything seemed consistent with his being the man who bloodily stabbed George Henry Storrs to death and then escaped through the jagged edges of a shattered scullery window.

Yet from the start he claimed an alibi. 'I lived at Joyce's lodging-house at Huddersfield from 16 October to 11 November,' he said, 'except for two nights when I was in Leeds. I returned from Leeds on 31 October and stayed in the lodging-house every night until 11 November when I came to Oldham.' That was the essence of his account given within hours of his arrest. It never varied throughout the months that followed.

The cuts on his legs and the bruises? He got those in an accident at Joyce's lodging-house shortly before he left. He denied vehemently that he was in Dukinfield or Stalybridge or anywhere near Gorse Hall on 1 November, the night of the murder.

But the police must have been very confident of their case. Or very desperate. At 2.30 that same afternoon – before he had attended a single identification parade – Howard was cautioned and charged with the murder. 'I have nothing to say,' he replied.

The following morning at Dukinfield police station identification parades were held. This really was putting the horse after the cart. Nevertheless, the police were not disappointed. Marion Lindley, the Storrs' niece, and the two maids identified Howard in a nine-man line-up without any difficulty – except that all three commented that on the night of the murder he had a slight moustache. Only Mrs Storrs was uncertain: she picked him out as 'somewhat like' the man. But could not be positively sure.

No matter. The police soon found two other witnesses before whom Cornelius Howard and eight other men were paraded. An Oldham lodging-house keeper picked him out as having stayed at her house on the night of the murder. An Oldham barber said that he was 'similar' to a young man who called at his shop the following morning – and had his slight moustache shaved off.

Howard was undeterred. He maintained that he had long ago shaved off his moustache. He stuck rigidly to his story that he had not been out of Huddersfield on the night of the murder.

'On that night I visited a public-house called the Ring-o'-Bells at Huddersfield about 9.00 pm,' he told Deputy Chief Constable Leah. 'I was there until about 10.30 pm. During that time I played the landlord of the house two games of dominoes for half a gallon of beer each game. There were three or four other men present.

'Three of the men were navvies, and as they had spent all their money and had not the price of their lodgings, the landlord gave them the price of their lodgings. He gave them 4d each and sent them to their lodgings. This was about 10.30 and I left the house about five minutes later.'

The pattern of the case was set: the strong positive identification of at least three eye-witnesses against a detailed alibi. Which was to prevail?

On 24 November 1909, the coroner's inquest – having heard the Gorse Hall eye-witnesses but without hearing any alibi witnesses – brought in a verdict of wilful murder against Howard. He was committed to stand his trial at the next Chester Assizes upon the coroner's warrant.

But the police were not content. They also asked the local magistrates to commit Howard for trial. And for two days in December, the crowded Dukinfield police court – presided over by the major and no fewer than seven other magistrates – heard the same evidence repeated.

Yet this time there was a difference. The prosecution also called John Henry Davies, the landlord of the Ring-o'-Bells, as a witness. They must have expected him to confirm the incident of the dominoes – which he did. They also expected him to say that this happened on the following night, 2 November, which he did not.

'Can you fix the date of the month when these games were played?' asked prosecuting counsel Sewell Pearce.

'I fix it by these men being in the house on that date.'
'How do you fix it?'
'By these three men asking if I had voted.'

'Was that the same night when you played the game with Howard?'

'Yes.'

'Can you fix the date?'

By now the prosecuting counsel must have been almost desperate. Nor did the answer help his well-being: 'Yes, it was the same date as voting day!'

No wonder the local paper described it as 'sensation in court'. Here was a principal prosecution witness corroborating the accused man's alibi!

Mr E. T. Nelson, Howard's coloured barrister – probably the first coloured man to practise at the English Bar – tried to press home his advantage. Instead of meekly accepting, as is usual, that there was a case for his client to answer, he called five witnesses to support Howard's story that he was in Huddersfield on both the 1st and 2nd of November – and that he then did not have a moustache.

But the local Bench could not believe that the three positive witnesses from Gorse Hall were mistaken. They, too, committed Howard to stand trial at the next Chester Assizes.

Nearly three months later, at 10.40 on the morning of 3 March 1910, Howard stepped into the dock at Chester Castle. 'Not guilty,' he said in a loud, clear voice.

Once again, and now for the third time, Marion Lindley and the two maids gave their evidence. Once again, they positively identified Cornelius Howard as the murderer.

This time, however, there was a fourth identifying witness. Mary Storrs, still in deepest mourning, was asked to look around the court and say if she saw her husband's assassin. 'That is the man!' she cried pointing at Howard.

Gone was all her former hesitation. 'That is the man. He is looking at me now in the same way as he did that night!'

What chance could Howard have after an identification like that? The atmosphere was electric, the tension almost unbearable.

Yet Davies, the Ring-o'-Bells landlord, stuck doggedly to his support of Howard's alibi. So much so that the judge allowed the prosecution, although they had called him, to treat him as a hostile witness.

One by one, Howard's alibi witnesses went into the witness-box. All came from a much lower station in life than the murdered man's widow: they were labourers, carpenters, in one case a fish, tripe and potato dealer. But at the end of a two-days' trial, the jury preferred their evidence.

The verdict after only a twenty-minute retirement: Not guilty. The judge ordered the prisoner to be discharged.

But that was not the end of the case. 'The police, it is hoped, will not relax their efforts,' thundered a local newspaper that weekend.

And, sure enough, five months later the police arrested a second man, a twenty-eight-year-old soldier called Mark Wilde, and charged him with the murder! The only time in the history of our courts that two men have been charged, one after the other, with the same murder.

The case against Wilde – such as it was – rested upon the fact that he was admittedly in the neighbourhood on the night of the murder. That he had bloodstains on his clothes: he said he had been involved in a public-house fight. And the fact that some of his fellow soldiers claimed to recognize the gun that was used on the night of the murder as being the same as one they had seen in his possession some years previously.

A ludicrously weak case. But once again the Gorse Hall eye-witnesses claimed to identify the accused man as George Henry Storrs's assailant. They were not as confident as they had been before, but nevertheless two said he 'resembled' the killer: the other two said he 'was like' the killer.

In a dramatic moment during Mark Wilde's trial in the autumn of 1910, Cornelius Howard came back into the court-room where he too had stood trial for murder. The two men stood side by side: and the jury were allowed to see how similar – or different – they were.

At 5.20 on the evening of 28 October 1910, Mark Wilde heard the same verdict as Cornelius Howard: Not guilty.

Over sixty years have passed since then. The police made no more arrests. The file was closed. But the case remains as big a mystery as ever.

What was the motive for the murder? Was there any connection between the earlier incident of 10 September and the killing itself? If so, what was it? How could four honest, intelligent women make the same mistake and independently pick out the same man? Why did George Henry Storrs die?

Soon after the joint acquittals, Cornelius Howard wrote in a magazine: 'Mark Wilde and I have been discharged, and only time can solve the baffling question: "Who murdered Mr Storrs?" ' Time has proved Howard wrong. No one will ever now know the answer to the Gorse Hall Mystery.

2   Frank Smith
Accidental Killer or Murderer?

The name of the house has altered. It is now no longer called, romantically, 'Stella Maris' – star of the sea. Otherwise its appearance has changed little in forty-seven years. It still stands, in odd contrast to its former name, prim and respectable in a row of tidy, suburban houses on a hill overlooking the sea at Tankerton, near Whitstable, Kent.

I peered into the front window. But I could see nothing. It was a cold, sunny morning and the panes of glass were misted over as I stood on the pavement outside.

At this spot on 12 August 1926, a passing neighbour looked through that same window and saw a struggle between two men. A struggle that ended in death, and led to a trial for murder that was the talking-point of the nation.

The dead man was forty-year-old John Derham, of good family and background. Son of a barrister, educated at Eton and Cambridge. An international sportsman, wealthy and gay.

The other man was the grandson of a millionaire. Also educated at Eton and Cambridge. An international playboy, who had got through a fortune of half a million. His name: Alfonso Francis Austin Smith – 'Frank' to his friends. His age: thirty-seven.

Strange contestants for a chintz-curtained front room in Tankerton. Where, as a local resident told me, 'most of the inhabitants – then as now – were quiet, middle-class folk mainly living on small or fixed incomes.'

What had brought these two larger-than-life characters there? The answer was classic: a beautiful woman. In this case, Kathleen Smith, Frank's pert, attractive wife, ten years his junior.

The marriage of Frank and Kathleen Smith had been happy enough. True Smith had drunk, gambled, and squandered most

of his money. But he still had no need to work. Kathleen had
£10,000 capital of her own, and they could still afford a nanny
for their three children.

Then came that day in January 1926. An introduction by a
mutual friend: 'Frank, do you know Jack Derham?' – 'Jack, do
you know Frank Smith?' – 'You two chaps must have met each
other at school.'

In fact, the three years' difference between them had sufficed
to keep them apart. Despite the same school and university. But
now their common background and interests quickly brought
them together.

Unlike the failing Smith, Derham was still at the peak of his
powers: handsome and charming. His wife had left him but
would not divorce him. But that did not occur to Smith as a
danger.

'You must meet my wife,' he said. 'I'm sure you'll like her.'
And soon all three were firm friends.

Kathleen Smith later claimed: 'There never was anything
between me and Jack Derham except the clean friendship that
can exist between a man and a woman.'

But Frank Smith did not agree. There were frequent rows
between him and Kathleen. Twice the two men came to blows.
In June 1926 Smith left home, a furnished house at Herne Bay,
and went to London.

Kathleen, the children, and nanny went to the country house
near Canterbury owned by Derham's father. But they observed
the proprieties: Derham did not remain under the same roof.
He, like Smith, went to London.

Kathleen seems to have intended her parting from Smith to
be permanent. A Canterbury solicitor drew up a separation
deed.

But Frank Smith was no complaisant husband. He was drinking more and more, becoming maudlin, tearful – and dangerous.

He forced his way in Derham's absence into Derham's
London rooms and snatched Kathleen's photographs from the
mantelpiece. He drove down to the house of Derham's father
and told the nanny: 'Get the children out of here! I'm going to
smash up the place and kill them both!'

Luckily Kathleen was out. But for fifteen minutes Smith went
berserk. Putting his fist through an oil painting, smashing china.

Then he stormed off to the Canterbury solicitor's office – and screamed at the clerk: 'I'm going to smash up Derham! I will kill them both! I don't care if I am arrested!'

His threats were not only oral:

You damned swine [he wrote to Derham] I only wish you had the courage to meet me... You dirty, white-livered fool. You lied to me and now you are going to suffer.

And to Kathleen:

I am going crazy in my misery. I tell you that I cannot go on living without you. I will deal with that damned cad Derham first... I shall come down and deal with you both in a fashion that can never be mended. Jackie [their son] won't want to have fingers pointed at him as the son of a murderer of an unfaithful wife and her lover, and a suicide. Come back to me, my girl, my little white heather.

The style may have been purest melodrama. But the intensity of feeling could not be ignored.

Kathleen moved out of the Derham family home. With her children, nanny and younger sister, she rented Stella Maris at Tankerton.

And there on Monday evening 9 August came her husband. Before leaving London, he had visited a friend and bought a Webley Service revolver and six cartridges.

Kathleen Smith was as changeable as she was pretty. On that Monday night, they sat up late. Smith showed her the gun, said he had bought it to kill himself. He protested yet again his love.

They slept in separate rooms. But the following morning she said: 'All right, I've decided I won't see Derham again!'

On Tuesday night they slept together. All seemed set for a second honeymoon of happiness.

But on Wednesday morning Kathleen appeared cooler. The postman brought a letter from Derham – which Smith tore up. Although she was in the house, he sat down and wrote her a letter himself. In his normal, 'East Lynne' style:

My own adorable little wife—You have made me happier than ever I hoped to be. I have been mad lately and in hell. Now you have given me glimpses of heaven. [But] do not throw a lifebelt to me and then draw it away at my last gasp. You have a great heart and courageous. I need it always and I want it.

But Kathleen had now reconsidered the whole matter. She

had changed her mind. 'You must go,' she told Smith.

He was distraught, imploring: he refused to leave. On Wednesday night he stayed at Stella Maris.

Then on Thursday morning, 12 August, he did an extraordinary thing: he sent Derham a telegram in Kathleen's name asking him to come down to Stella Maris. 'To have a discussion,' he afterwards claimed.

Derham arrived. Smith suggested that they both should not see Kathleen for three months. Kathleen and Derham countered that he should go – and permanently. For hours they argued.

Then at about nine o'clock they adjourned and all went off to a local hotel together. To have supper.

The other two ate while Smith sat morosely drinking champagne.

Then back to Stella Maris – where Kathleen began preparing a bed for Derham for the night. 'I will not have this lover of yours sleeping here!' said Smith angrily. But she only laughed.

In the front room, Derham began sorting out some playing cards. 'Will you join us?' they asked Smith calmly. He was almost in tears. 'No,' he cried. 'I'm going to shoot myself!' But to use his own words, 'it did not appear to distress them. They did not believe it.'

At that moment, James Browning Barton, a twenty-eight-year-old local builder, was walking up the road outside. On his way home. The lights were glaring in the front room at Stella Maris. The curtains were not drawn.

Mr Barton happened to glance in. He saw three people, Smith standing in the bay window with his back to the road. The others more or less facing him, a few feet away.

He moved on. But at that moment he heard a shot. He looked back through the window. Derham and Kathleen were now moving towards Smith. There was a struggle in which a window pane was broken. Smith fell to the ground. Derham struck him as he lay on the floor.

Kathleen screamed: 'Don't!' Then: 'Give me the revolver!'

There was a further scuffle. Then Derham staggered out into the road, clasping Smith's gun – and collapsed at Mr Barton's feet. Bleeding from a bullet-hole in his stomach.

'My wife kept inviting this man here, and one of us had to go,' a dazed and half-drunk Frank Smith told Mr Barton. In his pocket, when the police arrived, was yet another letter to Kathleen, this time undelivered: 'My dear girl,' it began, 'this problem can only be solved in one way: the removal of your lover Derham or myself.'

Yet, at the crunch, the will to survive is powerful – and sobering. Smith made no such reckless statement to the police. 'I intended to shoot myself,' he told Sergeant Quested. 'But in the struggle for the revolver it went off and shot Derham.'

When Derham died, twenty-four hours later, that was the basis of Smith's defence.

Accidental death. The trigger pulled during a struggle for the gun. It is one of the oldest – and most effective – defences in a murder trial.

And Frank Smith could afford the most brilliant defending counsel of the day to present it: Sir Edward Marshall Hall, KC, the Great Defender. He was in his late sixties, and his health failing – but he was still magnificent.

Smith was confident of acquittal. When his trial started at Maidstone Assizes on 25 November 1926 he had already chosen the menu for a 'freedom dinner' – scheduled for after the verdict.

For what was the evidence against him?

The scientific evidence was soon shown to be inconclusive. Dr Ernest Whitby, who conducted the post-mortem, conceded at once that Derham's injuries were consistent with the revolver's being fired accidentally.

Gun expert Robert Churchill maintained that a deliberate firing was more probable, but admitted that an accident was not impossible.

Smith's wild statements and letters? When analysed closely, they were not so damaging as might at first have appeared. They contained nearly as many threats to kill himself as to kill Derham.

But there was one rock-hard part of the Crown's case which, if the jury accepted it, meant that Smith must be guilty. The evidence of James Browning Barton, the young builder who looked into that front-room window at Stella Maris on the evening of 12 August.

For notice the timing of what Mr Barton heard and saw. It is absolutely vital. He said that he heard the gun-shot and then saw the struggle. Smith claimed there was a struggle and then the gun-shot.

If Mr Barton was right, the killing could only have been deliberate. There was no struggle until after the gun was fired.

Mr Ernest Ovenden is now a veteran reporter with a Kent newspaper. But in 1926 he covered the early stages of this case as a young reporter at Canterbury police court. He remembers James Browning Barton very well: 'A good old Whitstable type. Self-made, matter-of-fact, and down to earth. A good witness.'

Marshall Hall made the same assessment. He did not launch a frontal assault. There was none of the forensic fireworks that Frank Smith might have thought his 350 guineas brief fee (plus 'refreshers') entitled him to.

Instead – on the first afternoon of the trial – there was merely a gently worded 'suggestion' that 'the mental picture which you formed was a little wrong in time, if only a matter of a fraction of a second. I suggest that those two people jumped towards the prisoner before the shot went off.'

The reply was uncompromising: 'No. I was not looking when the shot was fired. When I looked round I saw that the two others were actually in contact with the prisoner.'

Marshall Hall was not going to budge this witness. Discreetly, he sat down. He knew that he still had his client to give evidence and his own powerful speech to make before the jury reached their verdict.

The judge – wizened Sir Horace Avory, known unaffectionately as 'Hanging Horace' – realized exactly why Marshall Hall had voluntarily forfeited his opportunity to lambast a prosecution witness.

He leaned forward in his seat. 'Were Derham and Mrs Smith moving towards the prisoner after the shot was fired?' he emphasized. 'Yes, my lord. They were still moving towards the prisoner, and they all had their hands up,' said Mr Barton.

Grimly, the judge made a note of the reply.

But the following day, Smith, a sprig of white heather in his buttonhole, strode purposefully into the witness-box. And emotion took over in that crowded, tense courtroom.

Marshall Hall read aloud, in his mellifluous voice, the 'Do-not-throw-a-lifebelt-to-me' letter written to Kathleen on the morning after their reconciliation. 'That was an honest expression of your feelings to your wife on Wednesday, 11 August 1926?' he asked.

Smith cracked. The tears rolled down his cheeks. His head bowed. 'It is,' he replied softly.

And then there was a shriek. One of the two women jurors screamed hysterically. Other women in court burst into sobs. The angry Mr Justice Avory had to adjourn the court 'until the ladies can compose themselves,' he said acidly. But the high-level voltage of the trial had been set. Smith's account of the firing of the gun was incoherent, almost incomprehensible: 'I went to get a chair. As I did so, I put my hand to unbutton the back pocket of my trousers to take out the revolver. The next thing that happened – there was a terrific struggle. I was struck on the head. The revolver went off.'

Holding the gun in his hand he said firmly: 'No finger of mine ever touched that trigger. That I will swear before God to my dying day!'

In his final speech, Marshall Hall kept up the emotional pressure:

Set free this man! [he urged the jury]

He begged his wife not to withdraw the lifebelt, which she had thrown him as he was struggling in the water. That lifebelt has been withdrawn once. Members of the jury, it is now for you to say whether you will throw him that lifebelt once more, give him the chance of grasping it and being pulled ashore to resume his old happy life with the woman he loves.

It was a Henry Irving performance: good, old-fashioned ham. And people in court cheered when the jury said, 'Not guilty.'

But Frank Smith still did not have his 'freedom dinner'. Everyone looked to the judge, expecting him to say, 'Let the prisoner be discharged.'

Instead, 'There is another charge on the calendar,' crackled Avory's voice. And there was! Everyone had forgotten a second, minor charge of unlawfully possessing a firearm with intent to endanger life.

Smith had to plead guilty. On his own evidence, he had the revolver in his possession to endanger his own life. 'You will go to prison for twelve months with hard labour,' said the judge. With obvious relish.

The sequel was tragic. Within three months the ageing

Marshall Hall was dead: his tired body unable to withstand the combined effects of influenza and bronchitis.

Frank Smith, when he came out of prison, did not resume 'his old happy life with the woman he loved'. Kathleen divorced him, their young son was burned to death in a school fire – and in November 1944, in a furnished room at Ilfracombe in Devon, he died. Poor and forgotten.

Was he guilty of murder?

Before answering, consider these three vital facts:

1. Kathleen was never called to give evidence. Why not? A wife cannot give evidence for the Crown against her husband. But she can always speak for him. Yet she spent the whole trial in the courtroom corridor. 'There were moments,' she later told a reporter, 'when I felt impelled to go inside. But I was persuaded not to do so.'

One can understand why. She had already given a statement to the police. If she said anything in the witness-box that contradicted what she had already told the police – she would have been mercilessly cross-examined.

2. Derham, before he died, also made a statement to the police which, too, they were unable to use. This has never been known before. But Mr Ovenden told me: 'I have always understood there was such a statement. It could not be used because Derham did not realize he was dying – and it, therefore, was not a "dying declaration."' (A genuine dying declaration, unlike other hearsay statements, is admissible in evidence.)

It is almost inconceivable that, if Derham had told the police that his death was accidental, they would yet have continued to prosecute Smith.

3. Perhaps most important of all: James Browning Barton is still alive. Living in retirement in Zambia, Central Africa. After all these years, he still maintains he was not mistaken. 'The evidence I gave was factual,' he has written me. 'I heard a loud report of a shot being fired. Glancing across I saw Derham approaching Smith, who was moving backward. They contacted and finished up in the corner of the bay-window where Derham took the revolver from Smith.'

These are words penned by a vital witness in a murder trial forty-two years after the event. And notice the sequence has remained the same: gunshot then the struggle.

Mr Barton's brother, Leonard, still lives in Whitstable: a

prosperous, stocky business man who took over and built up his brother's building concern. 'He wasn't the type to make a mistake,' he has told me. 'He would only have said in court what he actually saw and heard.'

Even the most careful and honest witness can make a mistake.

Did that happen here? Or is Mr Barton's recollection after more than four decades still a correct picture of the scene in that chintzy front room? If so, there can be no doubt: whatever the temptation, whatever the excuse – Frank Smith was a murderer.

3 *Alfred Moore*
Did an Innocent Man Hang?

The countryside below falls away steeply, then mounts again in a broad undulating slope towards a narrow, hedge-lined road. A chill wind blows across the open scene. It is Yorkshire, the West Riding. The view is from the road which climbs up out of the small village of Kirkheaton, near Huddersfield, towards the barren grandeur of the Pennine moors – a remote spot. Only isolated farm dwellings dot the landscape: today there is still a good deal of poultry, pig and cattle farming in the area, and in recent years wealthy business men have been buying some of the farms and sprucing them up.

Over twenty years ago, in the summer of 1951, the owner of one of these farms was a man called Alfred Moore. He was in his late thirties, and, outwardly, like many a local farmer of that time. He kept some pigs, some poultry. He had four daughters, aged two to ten, the two eldest at private, fee-paying schools.

Alfred Moore faced the eternal middle-class problem of making ends meet, yet somehow always managed to seem to do so.

But in one vital respect, Alfred Moore was different from his fellow local farmers. For by night, he was a thief, an accomplished burglar and plunderer of nearby mills and offices. He was that character straight out of fiction: a gentleman crook.

'A likeable criminal. You really couldn't help but like him,' someone who remembers him well has said. 'But the police had their suspicions. They had been trying to catch him for months.'

And on the night of Saturday, 14 July 1951, the hard-working local police force must have thought that, at last, they had caught up with him. By 11.45 pm – so they later said in court – a cordon of ten police officers had been thrown round Alfred Moore's hillside farm. All footpaths and ways of approach were watched.

They believed he was not at home. Where was he? If he was in fact out on a burglary that night, they would be bound to catch him, red-handed, returning to his farmhouse lair.

But these were British police. They were not armed. And some two hours later, at about 2 am on the morning of Sunday, 15 July 1951, five shots rang out murderously in the still night air.

A policeman – one of the cordon – ran towards the spot. Near a footpath leading up to Alfred Moore's farm he saw dimly two men lying on the ground. Forty-five-year-old Detective Inspector Duncan Alexander Fraser lay utterly motionless, Police Constable Gordon Jagger, aged forty-two, was still conscious. He was severely wounded in the stomach.

Police whistles sounded. Reinforcements arrived. Inspector Fraser and Police Constable Jagger were removed to the Royal Huddersfield Infirmary, where the former was found to be dead.

Warily, a horde of policemen, some now armed, watched the silent farmhouse on the hill. A light appeared for a while in an upstairs window. Later, puffs of smoke billowed from the chimney. Finally, just before 5 am, local CID chief George Metcalfe, unarmed but with a policeman with a revolver some feet behind him, approached Alfred Moore's farmhouse.

Whether Moore was guilty or innocent of the night's events, Metcalfe acted with a cool gallantry that later earned him an MBE. He spoke to Moore, cautioned him and told him that he was being arrested in connection with the shooting of two police officers earlier that morning.

'Oh, it's serious. It's awful,' said Moore. But, he claimed, he had no gun such as could have caused the two policemen's injuries – only a shotgun which the prosecution's own expert later said could not have done it.

Even so, it was a grim-faced Moore who was led off under armed escort to Huddersfield police station.

Meanwhile, doctors were fighting to try to save Police Constable Jagger's life. They performed an emergency operation. They gave him a blood transfusion.

At 8.15 on the Sunday morning Moore gave Metcalfe his first terse statement. It was to be the basis of his whole subsequent defence: 'I went to bed with Mrs Moore and Pat' (the eldest daughter) about 12 o'clock. I never got up again.' What about the later smoke from his chimney? 'If you must know, I got up to burn some rubbish. I'm not saying any more.'

He was obviously in distress: 'I want time to think,' he said. 'I'm in an awful spot. I think I'll have a solicitor. What's going to happen to my children?' Then: 'Oh, my head, I won't talk to you. I'm not forced to. I have my rights.'

As the Sunday wore on and Police Constable Jagger lay stricken on his hospital bed the police realized they must act promptly. They had only arrested Moore. He had still not actually been charged with murder.

His farmhouse and the surrounding country were already being searched for the elusive murder weapon. His daughter, 10-year-old Pat, had been taken to the police station for questioning. But these were only fringe matters.

There was one vital witness whose testimony must be obtained – before a higher court intervened for ever.

At 4.40 pm a hospital doctor examined Police Constable Jagger and pronounced his pulse 'of good volume' and his brain 'mentally alert'.

There then followed what I believe to be a unique incident in modern British criminal history: an identification parade was held in Police Constable Jagger's private hospital ward – with the dying policeman himself pointing the finger of accusation at the man who he said had shot him, from among the nine men standing before him.

The man he picked out: Alfred Moore. 'Are you satisfied with the conduct of the parade?' the officer in charge afterwards asked Moore.

'Yes,' was the reply. 'But it wasn't me.'

Now the police could act. At 5.20 pm Detective Chief Superintendent Metcalfe formally charged Moore with Detective Inspector Fraser's murder. 'How could it be me?' Moore doggedly replied. 'I have told you, I was in bed.'

Twenty minutes later, Moore once again stood at Police Constable Jagger's bedside. Also present was a senior local magistrate – and the hospital ward was converted into an emergency courtroom. For the last time in his twenty-one years of service, Police Constable Jagger gave evidence.

As a verbatim note was taken, he described what had happened when Inspector Fraser died and he had been wounded:

I first saw the accused at 2 am on 15 July. He was walking towards his home. As I got near to him, he must have heard my feet in the grass and he dashed under a hedge. I said 'Hello' and I shouted.

He said 'I thought it was a cow.' I shone my torch in his face and took hold of his left arm. I saw his face clearly in the light of the torch.

As I took hold of the accused's left arm Mr Fraser approached and shone his torch in the accused's face. Mr Fraser said, 'Are you Moore, Albert Moore?' He replied 'Yes.'

Mr Fraser said, 'We are police officers and you are coming with us.' He said 'No sir. Oh, no, sir.'

As soon as the accused said that he whipped his hand, his right hand, out of his overcoat pocket and shot me and Mr Fraser ...

Less than fifteen hours later Jagger was dead.

'I am on the spot. I know I am,' said Moore when charged with this second murder.

The search for the murder weapon went on. A cache of stolen goods was found hidden about Moore's house. Stolen postage stamps and dollar bills were discovered, half burned, in the grate. Police found no fewer than 159 skeleton keys – and a few empty cartridge shells.

But there was nothing substantially to incriminate Moore in the two policemen's murder. It was a thief's lair – not a killer's refuge.

Nothing was found that had been stolen that night – which was curious. The police must surely have had a tip-off that Moore was going on a raid. Why else the police cordon to catch him on his return?

And if he had not gone burgling that night, why should he have been carrying a gun when stopped by Fraser and Jagger?

Why would he have needed to shoot them? And if he had been burgling, where were the goods he was bearing home to the safety of his farmhouse? And where was his gun?

The search lasted for two weeks. The police called in Royal Engineers with mine detectors. Walls were demolished. All the grass on the farm was mowed down. Feeding troughs were drained, and the farmhouse and all its many cavities searched as thoroughly as human eye and hand could.

But never was a weapon – or any loot from that night – discovered.

The senior police officers conducting the investigation must have been disappointed. But, after all, they had the trump card of PC Jagger's death-bed identification and his sworn deposition. Let us, however, examine these a little.

The magistrate who took the deposition afterwards certified that Moore 'had full opportunity of cross-examining the witness.'

That was indeed true. Moore was allowed to ask what questions he liked. But he was a farmer-cum-burglar. He was no lawyer, and he had never asked anyone questions in court before.

All he could manage by way of 'cross-examination' was the inadequate 'Are you quite sure?' which secured the inevitable answer 'I am quite sure.'

Moore did not have the benefit of a lawyer's help until two days later, when Jagger was already dead. It was not his fault – nor that of the police. They had tried to contact the local solicitor who had handled his purchase of his farm, but without success. On that summer's Sunday he could not be found.

Only on the Tuesday did another local solicitor – the late Mr George Hutchinson, then in practice in Huddersfield – undertake the case. 'But by then,' I have been told, 'Mr Hutchinson was faced with an almost impossible task.'

Police Constable Jagger's evidence – under oath and within hours of his death – placed overwhelming difficulties in the path of any defender, however able.

Yet, if only an experienced defence lawyer could have represented Moore's interests at the death-bed court in that hospital ward, the deposition might well have read very differently.

Everyone, of course, must feel the greatest sympathy for Jagger, the brave police officer, lying in bed, his life force slowly ebbing away. But a lawyer has a duty to his client.

He would have asked Jagger if he had seen a photograph of Moore before he set out to watch his farm. Later, at the trial, Moore's counsel in fact established that a photograph of Moore was kept at the police station where Jagger and his colleagues assembled.

How had that affected his identification of the face he later saw highlighted briefly in the light of a torch against the dark background of a night sky?

Jagger said that Fraser had asked the man they accosted: 'Are you Moore, Albert Moore?' This Moore's first name was Alfred. Why the mistake?

Above all, an experienced lawyer would gently have probed Jagger's own condition at that time. Massive surgery had been undertaken in the effort to save his life. His evidence was given only hours after he had regained consciousness. Had he by then recovered fully from the effect of the anaesthetic?

All these matters, a lawyer would have explored. And, for better or worse, the answers would have been recorded for Moore's jury subsequently to consider. As it was, they had only: 'Are you quite sure?' – 'I am quite sure.'

Moore's trial opened at Leeds Assizes on Monday, 10 December 1951. Mr G. Raymond Hinchcliffe, KC – now a High Court judge – led for the Crown.

His opening speech was strong and certain: 'In the early hours of Sunday, 15 July, a most callous and shocking murder was committed. The prosecution submit that the person who committed this murder is the prisoner in the dock.'

Yet, despite such outward assurance, the prosecution did two strange things:

1. In the local magistrates' court they had subpoenaed as a witness against her father Patricia – to throw doubt on his story that he had gone to bed at about midnight at the same time as she and her mother. Her evidence – unsworn because of her age – had been, on balance, inconclusive.

But now no mention was made of her testimony to the jury. Nor was she called as a witness although the police had earlier thought her evidence of sufficient significance to warrant the issue of an official court subpoena against this schoolgirl.

2. They called as a witness a local villager who said that he had seen what looked like a 'Luger automatic revolver' in a box on Moore's farm. But the prosecution's own gun expert, while agreeing that the fatal bullets had probably been fired from a revolver, conceded in cross-examination by Mr Harry Hylton-Foster, Moore's KC, that the Luger firm had never manufactured a revolver.

Moore gave evidence, stolidly but well. He denied having owned a revolver. He said he was in bed from about 12 o'clock onwards on the night of 14 July.

He agreed that later he had heard some commotion outside. He realized it was the police and had tried to burn the stolen stamps and dollar bills in his possession – the 'rubbish' whose burning had sent puffs of smoke up his chimney. But that was all.

'Had you anything to do with the shooting of Inspector Fraser and Police Constable Jagger?' Mr Hylton-Foster asked him. 'No,' was the reply.

'Do you now know who shot them?' – 'I have no idea.'

'On the night when they were shot, were you yourself concerned with any crime at all?' – 'No.'

He claimed that he had walked his brother part of the way home after the brother had spent most of the day helping him on the farm. This was confirmed by the brother in the witness-box. Then he got back to the farmhouse 'between quarter to and twelve o'clock to the best of my knowledge', had a wash and went to bed.

Mr Hinchcliffe's cross-examination was short – and powerful. He knew full well the strength of his case. His last questions were about Jagger's death-bed testimony:

'Were you given an opportunity of cross-examining him?'
'Yes.'
'Was the question you put "Are you quite sure?"'
'It was, Sir.'
'And was the answer "I am quite sure"?'
'Yes.'

Mr Hinchcliffe sat down.

In his final speech, Mr Hinchcliffe made a further point to the jury: 'How could Moore be telling the truth about returning to the farm by about 11.45? At that hour, the police cordon had been fully set. How could he have got through without being seen?'

The jury took less than an hour to convict. 'My Lord, I protest my innocence. I am not guilty,' cried Moore before sentence of death.

His appeal was dismissed in less than thirty minutes. He could not escape the dying Jagger's identification. 'The real point in the case was as to identity,' said Lord Goddard, the Lord Chief Justice, in the Criminal Appeal Court. 'The evidence before the jury was that the police officer who was wounded, but died, positively identified the appellant as the man who fired the revolver.'

I have discussed the case with a friend of Moore's. 'To the end in the condemned cell, he protested his innocence,' I have been told.

Mr Hutchinson, his solicitor, petitioned Home Secretary Sir David Maxwell Fyfe, KC, for a reprieve. But Moore was a convicted police slayer. There was little hope of compassion.

At nine o'clock on the morning of 6 February 1952, he was hanged at Armley Jail, Leeds.

His wife and daughters left the district, changed their names, became enshrouded in a merciful obscurity. But did an innocent man die?

'I don't believe that he did it. I don't believe he was the sort of man who would use violence,' says his friend. 'In the pubs down Huddersfield you can sometimes hear the young tearaways of the time – now respectable and successful in their late thirties and forties – discussing the case. I have even heard some of them say they know who really did it.' The friend paused: 'But it's all guess-work – isn't it?'

I put forward one theory of my own. A theory that would get round the problem of how Moore 'got through the cordon' unseen – and explain why no loot from that night, nor any murder weapon were ever found on his farm.

It is a theory with the awesome implication that Alfred Moore was hanged for a crime he did not commit.

First, 'getting through the cordon': that is easy. A matter of a few minutes here or there. If the police officers' recollection of when they took up their stations was inaccurate by a few minutes out, there is no problem.

Moore could easily have got back to his house before the police cordon was fully set.

Secondly, the absence of loot and of the weapon: this can also be explained. The real killer – if my theory is correct – was not Moore returning to the farm from a burgling expedition but a 'fence', a receiver of stolen property, cutting across the fields by appointment to collect some of Moore's cache of stolen goods.

This receiver could very probably have been carrying a gun – for his own protection. When stopped by Fraser and Jagger and asked if he is Moore, of course he will say: 'Yes.' He is hardly likely to give his own name.

Then he shoots the two gallant police officers, and disappears into the night with the murder weapon. He goes the way he came – not up towards Moore's farm.

What about Jagger's identification? The man was dying. He genuinely believed it was Moore. Moore was the man they were expecting. Police Constable Jagger spoke in sincere good faith.

But so soon after major surgery and a blood transfusion, who can say that there was not the risk of error?

Home Secretary Sir David Maxwell Fyfe is now also dead. We will never know how he justified to himself the decision to let Alfred Moore hang. I am not saying that I believe Moore was innocent. That would be going much too far.

But I am glad his death is not on my conscience.

4 *Edward Black*
Condemned Before his Trial

Even when investigating a murder case over half a century old, something new can sometimes be discovered. It is a strange and thrilling experience, unearthing a vital fact that everyone else who has examined the case has overlooked.

Such was my feeling when, going through the official Register of Deaths for St Austell for the year 1921, I saw the following entry. Against the name of fifty-year-old Mrs Annie Black who had died on 11 November 1921, at the nearby village of Tregonissey, was written: 'Cause of death: Arsenical poisoning by Edward Ernest Black. Murder.'

What was so unusual about that? Husbands do murder their wives – in the nineteen-seventies as much as in the nineteen-twenties. It was the date of the entry that riveted my attention: 10 January 1922.

For that was twenty-two days before insurance agent Black went on trial for murder. Twenty-two days before the accused man entered the dock at Bodmin Assizes the Deputy Registrar for the district of St Austell had already written in the official records that one damning word: 'Murder'.

'And quite a few people would have known about it. For a start the local undertaker would have had a copy,' an old solicitor friend of mine told me. 'If I were defending Black now he'd be home and dry for an acquittal. Nowadays we don't pre-judge defendants.'

But in the early nineteen-twenties? In this distant corner of Cornwall what manner of justice was meted out to thirty-six-year-old Edward Ernest Black?

Annie Black was a popular Cornish woman. She kept the sweets shop in Tregonissey, then a small hamlet – now almost a suburb of St Austell.

In her youth, there had been some scandal. When she married

Edward Black, a handsome, presentable man, in August 1914, she already had a ten-year-old daughter Marion. 'My mother and Mr Black lived fairly well together,' Marion later said in court, 'although there was one occasion when there was a difference about money matters.'

Indeed money was tight in the Black household. Mrs Black's total estate, when she died, amounted to only £61 2s 10d. And Edward Black did not do too well out of his small-scale insurance agency.

Yet ... 'You would think he was very devoted to his wife if you saw them on Sunday nights,' an old lady who remembers them both, has told me. 'He would always walk to church with her and her daughter. I can see them in my mind's eye now. Like a picture. He was an attractive man. He used to go to dances a lot,' she laughed. 'I used to dance with him! Old-fashioned dances – veletas, old-fashioned waltzes. That sort of thing. No, his wife never used to come with him. She was nearly twenty years older than him, you know.

'But I never felt as if I was dancing with a possible murderer. Everyone looked up to him as an upright churchman.'

Even so, Edward Black had one major blemish, so far as his neighbours were concerned. He was not a Cornishman. He was born in Lancashire. 'Foreigners start at the River Tamar, the boundary between Devon and Cornwall,' my solicitor friend told me.

'I still think they are clannish, mind, even today,' said the old lady.

And when – on Wednesday, 8 November 1921 – Edward Black suddenly disappeared from the district, owing money to people who had paid for insurance policies and never received them, there were quite a few locals ready to say: 'I told you so! I never trusted that man!'

Local suspicion exploded into a crescendo of hatred when the startling news came three days later that Annie Black – 'that poor, dear woman' – had suddenly died.

Why had she died? What had happened? Admittedly, in the last few weeks there had been an epidemic of gastro-enteritis in the district. Could that be the cause?

Or was it something to do with her disappearing husband? Only just over a year previously, there had been a sensational murder case in South Wales when a man had been acquitted of poisoning his wife with arsenic.

In those distant days before radio or television, real-life murderers were the *Softly, Softly* of the age. They were almost a form of popular entertainment – discussed in the pubs like last night's television show is nowadays.

Was this sudden death of Mrs Black's a repeat performance of what many people believed had happened to the woman in South Wales?

Dr Edwin Andrew, the local GP who attended Annie Black in her last illness, seemed to think so. He had first treated her – for gastro-enteritis – on Monday, 31 October when she had been taken ill after breakfast with stomach pains. There was nothing unusual in that. But now, after eleven days, with intermittent vomiting and diarrhoea – she was dead. He refused to sign a death certificate.

'I did not at first suspect anything wrong,' he later explained at the coroner's court. 'But afterwards the combination of circumstances led me to refuse.'

On 12 November 1921, Dr John Gilchrist, the local police surgeon – not, it will be noted, an experienced pathologist – carried out the post-mortem. His assistant was a Dr Andrew. Two country doctors, in ordinary, everyday practice, carrying out a highly specialized task that should only be done by experts.

What sort of doctor was Dr Edwin Andrew, now long since dead? 'A good, old country doctor,' I was told. 'Honest. Helpful. Not all that brilliant, I think.'

The post-mortem's verdict was only provisional: there was no evidence of heart disease. The dead woman's kidneys showed clear signs of long-standing disease. But, as for arsenic – the substance always sought in suspected poisoning cases – the two do-it-yourself pathologists could not tell.

Arsenical poisoning does show itself in certain physical effects upon the outer skin and contents of the body. But in their subsequent evidence in court neither doctor referred to any such matters. They merely removed various internal organs and sent them up to Mr John Webster, the Home Office analyst, in London, for him to analyse.

They did not send for analysis the dead woman's fingernails or hair, although even by 1921 it was already well established that arsenic persists in nails and hair long after it has disappeared from the rest of the body.

This was an elementary error. The eminent modern pathologist, Professor Keith Simpson, in his classic text-book *Forensic Medicine*, states: 'Samples of hair and nails should be taken for analysis, as the poison is stored permanently in them.'

While the investigation was still in an early stage, Joseph Kelly, a Tregonissey butcher, received a startling and surprising letter from Edward Black. Black was then still missing, although a warrant was out for his arrest on a false pretences charge in connection with his insurance fiddles.

The letter bore a Liverpool postmark.

Joe, I am heart-broken [it read], and can't stand it any longer, so now I am going to Annie. God bless her: she will forgive me if nobody else will. So farewell to all my friends. I never thought you would have kicked me when I was down, but never mind, old friend, you can't hurt a dead man, and the people who are telling such horrible lies about me will have their day.

Well, Joe, for one thing, I can't understand. For God's sake why doesn't Dr Andrew tell the others the state of Annie's heart, *the same what he told it to me* [my italics]. Ask him to be a man and not a cad. What does he mean by suggesting arsenic. My God, Joe, you know me better than that.

So now farewell to you from a heartbroken, miserable man whom I hope God will forgive.

The letter of a highly religious man racked with eternal guilt at murdering his wife? Or the letter of a highly religious man sick at heart at having defrauded those who had become his friends, and cast down by the tragedy of his wife's death? Your estimate is as good as mine.

Black was eventually traced to a temperance hotel in Liverpool. At about midnight on 21 November 1921, a detective knocked on his third-floor bedroom door. 'Right, wait a minute,' Black called. The detective did not wait. He forced open the door.

The room was in darkness. By the light of his torch he saw Black sitting on his bed; his hand to his throat, blood pouring down through his fingers.

Black had tried to commit suicide.

Edward Black was rushed to hospital. Gradually the wound in his neck healed.

And while he was still in his hospital bed the inquest on his wife opened – hundreds of miles away in the lecture hall at St Austell. By now Home Office analytical chemist John Webster had reported on his examination of Annie Black's inner organs. He gave evidence before the coroner and his local jury.

What had he found? A total of one-seventeenth of a grain of arsenic in the body – although two grains is the minimum fatal dose. He explained that far more could, of course, have been administered to the woman in her lifetime – but he could not be certain of this. 'It is quite possible for all of it to disappear even if the deceased had had fatal doses,' he said.

What about the fact that Edward Black had left home three full days before his wife died? That, too, did not deter Mr Webster. He said that if sufficient damage to the dead woman's system had been caused before Black disappeared, she could well have lived on for a few days afterwards though it would have been unusual.

Moreover, this view has been confirmed to me by a modern pathologist.

But although both doctors Gilchrist and Andrew were later to say that 'undoubtedly', in their view, arsenical poisoning was the cause of death – Mr Webster was more guarded.

'It is not possible from the analysis itself to say that death was due to arsenical poisoning,' he said. They were fair words. And Edward Black sorely needed fairness.

The inquest was adjourned. Edward Black spent Christmas 1921 in a prison hospital bed in Liverpool. Three days later he was pronounced fit to travel.

When the inquest reconvened on 5 January 1922, Black was present in court. He had not yet been charged with her murder. He was in custody – but merely on the false pretence charge. He could hardly try to escape. He was still weak from his suicide attempt. He sat with bowed head, coughed and shivered and, to quote an eye-witness, 'appeared very unwell.'

Yet the authorities made him sit in court with a uniformed police sergeant on one side and a uniformed constable on the other. He had no lawyer to speak for him. No one to defend him. He looked as if he had already been tried – and found guilty.

Neighbours, Cornish folk, friends of his wife, gave evidence of Annie's last illness. How she was said to have complained of 'the beastly medicine' that Black had given her, prescribed by Dr Andrew.

How it was 'very funny' that when a woman neighbour gave her the medicine, it never seemed to hurt her – although she generally was ill after her husband gave it to her.

How she said to another neighbour: 'I will not take any more of this medicine if I am to die this minute.'

And how, after Black disappeared, she told another friend: 'If I come to the window and shout to you, will you come across and defend me in case Black comes back, as I will not have him in the house.'

It is not easily understood how the local coroner allowed the majority of this tittle-tattle to be given in evidence. Most of what the dead woman was alleged to have said was when Black was not present. It was hearsay – and should have been ruled legally inadmissible.

Yet it is not difficult to imagine its effect upon the local jury, sitting there spellbound.

For most of the time, Black was inert, silent. At one point, he fainted and had to be revived with a glass of water. At only one stage did he pull himself alert and listen attentively to the evidence.

This was when a local St Austell chemist was in the witness-box, giving evidence that 'at about 3.30 in the afternoon' on Saturday, 29 October 1921 – two days before Dr Andrew was called in to treat Annie's 'gastro-enteritis' – Edward Black was in his shop buying two ounces of arsenic.

'He said he wanted it for poisoning rats. He signed the poison book.' And the chemist produced the book – with the signature 'E. E. Black.'

This was deadly. This was not just village gossip. This was a vitally incriminating piece of evidence that could easily place the noose firmly round Edward Black's already damaged neck.

He struggled to his feet. Haltingly, he told the chemist that he was wrong. He had not bought any arsenic then—or ever.

'The signature is not mine,' he said.

At 4.15 pm the jury retired to consider their verdict. Suddenly, something again seems to have stirred in Black's misty consciousness.

He asked the coroner for permission to make a statement. 'I

want to take the oath,' he said. The coroner agreed. The jury were recalled.

In a long, rambling speech – at times, his voice so low that spectators had to crane forward to hear – Black protested his innocence.

Pointing at the chemist, he said: 'There is the man who says I purchased arsenic two days before they say my wife was ill. My wife was taken ill before then. There are witnesses in court who can say that she was taken ill at the dance on the previous Thursday night.'

He denied that he could physically have been in the chemist's shop at 3.30 on the Saturday afternoon: 'I want to say that I never left my wife by herself to go to St Austell to buy anything at all until the Saturday night at eight o'clock.' And then he only went to get some cigarettes for her shop.

'I was the man to call the doctor in, on the Monday,' he declared. 'Why should I want to do my wife any injury whatever? It is no gain to me. I am out to lose, not to gain. I did my best for her, as anybody can say. I want to ask if there is any man, woman or child who can point the finger at me and say I was ever cruel to my wife. I challenge them to do so now.'

It was a tense, dramatic moment. No one challenged the solitary, swaying figure pleading passionately for his good name – and his life.

The jury retired again. And returned less than fifteen minutes later with the unanimous verdict: 'Annie Black died from arsenical poisoning unlawfully, feloniously and with malice aforethought administered by Edward Black, her husband.'

The coroner committed Black for trial at the next Bodmin Assizes. Technically the jury's verdict was not the end of the story. It was not a definite court finding of guilt. It merely entitled the coroner to commit Black for trial and the police to charge Black formally with Annie's murder. Which they promptly did.

Legally, the inquest verdict was merely an episode in the tale. But so far as the locals were concerned, it merely confirmed what they were already saying: that Black was guilty.

The following Friday the local weekly newspaper *Cornish Guardian* published a photograph of Black sitting dispiritedly in court between a uniformed sergeant and constable: a photograph which could not now be legally taken.

And the St Austell Deputy Registrar wrote in the official Register of Deaths that revealing entry: 'Cause of death: Arsenical poisoning by Edward Ernest Black. Murder.'

Everyone seems to have forgotten the basic legal verity that a man is presumed innocent until his guilt is proved.

A new ordeal now began for Black. The Director of Public Prosecutions in London through his local representative, Penzance solicitor Mr J. Vivian Thomas, asked the St Austell magistrates to commit Black for trial as well.

The *Cornish Guardian* reported: 'In cold, relentless, and damaging terms Mr J. Vivian Thomas eloquently laid bare the facts upon which the prosecution hoped to bring home the crime of murder against Black.'

The magistrates' hearing took two whole days. Again, Black was alone. It was long before the days of the modern legal aid system and he had no lawyer to advise or defend him. The witnesses against him had another opportunity to perfect their evidence. And this time they were supported by the testimony of Sir William Willcox, Home Office consultant and one of the most eminent forensic experts in the country.

'In your opinion was death in this case caused by the administration of arsenic?' Mr J. Vivian Thomas asked him.

'Yes,' replied Sir William.

'Acting on the debilitated state of a patient suffering from kidney trouble?'

'Yes.'

'Would the death of the patient have occurred from the kidney trouble apart from the administration of arsenic?'

'No, certainly not!'

Firm answers. But the woman did have a weak kidney and there was a local epidemic of gastro-enteritis, which in extreme cases can cause death.

Can you imagine what Marshall Hall would have made of the case? Can you imagine what a really high-powered defender could have done with such testimony? With such a chink in the prosecution's armour to work on?

But the chairman of the St Austell Bench announced: 'We are quite satisfied a prima facie case has been made out against you, Black, on the capital charge.' For the second time he was committed for trial at the next Bodmin Assizes. No one was surprised.

The rest was anti-climax. Black's trial opened in Bodmin's grey-stoned assize court on 1 February 1922. Townsfolk from St Austell crowded into horse-drawn wagonettes to make the journey to witness the spectacle.

But it was no great courtroom epic. Black, at last, now had a barrister. But it was no spell-binding KC such as Marshall Hall or Sir Henry Curtis Bennett. Under the Poor Prisoners Defence Regulations, he was defended by John Lhind Pratt, a thirty-seven-year-old junior barrister with only thirteen years' experience behind him.

In later life Pratt, brother of famous actor Boris Karloff, was a London stipendiary magistrate. And as a young student I remember occasionally seeing him in court. He was then an old man, but still very much in command.

As a young barrister defending Black on a murder charge he did all he could. He put up a brave fight. In particular he elicited from Marion, Annie's seventeen-year-old daughter, that her mother 'was unwell with indigestion a few days before 29 October'.

On any objective view, that was crucial. It confirmed, from the dead woman's own child, that Black had been telling the truth when, in his outburst in the coroner's court, he had claimed that Annie had been ill before the day that the local chemist said he had bought arsenic.

But Pratt did not press the chemist on one important change in his testimony. Remember that in the coroner's court he had said that Black had visited his shop 'at about 3.30 in the afternoon', and Black had said that he had not gone out until about eight o'clock that evening?

Now the chemist gave as the time of Black's visit anything between noon and eight o'clock!

A new witness gave evidence. The chemist's young girl assistant. And she gave the time of the alleged visit as about ten past six in the evening.

Marshall Hall – or even any strong modern defender – would have exploded at such discrepancies. But Pratt just went quietly on.

On the other hand, the prosecution was not lacking in strength, Holman Gregory, KC, later an Old Bailey judge, led for the Crown. He did not bother too much about any absence of motive: 'In consequence of this man wickedly desiring his wife's end—because she was an old woman *or some other reason* [my italics]—he decided to kill her,' he airily told the jury.

Home Office analyst John Webster and distinguished consultant Sir William Willcox repeated their former evidence. And the judge, Mr Justice Rowlatt, gave the jury a clear indication as to where their duty lay:

> You have had a very great deal of scientific evidence, the best that can be got [he said]. Sir William Willcox and Mr Webster are among the most eminent gentlemen in the kingdom that could give it. To persons like you and me, who are not medical men, or chemists, their arguments and conclusions were sometimes difficult to follow and criticize, and you have to take a certain amount for granted.

Sir Sidney Rowlatt was a judge of the old school. In the words of his biographer, 'He rarely reserved, and almost never wrote, a judgement.' Crisp and to the point, he, in effect, told the jury to touch their forelocks and do as the gentry told them.

Which they did. After a two-day trial, the jury took only forty minutes to return a verdict of Guilty.

Asked if he had anything to say before sentence of death, Black stood silent in the dock. It seemed as if he had not heard the question. Without further preamble, Mr Justice Rowlatt passed sentence.

John Pratt appealed to the Court of Criminal Appeal in London on behalf of his client. He complained that Mr Justice Rowlatt had totally omitted to remind the jury, in his summing up, of Marion's evidence that her mother had been unwell before Black's alleged visit to the chemist's shop. And he attacked Rowlatt's decision to allow the neighbours' largely hearsay evidence to be given.

But the Court ruled: 'There has been no misdirection. There are no grounds for the appeal and it must be dismissed.'

No one got very upset about what was happening in a remote part of the West Country. There was no nationwide petition for a reprieve. No Press campaign for mercy. On 24 March 1922, Edward Black was hanged.

It is impossible to consider this case without a feeling of sadness. And of anger.

There was only one piece of really solid evidence against

Black – the purchase of arsenic sworn to by the chemist and his assistant, corroborated by his apparent signature in the poisons book. The rest was all tittle-tattle, surmise – and prejudice.

One must concede that he could have been guilty. Yet he did not get a fair deal. He never stood a decent chance of defending himself.

And there persists the awful, nagging doubt that, in truth, he was innocent. I pose these five vital questions – and we can each give our own answers:

1. Was it safe to convict – let alone hang – the man when only a minute portion of a fatal dose was found in the dead woman's body?

2. Is there no possibility of doubt, when one remembers that he left home three days before she died?

3. Is it feasible that he would visit the chemist in a small country town, where the staff knew him, to buy the fatal arsenic, and meekly sign his name in the poisons book? Doesn't the time discrepancy in the chemist's evidence help to show a possible mistake?

4. Why was no handwriting expert called by the Crown to prove that the signature in the poisons book was his?

5. Above all, how could you safely hang the man when the prosecution itself could not suggest a valid motive for the crime?

But they did hang him. They hanged a man who had been formally pronounced guilty of murder even before he stepped into the dock.

5 *Devlin and Burns*
The Strange Alibi

Wavertree, not far from the centre of Liverpool, is a complex of terraced, Coronation Street-type houses: neat, well painted, solidly working class – but some with cars parked outside.

Neighbour still knows neighbour. As they did in the summer of 1951 when a fifty-two-year-old widow named Mrs Beatrice Alice Rimmer lived in Cranbourne Road.

'Oh, yes, I remember her,' an elderly resident told me. 'She was a bit of a recluse. Lived alone. Kept herself to herself. She didn't go out to work and they said her husband must have left her some money. They said she used to keep it round the house.'

This local belief in the wealth of Mrs Rimmer in her little, two-storey house led to her murder.

At about ten o'clock on the evening of Sunday, 19 August 1951, Mrs Rimmer turned into Cranbourne Road. Then, as now, the street lighting was not too good.

She had been visiting her younger married son, an ex-policeman. She was holding some flowers he had given her as she inserted her key in her front door, and walked alone into the darkness.

Next day, her neighbour noticed Mrs Rimmer's milk uncollected on the doorstep. Her newspaper remained in the letterbox.

At 7.15 pm her son called to see her. He rang the bell. There was no reply. He pushed the newspaper through the letterbox – and saw his mother's body lying crumpled in the hall. She still had her outdoor clothes on. The flowers had fallen from her hand and lay scattered beside her. She was covered in blood.

There were fifteen wounds on the back of her head. Some had been caused by a light instrument with a sharp cutting edge, others by a blunter instrument which had broken the scalp.

This appalling violence had not resulted in her immediate death. She had lingered for hours, lying alone in her own hall as life ebbed away.

Robbery could be the only possible motive. But nothing was missing.

It looked as if Mrs Rimmer's two assailants – the different instruments indicated two men – must have got in through a broken rear window. Then, it was assumed, they waited for her return, intending to make her tell them where she kept her money hidden. But they must have hit her too hard, panicked, gone on hitting her as she lay defenceless on the ground – and then fled.

But who were these assailants? Detectives found many fingerprints but they were all Mrs Rimmer's.

There were no missing articles to trace through the small-time 'fences' of Liverpool's seedy underworld.

Some youths were arrested and charged with house-breaking in the area, also through a broken rear window. But blood on their clothes turned out to be a different group from Mrs Rimmer's.

Weeks went by. Detectives scoured the billiard halls, public houses, all-night cafes, dance halls, and lodging houses of central Liverpool. But the case seemed insoluble. There simply were no leads.

In charge of the investigation was the late Chief Superintendent 'Bert' Balmer. I knew Balmer. He was the finest kind of senior police officer – honest, hard-working; relying as much upon his experience and intimate knowledge of his area as upon the methods of modern forensic science.

He was popular even among crooks. And towards the end of September 1951, more than a month after the murder of Mrs Rimmer, he had a tip-off: 'There's a prisoner in Walton Jail [Liverpool's prison] who knows who the murderers are.'

Soon Balmer was talking to a young house-breaker aged nineteen. There is no point in my giving his name. He may now be leading an honest life. Then he was a thoroughly dishonest character – with a criminal record which had started at the age of nine.

But the police cannot ignore evidence because the witness is not of high moral character. They have to take what help they can – from wherever it comes.

The youth was not anxious to talk. 'I'm no squealer,' he said. But under Balmer's gentle probing he told how about a week before the murder he had met two men in an all-night cafe. 'They wanted to do a job and said they had a good one specked in Cranbourne Road. It was a woman who lived there by herself.' If necessary, said the youth in jail, she would be 'attended to'. He agreed to join them, and the job was set for the weekend Mrs Rimmer died.

But on the Friday he was arrested as an Army deserter – and was in jail at the time of the murder. The two men did the job without him.

They were not Liverpool men. They came from Manchester, over thirty miles away. He named them: 'A man called Alf Burns and another named Ted Devlin.'

At last, Balmer had his first real break.

The word of a man in jail, though not sufficient for an instant arrest, concentrated the inquiries on two suspects – and their associates. Balmer and his Liverpool detectives, working closely with the Manchester police, traced two girls: seventeen-year-old 'Chinese Marie', who hung around Liverpool's all-night cafes, and a twenty-one-year-old Manchester girl of similar habits.

Their statements to Balmer – if true – were damning against the two men named by the Walton Jail prisoner. The Manchester girl, who was Devlin's latest girl friend, told how they had plotted 'a job with an old woman in Liverpool', but she had refused to help them as a look-out.

'Chinese Marie', who had recently teamed up with Burns, admitted she had agreed to help them and had actually driven with them to Wavertree in a taxi the night Mrs Rimmer died. But at the last moment they had said they did not need her and she had met them afterwards.

Then – so she said – they were both 'very nervous': 'Will the woman live?' asked Devlin. 'To Hell with the woman. We'll be out of Liverpool before long,' said Burns.

Probably with 'Chinese Marie's' help, Balmer also interviewed a young Liverpool man who said that on the Friday before the murder—after the Walton Jail prisoner had been arrested—he had met Burns and Devlin with 'Chinese Marie' outside Liverpool's Central Station.

And, said the informant, Devlin had asked him to 'do a job' with them that weekend—in Wavertree. At first, he had said 'Yes'. Then he had changed his mind.

Who were these two men, Burns and Devlin? Police records

quickly showed they were Manchester house-breakers with a string of convictions. Both were still in their early twenties.

Balmer decided the time had come to pull them in.

At about 8.15 pm on 10 October 1951, nearly two months after Mrs Rimmer's death, Edward Francis Devlin was arrested as he entered a Manchester milk bar.

Immediately – and always thereafter – he denied his guilt: 'I was not in Liverpool at the time of the murder and I did not hear of a murder while I was there or since until tonight,' he said in a written statement.

At once, he gave an alibi – or an alibi of sorts: 'Round about the time of the murder I was doing screwing jobs [breakings-in] at Manchester, Hulme, Deansgate, and other places.... I was screwing on 10 August to the end of the month, and I was probably screwing a gaff on 19 August.'

That was the night Mrs Rimmer was killed. These words were later to prove of crucial importance.

Alfred Burns was traced the following day – in Manchester's Strangeways Prison, where he had been taken some days before as an absconder from Borstal.

He, too, immediately protested his innocence – 'I didn't do the murder' – but was not so specific as Devlin about a possible alibi.

He said: 'All the time from the day we first met the girls and for the next two or three weeks I was with Devlin all the time. I can't say exactly where I was, but my mother will be able to give me an idea.'

Their clothing was sent for analysis by forensic experts. But the report was none too encouraging for the police: some stains were found. But both sets of clothes had recently been cleaned, and there was insufficient evidence to say positively if the stains were human blood, let alone if they came from Mrs Rimmer's blood group.

The young Liverpool man who claimed he had been approached on the Friday to help in the 'Wavertree job' failed to pick them out at an identification parade — although he afterwards said he was too 'nervous' to do so.

The Walton Jail prisoner readily identified them – but the taxi driver who had driven 'Chinese Marie' and two young men to the Wavertree district on the day Mrs Rimmer died said he had not seen their faces.

No murder weapon had been found. There were no incriminating bloodstains or fingerprints. The case against these two young members of the underworld depended almost entirely on the evidence of a man already in prison, another man who admitted he had initially agreed to be party to a house-breaking and on the story of two girls of obviously low moral character.

Basically, it was word against word. And for all Balmer's outward confidence, he must have had considerable inner doubts as to whether his case would stand up in court.

Richard Whittington Egan was then one of the leading crime reporters in Liverpool. 'I was present at the magistrates' court during the committal proceedings,' he told me.

'Devlin was insolent – whispering and sniggering to his companion in the dock. I never saw two people on a serious charge so unaffected by the circumstances in which they found themselves.

'I was later to see them at the trial. I expected to see a change in their demeanour after their long weeks in prison.

'But they were still as cocky as ever. They saw themselves as gangster heroes.'

Two unpleasant young men. But were they murderers? And could the Crown prove its case?

The trial opened at Liverpool Assizes on 13 December 1951. It unfolded slowly. The girls and other prosecution witnesses gave their evidence and were cross-examined strongly and with high ability by Miss Rose Heilbron, KC for Devlin and by Sir Noel Goldie, KC for Burns.

There was no untoward incident until about halfway through the fourth day, when Sir Noel Goldie asked a Liverpool detective inspector: 'Am I right in saying that on the night of the alleged murder a burglary and breaking-in was committed at the Sun Blinds Ltd, 6 Great Jackson Street, Manchester?'

What had this to do with the case? At once, Basil Nield, KC for the Crown – now a High Court judge – rose to object that the question was irrelevant. But Sir Noel brushed the objection aside: 'I don't want it to be said at a later stage that I am taking my learned friend by surprise,' he commented.

For when the two young defendants went into the witness-box they proceeded to give what must surely be one of the most unusual defences to a murder charge ever presented in a modern criminal court.

They claimed that they could not have been in Liverpool on the night of 19 August 1951, murdering Mrs Rimmer – because they were in Manchester on that night burgling the Sun Blinds Ltd's warehouse!

Mr Harry Livermore was Devlin's solicitor. I have discussed the case with him. Now, more than 20 years later, he says: 'It was a very risky alibi to put forward. Indeed if it was a fake alibi, they could have thought up a better one, I would have thought. One wonders why they should choose so damaging an alibi – unless there was some truth in it.'

In any event, he remembers 'having terrible qualms about the allegation and the effect it would have on the jury. I discussed it with counsel. But those were Devlin's instructions, and – together with Burns's representatives – I had no alternative but to put it forward.'

The defence did more than just rely on the two young men's own words that they had done the warehouse breaking. They called as a defence witness – from prison – a man who had been convicted of the crime.

And he claimed under oath that he had not done it alone – but with the two men in the dock.

Obviously a crucial question was: Just how much did Burns and Devlin know about the Manchester break-in? Was their knowledge sufficiently detailed to convince the jury that they had been there?

This issue was probed at the trial, but no conclusive picture emerged. Both men had some knowledge of the Manchester raid – but it might have resulted from direct participation, or from what they had heard about it from criminal contacts.

In his final speech, Basil Nield, KC, called the alibi 'a manufactured alibi' and asked the jury to ignore it.

Sir Noel Goldie, KC, countered: 'Far from being manufactured, it is proved absolutely up to the hilt. I submit to you with the utmost confidence that it would be most dangerous to convict in this case on the evidence which has been called before you.'

It was left to the judge, Mr Justice Finnemore, to point out quietly in his four-and-a-half hour summing up that both the prosecution's case and the defence claim that the men had been in the Manchester raid could be true.

No one had been able to pinpoint the hour of the break-in. Burns and Devlin could have got back to Manchester from Liverpool in time to do it that same night. The case was back to which set of witnesses the jury were prepared to believe: those who gave evidence for the prosecution – or the defence?

After a ten-day trial, the jury took only seventy-five minutes to convict both men of murder.

Devlin gripped the dock rail for support. 'My Lord,' he told the judge. 'I would like to stress that it means the police are not infallible to tell lies. Everything I said in the court is true.'

Burns was less polite: 'As far as the evidence is concerned, I think it has been a fair trial,' he said. 'But as far as the judge is concerned, I think he has given a prejudiced view of the case.'

Mr Justice Finnemore sentenced them both to death.

Mr Livermore and Mr Joseph Norton, Burns's solicitor, announced that there would be an appeal. The hearing was fixed for Monday, 31 March 1952. But three days before the court sat, a Liverpool newspaper reported: 'There may be a surprise development at the hearing in the Court of Criminal Appeal.'

And there was!

Before starting her legal argument that Mr Justice Finnemore had misdirected the jury, Miss Rose Heilbron, QC, asked Lord Goddard, the Lord Chief Justice, and his two fellow appeal judges to allow her to call new evidence – a procedure almost never permitted in the Court of Criminal Appeal.

The new evidence? A fifteen-year-old girl had come forward to say that after the trial, Devlin's Manchester girl friend, who had given such damning evidence against him, had told her that she had not spoken the truth when she said that Devlin and Burns plotted the robbery and asked her to join in.

The true murderer was the father of her child, Devlin's girl was alleged to have told the fifteen-year-old.

If Devlin's girl really had said this, how could the appeal court uphold the convictions? Surely, there must be a doubt? But Lord Goddard refused Miss Heilbron's application: 'If necessary, that matter can be submitted to those whose duty it is to advise the Crown in these matters. It is not a matter which this court can go into.' The appeal judges dismissed the appeal.

Miss Heilbron took Lord Goddard's hint about 'those whose

duty is to advise the Crown in these matters'. After the court rose, she hurried round to see Sir Lionel Heald, QC, the Attorney General, who then approached Sir David Maxwell Fyfe, QC, the Home Secretary.

Two days later, legal history was made. The Home Office announced that Mr Denis Gerrard, a leading QC on the Northern Circuit, and later a High Court judge, was to conduct an immediate inquiry into the reliability of the new evidence: to 'consider any further relevant information laid before him and to report whether, in his opinion, the result of his investigation affords any reasonable grounds for thinking that there has been or may have been a miscarriage of justice.' The execution date had already been fixed for 18 April 1952.

Working in secrecy and against the clock, Mr Gerrard examined a succession of witnesses who were called before him. The Manchester girl gave evidence. So did Devlin, but not Burns, possibly because he was not so directly involved in the 'new evidence' issue as Devlin was. Devlin questioned many of the people who had already given evidence at the trial, and others besides. The condemned men's counsel were present, but Mr Gerrard did all the questioning.

Finally, on 21 April – four days before the execution date – Mr Gerrard published his report. He accepted that the Manchester girl had said afterwards that her trial evidence was false and the true murderer was the father of her child – but in front of him she had gone back on that. She said she had spoken the truth when under oath at the trial.

So why had she lied to the fifteen-year-old girl? 'Her motives for making the untrue statements are a matter of speculation only,' said Mr Gerrard.

After considering carefully all the evidence, he reported that in his opinion 'there has been no miscarriage of justice.'

The desperate battle to save these two young men's lives continued. Their solicitors, with the help of Miss Heilbron and her junior counsel, drafted a memorandum, setting out grounds for a reprieve. This document was rushed to Home Secretary Sir David Maxwell Fyfe. The widowed mothers of the two condemned men gathered signatures for a petition, and wrote pleading for mercy to the Queen.

But at 9.00 am on Friday, 25 April 1952, the two men were hanged at Walton Jail.

Some weeks later Lord Goddard made legal history. He initiated a debate in the House of Lords using the Burns and Devlin case as an argument for giving the Court of Criminal Appeal the right to order a new trial – a complete re-hearing of a case in front of a fresh judge and jury.

He made it clear that he was in no way criticizing Denis Gerrard, QC, for the way in which he had conducted the inquiry. But the whole procedure was wrong. 'There was,' he said, 'no power to order a new trial, but what is in fact a new trial took place without oath, without counsel and in private.'

In due course, this pronouncement from the Lord Chief Justice of England had its effect. The Home Secretary set up a special committee to investigate the powers of the Court of Criminal Appeal.

And eventually – thirteen years after the trial of Burns and Devlin – the 1964 Criminal Justice Act gave the court the power to order a new trial. There would be no more secret prison inquiries with a distinguished QC trying to grapple with the problem of an accused man's guilt or innocence.

Burns and Devlin were two baby-faced young villains. But should they have died a dishonourable death within the walls of prison?

I leave the last word with Devlin's solicitor, Mr Livermore: 'A capital charge which found the Court of Criminal Appeal in some difficulty and which resulted in (1) an independent inquiry being carried out and (2) the Court of Criminal Appeal being ultimately empowered to order a new trial in suitable cases, must inevitably raise a feeling of doubt.'

6   *John Williams*
Conviction by a Trick

The wooden seat is still there. It is painted green and white and faces out to sea at the western end of Eastbourne seafront, where the ground starts to rise towards Beachy Head. Away to the left stretch the cliffs of Hastings; beneath, the grey waters of the Channel.

On the same seat sixty years ago a young girl named Florence Seymour had sat and waited for her lover. They had been out for a walk. Then he had excused himself, saying he had 'business' to do near by. After about twenty minutes he returned and they wandered back together down to the town.

They made an affectionate, tender couple. She leaned on his arm – for, although they were not married, she was pregnant with his child.

Her companion's name was John Williams. He was the twenty-nine-year-old son of a Scottish clergyman. He was of good family and education, but he had lived a life of crime ... larceny, house-breaking, burglary. Later he claimed that he had given up crime. He was to say: 'I have gone straight because of Florence.'

But was this true? And what was he doing while his 'wife' – as he called her – sat and waited on that seat on the seafront?'

For many years Eastbourne has been a prosperous town: a leading South Coast resort with a mild climate, making it popular both with summer visitors and comfortably-off, all-year-round residents.

In October 1912 one such resident was middle-aged Countess Sztaray, daughter of an Hungarian nobleman and an English mother. She lived, in some style, in a three-storeyed house in South Cliff Avenue ... near where Florence Seymour sat looking out to sea.

At about 7.15 on the evening of Wednesday, 9 October 1912, the countess's coachman waited outside her door. He was due to take her to a nearby hotel for dinner.

It was dark and the street had little lighting. But suddenly the coachman saw the shape of a man lying silently on the flat porch over the door.

The coachman did not panic. When the countess came out, he drove off. Then in the next road, he stopped and told her what had happened.

She must have been a courageous woman. She told him to turn back. Then she calmly walked back into the house – with the black outline of the intruder still lurking on the porch.

She telephoned the police. Within minutes, forty-four-year-old Inspector Albert Walls – moustached, highly respected, over twenty years in the force – arrived.

The waiting coachman saw him enter the front garden. 'Here, old chap, come down!' called the inspector. The man on the porch moved. A gun flared. The inspector staggered back.

The coach horse bolted in fear. By the time the coachman managed to control it and return to the house Inspector Walls was dead. He had been shot through the heart.

The man from the porch had disappeared. But a neighbour picked up a grey trilby hat, lying in the gutter. 'It must have been his,' he said. It was the only clue.

Inspector Walls was a popular policeman, well known in the town. And Eastbourne, not accustomed to violence, was shocked.

The local police had little experience of murder investigation and that night Scotland Yard was called in. Before lunch the next day Chief Inspector Eli Bower stepped off the London train.

A policeman had been killed. And there is always an extra edge to a murder investigation when the victim is a fellow police officer. Bower – grim, experienced – was the man to hunt down remorselessly a colleague's killer, and not be too particular how he did it.

Routine measures were taken: the porch was searched for fingerprints. A mould of footprints was taken from the countess's front garden. Inquiries started into tracing ownership of the hat found in the gutter. But none of these obvious ploys looked too hopeful.

Then at about five o'clock on the first afternoon, within twenty-four hours of the murder, a swarthy young man walked into Eastbourne police station and asked to see Chief Inspector Bower.

'My name is Edgar Power,' he said. He had both a story to tell – and a proposition to make.

His story: that he knew who the murderer was. The killer, he said, was a friend of his: 'a burglar named John Williams.' Williams, according to Power, had been in Eastbourne for a few days with his girl friend, Florence Seymour.

That morning (said Power) Williams's brother, who lived in London, had received an urgent letter-card posted the previous night, asking him to 'save my life' by coming down at once with some money.

The brother had contacted Power and the two had travelled from London to Eastbourne together. The brother was at that moment already on the train back to London with John Williams. 'I am going back now to collect Florence Seymour and her luggage and take her as well,' Power told Chief Inspector Bower.

His proposition was that he would help the police track down John Williams. If they were prepared to co-operate, he would lead them to their man.

What motive would this self-described friend of Williams have for such an action? One still does not know. It has been suggested that it was jealousy – that he was himself in love with Florence Seymour and wanted Williams out of the way.

It was an extremely odd situation. But Bower eagerly accepted the chance it offered. He must surely have known, or at least suspected, that Power too had a criminal record. But, the saying goes, 'Set a thief to catch a thief.'

Power – followed by detectives – went back for Florence Seymour. He travelled with her to London, booked her in at an hotel, and then made an appointment with John Williams to meet him the following afternoon at Moorgate Underground station.

At 4.45 pm on Friday, 11 October 1912, Chief Inspector Bower arrested Williams at Moorgate station as he was talking earnestly with his 'friend' Edgar Power.

Charged with Inspector Wall's murder, Williams said: 'I am perfectly innocent of this. I would not do such a thing.' The young man who now faced a murder charge was well dressed, calm, clean-featured.

The following day, in the train to Eastbourne with Bower, Williams said: 'Do you think if I had done that, I should have the cheek to lie on that small piece of board while the countess was dressing?

'Wouldn't it have been easier to have watched the lights go down and the lady leave – and then go in?' It was perhaps a telling point for a professional – or ex-professional – burglar to make.

And he gave an alibi: 'On Wednesday evening' – the night of the murder – 'I went with my wife to the picture palace to see *Danie*. There was a fellow there who sang a song which I don't remember.'

Why had he left Eastbourne so suddenly after the shooting? Because he was frightened that the police, knowing of his record, might pick him up.

The authorities were taking no chances. On Williams's arrival, Eastbourne railway station was closed to the public. He was taken to the police station with a hood over his head, so that later no defence counsel could complain that any identifying witness had been influenced by seeing his picture in the newspapers.

'The Hooded Man' was the name the Press gave from then on to John Williams.

The investigation soon hit snags. That Saturday night Williams stood in line with eight other men but neither the Countess Sztaray nor her coachman picked him out. In the dark neither had caught a clear glimpse of the intruder's face.

Where did that leave Chief Inspector Bower? He had made a highly publicized arrest. And now all he had against Williams was suspicion because he had suddenly left town and the accusation of an informer with a criminal record.

Although one will never know for sure, it seems almost certain that Bower called in Edgar Power to see him again. Could he be of any further help? What about the girl, Florence Seymour – was there any possibility there?

Now came a strange development. On the following Tuesday morning Edgar Power and Florence Seymour travelled from London to Eastbourne together by train. They went to a part of the beach by the Redoubt, an old Martello tower that still stands.

There they began to search the shingle, and while doing so they were both arrested by policemen who had been waiting for them. The police had, in fact, been tipped off to be there by Power.

Florence wept and screamed. The police probed among the stones. And they found a gun – John Williams's gun.

For five hours Florence was interrogated by Chief Inspector Bower. She was terrified and hysterical. She signed a statement that on the night of the murder she waited on that seat on the front while John Williams went off, and then returned without his hat. Next day, according to Florence, Williams saw the announcement of Inspector Walls's shooting 'by a burglar' in a shop window and sent the urgent letter-card to his brother.

Then, she said, he took out his gun, wiped it free of fingerprints and the following morning they buried it together on the beach.

If that statement stood up in court it was enough to hang John Williams. It proved conclusively that on the night of the murder – and round about the time of the murder – this convicted burglar, armed with a gun, was in the immediate vicinity where Inspector Walls was shot.

If the purpose of staging that dramatic scene on the beach was to force Florence into admissions she might have withheld under less tense circumstances, Chief Inspector Bower and Ed Power (who was released soon after his 'arrest') must have felt satisfied with their work.

Next day, the weekly *Eastbourne Gazette* assured its readers:

> It is one of the most honourable characteristics of the Eastbourne authorities that they aim not at straining the law against any accused person, but at arriving at the truth. The suspect now in custody will have every opportunity of making his defence, and the police have already taken exceptional provisions to guard against anything remotely approaching unfairness.

It is certain that such a claim would be true today. But when one considers the John Williams case, one has doubts about its truth in October 1912.

A few days after Florence had tearfully signed her statement and been allowed, at last, to go home, the telephone rang in the Temple chambers of Cecil Whiteley, aquiline, resourceful prosecuting counsel.

The Director of Public Prosecutions was speaking: 'Willie Mathews here,' he said. 'Put yourself in a taxi and come round and see me. I want you to appear for the prosecution in the Eastbourne murder.'

Many years later, Whiteley related in his memoirs how Mathews – 'standing in front of the fire in his characteristic attitude with legs apart and smoking a cigarette in a long holder' – told him that, in the absence of any identification at the scene of the crime, 'Florence Seymour's evidence would be vital for the prosecution.

'She is in love with this man, my dear Cecil, and is pregnant by him. When you call her into the witness-box and she sees him in the dock, she will either faint or have her baby – but whatever happens, you must get her evidence on the dispositions.'

And, like a competent prosecutor, Whiteley did that, despite Florence's tears and entreaties, and moaned exclamations of 'Oh God! Oh God!' as she stood in the witness-box at Eastbourne police court, with her lover and the father of her unborn child in the dock a few feet away from her.

But despite all Whiteley's skills, there were still some gaps in Florence's evidence. When he asked her, 'Did you go out in the evening?' the reply was: 'Yes, on that evening or the evening of the preceding day – I am not positive which – we went out about 6.30.'

And again: 'When he came back had he a hat?' – 'No, he had no hat on then, but he was always in the habit of putting it in his pocket.'

But most important of all, she said: 'We went straight along the front towards Beachy Head. We sat on a seat near the top of South Cliff Avenue. I am not sure of the night. I can't remember distinctly, but I know it was the night we spoke to a lady about a baby crying.'

And that, as was later established, meant not the night of the murder, but the previous night.

Now remember Florence had not seen her lover since he had left for London with his brother the day after the murder. There had been no communication between them. No opportunity for them to concoct an invented story. Yet there she is frightened and almost fainting in the box – talking about the possibility of the whole incident having occurred the previous night, when it would have had no relevance to the murder.

Despite the *Eastbourne Gazette*'s assertions of fairness, John Williams had no lawyer to defend him in court. Nowadays, there is legal aid. Then, there was merely rough justice – at least in the lower courts. Yet Florence Seymour's evidence was crucial. It had to be questioned at the earliest possible instance.

Williams – alone, untrained, with nine magistrates looking down at him – stood up and faced the court. 'I know that she is in a delicate condition, and I would have preferred not to question her now,' he told the chairman of the Bench.

'But it is a vital matter to me and I must.'

Slowly, gently he questioned Florence Seymour. He asked her about the evening she sat and waited for him: 'Was it the evening we spoke to the lady about the crying baby?'

'Yes,' she said.

He asked her about the gun: 'When I cleaned it, did I only rub it or clean out all the chambers?'

'I saw you just rub it,' said the girl. 'I'll swear my life you did not clean it out.'

The inference was obvious: she was confirming that he had not needed to clean it out. It had not recently been fired.

Quietly, Williams had made two telling points – if only the world would listen.

After Florence left the witness-box, during the luncheon adjournment, he said to a police constable: 'I cannot see how they can keep me after this. But still circumstantial evidence is a funny thing. If I hang I shall hang like a man.'

Of course, they did keep him. There were two more hearings in the Eastbourne police court before the magistrates committed him for trial at Lewes Assizes. 'All that I have to say is that I am innocent of this charge,' he said.

And to his brother he wrote: 'You see they have not got the right fellow, and to pacify the public picked out a poor devil known to the police. I can prove my innocence to the smallest detail.'

It was a confident assertion. At least now he had a lawyer to help him, Harold Glenester, a local solicitor. It still is a mystery where Williams got the money from to pay his fees, but it seems probable that his brother and friends clubbed together.

Yet their funds were not great. They could not afford a KC to lead for the defence. They had to go to a young, comparatively inexperienced – and inexpensive – junior barrister. His name: Patrick Hastings.

In later life, Pat Hastings became probably the most famous

and successful advocate in the country.

'He was brilliant, lucid and calm,' says a retired QC who knew him well. 'But as a young man' – he paused – 'he must have been a terrier!'

Hastings threw himself into this, his first murder defence. He broke his usual rule of not seeing the accused man in prison before the hearing and geared himself to the 'thoroughly unpleasant experience' of an interview with Williams at Lewes Jail:

It was impossible to see Williams for the first time without some slight feeling of admiration [he later wrote in his autobiography]. He was possessed of the quality of unflinching courage. He showed not the faintest sign of fear or even anxiety. He said nothing about the facts of the case except to deny explicitly that he knew anything whatever about the murder.

Hastings asked if he wanted him to try for a manslaughter verdict on the basis that the shot had been fired without any intention to kill. Williams refused: 'I did not fire that shot,' he said. 'I've been in prison before and, although I am completely innocent, I'd rather be hanged than go to prison for another twelve months.'

On 13 December 1912, Williams walked with an alert step into the dock at Lewes Assize Court. 'Not guilty, my lord,' he said in a firm voice.

Sir Frederick Low, KC, MP – ponderous, large and florid of countenance – rose to lead for the prosecution. He had Whiteley as his junior. All the power of the State was summoned up against the accused.

Yet the really vital danger to him came from one sole witness, Florence Seymour, now only days off her confinement, pale, trembling and on the brink of tears as she took the oath to tell 'the truth, the whole truth and nothing but the truth'.

She looked at the maps and the photographs which the jurymen were studying. She smiled faintly at the man in the dock. She agreed she went out one evening in October last with 'my husband'.

The description worried Sir Frederick Low. 'I must ask you the question,' he said. 'You are not, in fact, married?' 'No,' replied Florence, quietly.

Then came the thunderclap. She would say nothing. She

could give no evidence. She knew nothing whatever about the murder.

'But your statement to the police! Your evidence before the magistrates!' spluttered Low.

'They are all untrue,' she cried. 'Inspector Bower told me that if I didn't say differently I would be accused of murder too.'

Normally, a barrister cannot cross-examine his own witness. He cannot ask him leading questions. He cannot seek to probe the answers of the person whom, after all, he has brought into the witness-box.

But with the judge's leave, you can cross-examine your own witness — if he proves to be 'hostile'. Readily Mr Justice Channell accepted Low's submission that he could treat the now near-hysterical Florence as hostile.

For nearly an hour, the leading prosecuting counsel cross-examined the girl in the witness-box heavy with the accused man's child, in an attempt to make her return to her earlier evidence, and to restore the linchpin to the prosecution case.

Yet despite the tears and the drama, Florence seemed to gain strength through her ordeal. Yes, she had been out with Williams along that part of the Eastbourne sea-front — but it was the night before: 'the night when the baby cried in South Cliff Avenue.'

Remember that phrase. Remember how even at the police court she had said: 'I am not sure of the night. I can't remember distinctly, but I know it was the night we spoke to a lady about a baby crying.'

Low could do nothing with her. 'I will not tell anybody anything but the truth,' she said. The tears poured down her face. She gripped tightly the edge of the witness-box.

Hastings had few questions for her. What need was there? In court, as anywhere else, you do not try to gild the lily.

And what about Williams's gun, found on the beach? Why had he taken it down to Eastbourne if he did not intend to use it?

'I would not part with it for anything. I had it with me in Africa,' he had told a policeman. And he claimed the gun was not in working order.

Robert Churchill, the famous gun expert then starting his long and distinguished career, confirmed under Hastings's probing questioning that this might be so. Williams had broken the gun in two pieces before burying it. The hammer and springs were never found – and Churchill had to fix new ones before he could fire it.

This could mean that the missing parts were lost for ever beneath the shingle of Eastbourne beach – or that Williams was telling the truth when he said the gun was unusable before burying it.

Churchill also admitted that the gun was one of the commonest types sold. Although he claimed that the bullet that killed Inspector Walls could have come from that make, he agreed that he could not say – at that stage of scientific knowledge (unlike now) – that it had come from that specific gun.

The gun evidence, therefore, was totally neutral. It neither proved nor disproved Williams's guilt.

Hastings made five other telling points in his cross-examination of the prosecution witnesses:

1. No jury should place any reliance on the evidence of a man such as Edgar Power. Mr Justice Channell agreed. He tersely cut short Hastings's cross-examination: 'The position of this witness is clear.'
2. The prosecution lay great stress on the grey trilby hat found beside the murdered man. But the police confirmed that in Williams's belongings they had found a silk top hat, a yachting cap, a bowler – and a green trilby. Why would he need two trilbys? Was the hat in the gutter his – even though it did fit him?
3. Not one prosecution witness could say they had seen Williams wearing a grey trilby.
4. Williams had not taken his house-breaking gear with him to Eastbourne. The police had found it in the cloakroom at Victoria Station – deposited before he left London.
5. Most vital of all: Chief Inspector Bower agreed that police inquiries had confirmed a baby had been crying in South Cliff Avenue on the night before the murder!

By the time John Williams strode into the witness-box, the case against him – on any objective view – had substantially weakened.

But although he was confident and relaxed as a witness, there was one gaping-wide hole in his testimony. Why was he in South Cliff Avenue the night before the murder? Even if Florence Seymour was right and it was that night, what possible motive could there be for leaving her sitting on the front and going off to explore this perfectly ordinary residential road?

His answer could not have been very satisfactory to the solid Lewes jury: he was examining the road for some friends – who wanted to do a burglary there. 'It wasn't anything to do with me. But I'd met them in Eastbourne, and they had asked me to look around for them.'

'Then it was a sort of reconnaissance that you were making in South Cliff Avenue?' asked Sir Frederick Low. 'Oh, naturally!' replied Williams easily. A shade too easily perhaps for the citizens of Lewes in that jury box.

At 6.25 on the evening of Saturday, 14 December 1912 – at an hour no modern judge would send out a jury – Mr Justice Channell said: 'Gentlemen of the jury, consider your verdict.' It took the jurors only fifteen minutes to return into court. 'Guilty, my lord,' said the foreman.

'I should like to say once again that I am innocent,' cried Williams.

'The sentence I have to pass on you is not my sentence,' said the quavering voice of the seventy-four-year-old judge. 'It is the sentence of the law.'

Florence Seymour fainted as Williams was sentenced to death. A few days later she had her baby. A little girl. Florence was destitute. She had no money, no hospital would take her in. Patrick Hastings and his wife provided for her confinement.

And it was Hastings who argued a passionate two-and-a-half-hour-long speech in the Court of Criminal Appeal to try to persuade sixty-eight-year-old Lord Alverstone, the Lord Chief Justice of England, and two fellow judges to quash John Williams's conviction. But – as Hastings later wrote – 'I was not greatly impressed by Alverstone's acumen. From the outset of the hearing it was apparent that he was satisfied of the prisoner's guilt, and no legal argument seemed to make the least impression upon him.'

The appeal was dismissed, without Sir Frederick Low even being called upon to reply for the prosecution. 'It is quite impossible for us to come to the conclusion that there was not strong, and even conclusive proof to justify the verdict,' said Lord Alverstone.

Hastings tried to take the fight further – to the House of Lords, but the Attorney-General refused leave to do so.

Williams's only hope lay in the possibility of a reprieve.

'I am sure to get reprieved,' he wrote to his brother. 'They cannot hang an innocent man.' And to Florence: 'My Darling Wife – God bless you, darling one. I am in good heart.'

Thirty-five thousand people throughout the country signed a petition pleading for mercy. There was an emergency debate in the House of Commons by MPs anxious to make Home Secretary Reginald McKenna show compassion. But this dour politician who had refused Florence Seymour's post-conviction request to marry Williams in the condemned cell, now refused to save his life.

'The Home Secretary has declined to interfere with the sentence of death pronounced upon John Williams' announced the Home Office on 27 January 1913.

With her baby in her arms, Florence Seymour paid her last visit to her 'husband'. He took the child in his arms, kissed her affectionately – and pressed a small piece of prison bread into her hands. 'Now nobody can ever say that your father has not given you anything,' he said.

At eight o'clock the next day, he was hanged. 'There was no last-minute confession of guilt,' the prison governor afterwards told the coroner.

Was John Williams guilty? Did he fire the shot that killed Inspector Walls? It is very unlikely that we will ever now know. But one thing is certain: according to modern ideas of police fairness and prosecution standards, his guilt was never proved.

And it is sadly ironic that, if only he had married Florence Seymour before they ever went to Eastbourne, he could never have been convicted – even in 1912.

Because without her evidence there was not the start of a case against him. And, of course, a wife cannot be made to give evidence against her husband.

7 Probert and Parker
Hanged for £6

In all the years I have been investigating murder cases from the past, this was a unique experience. I was talking to three men who were giving me a first-hand description of a night nearly forty years ago when each played a vital part in the discovery of an appalling crime.

We were in the saloon bar of the Railway Inn at Portslade, on the outskirts of Brighton. The crime we were discussing was committed just round the corner.

There in his little junk shop eighty-year-old Mr Joseph Bedford was brutally murdered.

'The kids loved him,' said ex-Police Constable Harry Peters. 'He used to give them coppers. But you might call him eccentric. Always wore an old-fashioned high-crown bowler, which he never took off, even indoors. He lived alone. Hardly ever went out. People used to think he was a miser. With buckets of money stashed away about the place.'

Here are their accounts of that cold Monday night in November 1933: Said Mr Peters, 'I was patrolling North Street. It was ten past ten. I had got to the corner of Clarence Street. I saw old Joe hadn't put away his pots and things from outside his shop. Usually he took them in promptly at eight o'clock.

'Eddie Myers, the licensee's son from this pub, came by. I said: "I think something's wrong with old Joe." I sent him to phone for help.'

Bert Myers, present licensee of the Railway Inn, took up the narrative: 'I met my brother Eddie coming back. He told me something was up with old Joe – we all knew him – and I hurried off to help.'

By now Police Constable Peters had flashed his torch through a chink in the glass door. And amid the clutter of junk and general goods he could just make out Joseph Bedford staggering around in the dark: 'He looked horrible. His face was covered with blood. All swollen up. The door was bolted. I broke it down and as I did so he collapsed among a lot of broken glass. I could see at once that there had been a violent struggle.'

He did what he could for the old man who was still breathing but unconscious. Then he checked that the back door was locked. Next he went upstairs, leaving young Bert Myers on guard in the shop.

'There was blood on the floor at the back, on the stairs and on Joe's bed. Obviously the old man, after being attacked, had bolted up the shop, put out the lights, gone upstairs, lain on the bed, got up, come down again, seen me and my torch at the door and tried to come to me – all in a semi-conscious state. He must have been a tough old boy.'

It was glaringly obvious to young Police Constable Peters that old Joe had been savagely attacked.

But his superiors – impressed by the fact that the shop was bolted both back and front from the inside – preferred to consider it an accident. 'The old man must have fallen,' they said. There are many hard edges in the shop on which he could easily have banged his head.

At Hove General Hospital Police Constable Peters sat into the night with the old man. He was dying. For one brief moment he rallied. Peters spoke: 'Joe, it's Harry – Harry Peters. Tell me what happened.'

The old man could only gasp: 'They came in the shop....' His eyes closed again. At 6 am he died. Yet Peters's superiors still, amazingly, treated the case as accidental death.

Then another young policeman came into the story, Detective Constable Holt. He is now ex-Chief Inspector Holt and was the third man to whom I talked in the Portslade public house. 'A doctor at Hove General rang me and said he had a dead man there. Something to do with Portslade. I was Coroner's Officer at the time, and it was my duty to report on sudden deaths to the East Sussex coroner.'

Holt visited Portslade police station, and was told the death seemed accidental. But Harry Peters was a friend of his. The two keen young officers went round to the shop. There – to them – was incontrovertible evidence that Joe Bedford's death was no accident.

Said Mr Holt: 'Coppers were scattered all over the floor. An old chocolate box that Joe used as his till was lying at the back of the counter. Empty.' And Peters found Joe's treasured old bowler hat. It was stove in like a trilby – as if the old man had been struck a tremendous blow on the top of the head.

Nor was that all: amid the junk and rubbish keen-eyed 'Bob' Holt found a black overcoat button, with thread still hanging from it ... as if it had been torn off during a struggle.

Holt reported back to East Sussex coroner Dr E. F. Hoare: 'I'm not satisfied, sir.' 'Right!' said the coroner. 'I'll order a post-mortem.'

A local doctor carried it out. His verdict: death due to a fractured skull causing haemorrhage of the brain, accelerated by shock. The old man had two black eyes and a broken nose. If these injuries had been received in an accident, it must certainly have been some fall! It was another officer's vigilance, plus a large element of chance, that finally put the investigation on a murder basis.

The following day, at Worthing, eight miles along the Sussex coast, Inspector Leonard Lewis looked out of the police station window and noticed two young men – one burly, the other slight – walking along. He had not seen them before. And this was a time, with over two million unemployed, when young men roamed the country. Some of these penniless, rootless youths were on the look-out for what they could steal.

'Do you know them?' he asked his sergeant. 'No, sir.'

'Just keep an eye on them, will you.'

The sergeant left the station and followed them up the road. They came to a tobacconist's. He saw the burly one go on. The other waited outside.

He went up to him. 'Where do you come from?' – 'Folkestone.' Just then the other man came out of the shop – and walked right past them. Why should he do that, unless the sight of a policeman talking to his friend alarmed him?

'That's odd. Your pal doesn't seem to know you,' said the sergeant. 'Wait a minute!' he called out. The other man turned: 'Why don't you want to see your pal?'

'What pal?'

The sergeant sighed: 'I think you'd both better come along with me.'

And so the two men — giving their names as 'Frederick Smith' and 'Jack Williams' – were invited to come to the police station. It looked like just another 'loitering with intent' charge: spotted by a vigilant police inspector and his sergeant.

But at the station 'Frederick Smith', the smaller of the two, suddenly said: 'How's the old man at Portslade?'

What old man? The Worthing police knew nothing about it. Inspector Lewis telephoned the Portslade station. 'I was there when the call came through,' remembers Harry Peters. 'There's a young villain here asking about an old man,' said the inspector. 'You had any trouble lately?'

The two men were searched. 'Smith' admitted that his real name was Frederick William Parker: 'Williams' that he was really Albert Probert. Their clothing was taken away: Parker's was clean, but what looked like bloodstains were on Probert's suit. And in Parker's pockets were twenty-seven farthings – of which Joseph Bedford was known to have been a hoarder.

The two men were questioned closely by Inspector Lewis. And at once a difference in their character – and mutual loyalty – was revealed.

'I don't see why I shouldn't tell you,' said Parker. 'We knocked an old man out in a shop at Portslade on Monday night. We took the money from the till.'

'Do you realize the seriousness of what you're saying?' asked the inspector.

'Yes, I want to get it off my mind,' replied Parker. And he told a detailed tale of how 'we' held up the old man. At that stage he refused to say who 'we' were – 'I don't see why I should give someone else away.' But what he said was enough to damn himself:

'We walked into the shop and spoke to the old shopkeeper. I turned and locked the door. No one was passing at the time, and I brought my revolver into play. The gun was not loaded, but I had no other choice of making the old shopkeeper put up his hands.

'I held him up and the other chap with me – I don't want to mention his name – went round the counter and just knocked him out. I went to the boxes, and we both took money out and put it in our pockets. Those farthings you found on me are some I took from the till. It was somewhere about £6 that we got.'

Probert was much more taciturn. When Inspector Lewis read him Parker's statement, he merely said: 'I don't desire to say anything.'

Scotland Yard was alerted. Famous pathologist Sir Bernard

Spilsbury came down from London to perform a second post-mortem. His findings were formidable: multiple injuries to the head and face. A violent blow to the top of the head, probably heavy fist injuries to the nose, cheek bones, and upper jaw, neck injuries possibly caused by a hand grasping the throat. The picture was not pretty.

Within hours, Chief Inspector Askew, of Scotland Yard, was at Worthing police station. He saw Parker and Probert separately. For the first time, the two men were told that Joseph Bedford was dead.

Said Parker: 'Then I'll tell you what happened. I didn't want him hurt. Now I know he's dead I'll tell you who the other man was. It was the man who is charged with me.' And he gave the Scotland Yard man a more detailed version of much the same statement as he had previously given Inspector Lewis.

But now he added: 'I only told Probert to hit him gently.... He didn't take any notice of what I said.' He also claimed that, whereas he merely had an unloaded gun, Probert was carrying a heavy tyre lever. Just the sort of weapon that might have stove in old Joe Bedford's hat – and skull.

Probert took a totally different tack. He did not say, as usual when two assailants fall out, 'Parker hit him. I didn't. I merely watched.' Or 'I tried to stop him.' Or whatever phrase comes easily to mind.

Instead he denied altogether that he was even there: 'The statement made by Parker in which he refers to me being with him at the shop of Mr Bedford is absolutely untrue. I have been asked where I was on Monday evening, 13 November, and I have nothing to say.'

But he must have thought more about it overnight. Next morning Inspector Lewis got a message that Probert wanted to see him in the cells. 'If Parker says we did it with the tyre lever, he is a liar,' he said. 'I can prove that. I was there.' It was a remarkable statement. And the inspector took it down at once in his notebook. Later it was to prove of vital significance.

Yet all the time this was going on, the two men had not even been charged with murder! They were still being held at Worthing on the loitering charge.

On 23 November 1933, nine days after Mr Bedford's death, they were formally put up at Worthing Police Court and sentenced to a day's imprisonment. Leonard Knowles, then a local crime reporter, was present in court.

Today, Mr Knowles is an alderman and a leading member of Brighton's Town Council. But he still vividly recalls that day in court thirty-six years ago. He tells me that – despite the handcuffs on the two men in the dock and the hordes of uniformed policemen in court – another local journalist assured him that the two prisoners had absolutely nothing to do with Mr Bedford's death.

'He bet me five shillings that he was right,' says Alderman Knowles. 'I'm still waiting for that five shillings!'

Straight from the Worthing court, the two men were bundled into police cars – Arthur Probert handcuffed to Police Constable Peters – and driven to Portslade police station, where they were formally charged with murder.

'I was travelling behind them,' says Alderman Knowles. 'And through the back window I could see Parker suddenly slump to one side.' It was to be the first of several occasions during his subsequent court appearances when, without warning or explanation, he suddenly fainted. 'It was nerves,' so I was told by Mr Stanley Cushman, the local solicitor who defended Parker and did all he could to make the best of a hopeless case. And it was hopeless. 'Faced with his statements to the police,' Mr Cushman told me – the papers from his old file spread out on his office carpet – 'the best we could hope for was a manslaughter verdict. 'Jimmy' Cassels, later Mr Justice Cassels, who led for the defence, attempted to argue that Bedford's death was unrelated to the earlier blows: 'He put up a case that what actually killed Mr Bedford was a crack on the head that he received when Constable Peters saw him fall. This was some hour and a quarter after the two assailants had left.'

'A bit thin!' I commented.

He agreed. 'But, of course, in a murder trial it is proper to put forward all possible available defences. If the jury had accepted that the fall caused Mr Bedford's death, we were out completely. Even if we failed to establish this claim, but the jury thought that Parker had, when actually in the shop, called off his previous criminal intent, he stood, at least, a chance of reducing the charge to manslaughter. And on this issue I believed my client.'

Why? Because of a significant fact that has never before been publicly revealed.

Consider the stage that had now been reached: the police court hearing – after the men's formal charging at Portslade police station – was over. Parker and Probert were at Lewes Prison awaiting their trial. Mr Cushman then interviewed Parker at the prison. 'He told me that he had tried to stop Probert striking the old man. He said that Probert was grabbing Bedford by the wrist. He picked up a cup and hit Probert with it to try to break his grip. But the cup broke on Probert's gloved hand, and fell to the floor.

'I got in touch with Gerald Paling, who was prosecuting for the Director of Public Prosecutions, and said I wanted to go to the shop. I went there with the police – and, exactly where Parker said I would find it, I found pieces of a cracked cup on the floor!'

'He was telling me the truth.'

But it would need more than a few pieces of cracked china to save Parker from conviction. Mr Justice Roche, the astute judge who presided over the trial, was unimpressed by Parker's tale.

In truth, as one reads accounts of the trial, it becomes clear that Parker, in his understandable fear (he was only just twenty-one), pushed his claims a bit too far.

His evidence in the witness-box was full of phrases like: 'I told Probert to turn it in'; 'I tried to separate him and the old man'; 'I told him he had gone far enough'; 'I didn't expect he would do that'.

Sir Adair Roche – who did not allow his onerous duties as assize judge to prevent him from hunting to hounds while at Lewes – remained clearly unconvinced.

Towards the end of his testimony, Parker said: 'We both emptied the till between us and put the money in our pockets. We took some money from a chocolate box and left.'

Roche intervened: 'Was the old man quiet then?'

'I made an effort to get into the kitchen to see what I could do for him,' replied Parker. 'But Probert barred the way.'

'I asked you, was he quiet?' said the judge grimly.

'I think so,' came the muted response.

The point was not lost on the Lewes jury. Even if young Parker truly had misgivings about Probert's excessive violence, they had not gone very deep.

It was also the judge who blocked any possible chance of

acquittal for Probert. His was a 'neck or nothing' defence, as murder lawyers used to say. If the jury accepted that he was not there, he must be innocent. If they thought he was there, he must be guilty — of nothing less than murder.

Although earlier refusing to account to the police for movements on the fatal night, Probert claimed in the witness-box that he had left Parker earlier that evening. And met him again later, after the robbery.

All hinged on that vital short statement to Inspector Lewis: 'If Parker says we did it with the tyre lever, he is a liar. I can prove that. I was there.' The significance was this: the sense of these words depended on their punctuation. In Inspector Lewis's notebook they appeared without punctuation at all.

Probert denied he had said any of it.

Mr John Flowers, KC, defending Probert, claimed that the two final phrases in the inspector's book should be read together, without any full stop, thus producing the statement: 'I can prove that I was there.'

Why on earth should an accused man facing — and denying — a murder charge tell the police he could prove that he was there? Not even the most dullwitted murderer would make such a statement. Flowers argued that the very stupidity of it helped his contention that the words were never said.

Mr Justice Roche paid keen attention when Probert was in the witness-box. As he later told the jury, he noticed that Probert used the phrase 'I can prove that' no fewer than five times when giving evidence! It was a telling point. It showed conclusively that Probert had made the statement. He had unwittingly admitted to the police inspector that he was there. And if he was there, he was undeniably guilty of murder.

After a two-day hearing it took the jury only thirty-five minutes to convict both men. As everyone else stood, the judge's clerk placed the dread black cap on the seated Mr Justice Roche's head. He started to intone the words of the death sentence — and Parker slumped to his seat. He is one of the few men to receive the death sentence sitting down.

Both men appealed. But it was hopeless. The execution date was announced.

There was little public sympathy for twenty-six-year-old Probert. 'He was a thug. The bruiser type,' says Alderman Knowles. But Parker was in a different category. He had struck no blows. He was at the other side of the shop: so far away from Bedford that blood had not even splashed on his clothes. And until he knew their victim was dead, he had manfully refused to inform on his accomplice.

Nearly 3,000 people signed a petition for his reprieve. 'I believed then, and I believe now,' says solicitor Mr Cushman, 'that he was not the sort of man who had it in him to commit such acts of violence. A man easily lead and easily directed by a person of stronger personality – such as Probert.'

But there was no mercy. On 4 May 1934, within minutes of each other, both men were hanged at Wandsworth Prison. At the end, Probert – the 'strong-arm' man – cracked and was frightened. Frederick William Parker walked firmly to his death.

Three men dead. Aged Joseph Bedford. Parker and Probert, both in their early prime. And all for £6.

'They thought the old man had bags of money. And so he did,' says ex-Police Constable Harry Peters. 'But he didn't keep it in the shop. I'm probably the only man who knew that he used to leave the place once a week. To take the money to the bank!'

When Joseph Bedford's will was published six months later it was discovered that the little old junk man had left £2,480.

8 David Greenwood
Convicted by a Button

The ground was soft and muddy beneath my feet as I approached the spot, half-hidden by trees from the nearby road, where over fifty years ago an attractive young girl had been brutally murdered. I was on Eltham Common, a huge splash of greenness amid the built-up mass of suburban South-East London. It was a bright spring morning. But there had been heavy rain all night. Hence the muddy turf.

At this same spot, on a morning in February 1918, the grass had been like that – muddy and churned up. Then too there had been rain. But on that occasion there was an extra reason for the battered condition of the ground. It had been the scene of a violent conflict.

'This unfortunate young woman was most foully murdered after putting up a tremendous struggle for her honour and her life,' said prosecuting counsel, Travers Humphreys—later a famous judge – at the trial of the man charged with the crime.

It was a strange case. A case in which coincidence and chance allied to bring a man into the dock. A case which the judge, Mr Justice Atkin, told the jury was 'entirely circumstantial'. A case in which the two most powerful witnesses for the prosecution were two silent inanimate objects: a badge and a button.

It was, in fact, the case which became famous as 'The Badge and Button Murder'.

The young girl's name was Nellie Trew. She was sixteen. Bright, pretty, a little on the serious side. She worked, like her father, at nearby Woolwich Arsenal. 'She was a very nice girl, a very respectable girl. Not a fast girl,' a man who remembers her and her family has told me.

It was the last year of the First World War. In February 1918 the situation was grim. London had endured—for the first time in its history – bombardment from the air. The Germans were about to launch a massive new onslaught on the Western Front. Meat, butter and eggs were that month, for the first time ever, placed on ration for the civilian population.

It seemed as if almost the entire area of London around the Arsenal was devoted to the war effort and mainly to the manufacture of munitions.

Nellie Trew and her family lived in the quaintly named Juno Terrace, temporary hutments built backing on to the Eltham Common by the Government specifically for munition workers. You cannot find them now. They have long since disappeared to make way for the gleaming, red-brick houses of a modern estate.

But in those days the area was remote. A little cut off. And it was very dark on the common when at sometime after nine o'clock on the Saturday evening, 9 February 1918, Nellie stepped off the tram in nearby Well Hall Road and turned on to a cinder track. She was crossing the edge of the common to the warm safety of her home.

She had come from the public library in Plumstead High Street, some two and a half miles away. She had made her regular Saturday night journey to change her library book.

'She was never out after nine o'clock in the evening,' her mother later sobbed to the coroner. 'She just lived for her home. She was everything to me.'

When ten o'clock came and she had not returned, Mr and Mrs Trew were anxious. By midnight they were beside themselves with worry.

Mr Trew put on his hat and coat, and went out into the 'boisterous night' – his own description. Head downwards against the driving rain, he hurried across the common to the nearest police station, which was only two hundred yards or so away.

The police were sympathetic. Hot tea was brought. The situation of a young girl missing from home had not yet become the commonplace thing it is today. They phoned the neighbouring stations. But by 3 am the girl had still not been found.

Distraught, the father staggered back through the night to report to his wife. Not knowing he was passing within a few yards of where the murdered body of his daughter lay face upwards to the storm.

The following morning, at approximately 8.20, they found her. Some local people out for a brisk stroll on the common spotted the body. It was half protruding from under a clump of trees. She had been pulled there from the track.

Soon uniformed policemen and curious onlookers thronged the common. Twenty or thirty people, perhaps more, stamped around near that spot within the first hour or so. And this was later to prove a significant fact.

But the mill of people did not prevent an experienced police officer almost at once finding, some six or seven yards from the body, the girl's hair slide, a 3d piece – and what looked like the cheap replica of an Army badge.

Dr Milton, the local police surgeon, arrived. He carried out a preliminary examination. It revealed that Nellie had fought bravely. Her face and clothing was spattered with blood and mud. But she had been brutally assaulted, raped – then strangled.

Time of death: eight or ten hours before – not so long as twelve hours. This would tie in with death as she was cutting home across the darkened common.

The badge was not hers. Clearly it was her murderer's – grabbed by the girl in her last desperate battle. There could be little doubt about that. Its presence beside the girl's hair slide, so close to her body, practically ruled out any other explanation.

An hour and a half later, another clue was discovered. This time, some forty-seven yards from the body and after the ground had been tramped over by people ebbing and flowing across the common. It was a black overcoat button. A member of the public picked it up off the ground, and handed it to a policeman. It had one unusual feature. Through two of its four holes was threaded a piece of thin metal wire.

Was it – like the badge – the murderer's, possibly torn from his coat? Or was it nothing to do with the killing at all, but a button that had dropped accidentally off the coat of one of the curious bystanders?

When wing-collared Chief Inspector Francis Carlin took over the inquiry three days later he had no doubt about the relevance of both the badge and the button.

No further clues had been discovered. There was no other possible line on the killer. At once he ordered that photographs of the badge and the button be circulated to the Press: 'Any information to the Criminal Investigation Department, New Scotland Yard, or any police station, will be welcomed.'

The photographs appeared in all the daily papers on the

morning of Thursday, 14 February 1918. And at once it led to a development.

A twenty-one-year-old turner in an airplane parts factory near Tottenham Court Road in Central London walked into the Tottenham Court Road police station, with a mate from work, and said: 'I've seen the photographs in the paper. That badge looks like mine. It used to belong to me. I sold it to a man on board a tram travelling between Well Hall and Woolwich.'

The sergeant in charge asked his name: 'David Greenwood,' he replied. He gave his address: Jupiter Terrace, not a hundred yards from Juno Terrace where the murdered girl had lived. It too was a row of hutments backing on to Eltham Common.

In a written statement Greenwood specified the time when he said he had sold the badge: 'On Saturday, 9 February, between 4 and 5 pm.' It was for 2s. And he gave a description of the buyer: 'This man, to the best of my recollection, was about thirty-five, 5 ft 6 in and wore a black overcoat and bowler hat. His accent appeared to me as though he came from Belfast. I should say he was a man that had had an outdoor life.'

Fine! This young man had voluntarily come forward to help the police. He was allowed to go. But immediately the sergeant telephoned Scotland Yard and spoke to Chief Inspector Carlin. 'I want him brought in for further questioning,' said the chief inspector.

'That is my badge!' said Greenwood, when Detective Inspector Brown, Carlin's emissary, came to fetch him to Scotland Yard, and showed him the murder clue at his factory. So at least there was no doubt about that. But Greenwood explained again that he had sold it on the previous Saturday afternoon – before Nellie Trew was killed. Although apparently now he had changed his mind about the accent of the man who had bought it. It was that of Dublin, rather than Belfast.

'I'd like you to come with me to Scotland Yard to assist us in our inquiries,' said Brown. And as the young man put on his overcoat, the detective noticed a very strange thing: all his overcoat buttons were missing.

Where were they? 'They have been off for a long time,' said Greenwood. But the detective noticed something more; the bottom button but one was not only missing. A ragged hole was left where the button had been torn away. He pointed this out.

'That's where it was pulled out, I suppose,' said Greenwood lamely.

But, in Chief Inspector Carlin's office at Scotland Yard, Carlin picked up the button found on Eltham Common and – to quote his memoirs – 'applied it to the vacant hole. It fitted, if one may use the expression here, exactly.'

David Greenwood was asked to wait at the Yard. Carlin and Detective Inspector Brown hurried to the factory where he worked. There they quickly discovered his background. It was entirely worthy of praise. He had volunteered for the Army at the age of eighteen, as soon as war broke out; he had been in the RAMC, attached to the Leicestershire Regiment. He had served bravely on the Western Front, been badly shell-shocked and invalided out in November 1917, with a disordered heart condition and neurasthenia. He had been working in the factory for several weeks.

He was proud of his Army career. That was why he wore this particular badge – a replica of the famous tiger of the Leicestershires.

The work-mate who had accompanied him to Tottenham Court Road police station that morning explained that they had gone after a discussion between Greenwood and some of the other men working in the factory. They too had recognized the badge in the morning papers. Perhaps Greenwood felt he had to go?

In fact, this man had noticed the previous Monday that Greenwood's normal tiger badge was missing and had asked him what had happened to it. 'I got rid of it over the weekend,' was the reply. That, of course, was the weekend during which the girl was killed.

It was undoubtedly highly suspicious. But Greenwood was a man with an excellent war record. Everyone spoke well of him. Could he possibly be the sort of person who would outrage an innocent girl and then brutally take her life?

Carlin, with nearly thirty years' experience in the force, nearing his retirement, full of honour and achievement, was a cynic. You only have to read his memoirs to realize that, from the moment he knew that Greenwood was admitting the badge was his and he had himself checked the gaping hole in his overcoat from where a button had been ripped, the young man was guilty, in his book. But he had to prove it.

To this end, he performed a simple – but, it must be admitted, most impressive – experiment. He had noticed that thin wire was in use at the factory. 'Could you unfailingly identify your own wire?' he asked John Charles Gibson, the manager. 'Certainly,' was the reply.

So Carlin asked him to go out of the room for a moment, then laid on the table the piece of wire attached to the button found on the common. Beside it he put several pieces of wire picked up haphazardly in the factory. Then he called back to Mr Gibson – and asked him to say which pieces of wire were his.

The manager looked carefully at each individual piece of wire. His answer: 'All of them.'

With those words, Carlin knew he had a case to put before a judge and jury. All right! If the badge was the only clue, perhaps Greenwood, with his exemplary war record, might be given the benefit of the doubt. But how could he also explain away the button and the wire? Carlin and Brown did not go straight back to Scotland Yard. They drove over to South-East London to interview Greenwood's family.

Again there was the same picture of a fine young man. His health blasted by the war – but with nothing against his character. His movements on Saturday night? He went out late for supper and was back some time after eleven. The timings were such that, allowing a few minutes either way, he could have done the murder.

But they were adamant about two things: one, he had gone out without his overcoat; two, when he returned there was nothing unusual about his manner – or his clothing. And remember that the murdered girl was spattered with mud and blood; her murderer must have been in a similar state.

But, as Carlin later wrote in his memoirs: 'It is not a case of telling falsehoods. The really strange thing would be if those to whom a man is nearest and dearest should not see the case in the manner which is most likely to prove that he is innocent.'

He was not deterred. He drove back to Scotland Yard and resumed his questioning of David Greenwood. The youth gave a detailed account of his movements on the previous Saturday. He had left work at one pm, arrived home about three. Gone to the Woolwich public baths in the afternoon, returned home. Then, as it was getting dark, gone back to Woolwich to buy some overalls, and it was on the tram that he met the man to whom he sold the Leicestershire badge he wore in his buttonhole – because 'he had a son in the Leicestershires'.

Then back home again, and he had finally gone out at about a quarter to ten for a third journey to Woolwich, where he had supper at the YMCA before catching the last tram home.

Why so late? Greenwood explained that he had got chatting with a stranger at the YMCA, and stayed talking to him until about 11.20 pm.

The buttons missing from his overcoat? 'They have been broken off one by one so far as I can remember. The last one came off about two weeks ago. I should think for about two weeks I haven't had a button on the coat.'

All this was taken down, and Greenwood asked to sign it. As he straightened up after signing his name, there occurred – according to Carlin and Brown – a dramatic incident. Greenwood always denied it even happened.

The youth, according to the two policemen, picked up the vital button clue from Carlin's desk, held it for a moment, and said: 'If I say it is my button, what will it mean?'

'I cannot tell you,' replied Carlin.

Greenwood stared hard at the button. 'Well, I won't say it then,' he said. And put it down.

Shortly afterwards he was charged with murder.

That spring was a grim season of the year. The heavy guns continued to pound across the mud-churned fields of France. Men slithered and died. The plight of a young shell-shocked, ex-soldier went almost unnoticed by the world.

Greenwood's mother was separated from his father. She had two sons and two daughters. They had precious little money. They could not afford a lawyer to represent Greenwood at the police court hearing or the coroner's inquest.

The man who had fought for homes fit for heroes to live in was unaided by the State in the early stages of his battle against the hangman's rope. Yet Greenwood would seem to have been no fool.

At the inquest, he stood up and asked the one vital question that an experienced lawyer would have put on his behalf. After a uniformed policeman had given evidence of an onlooker handing to him the button found on the Common, Greenwood said: 'I would like to ask whether the button was picked up before or after the twenty or thirty people had walked over the common?'

It was a vital point. And the policeman could only give one reply: 'After.'

But the total weight of the Crown's evidence was too great. The coroner's inquest brought in a verdict of 'Wilful murder.' The local police court found there was a prima facie case. By both courts, David Greenwood was committed to stand his trial at the Old Bailey.

On Wednesday, 24 April 1918, Greenwood stood to attention in the large wooden dock of No. 1 Court. And, in a firm voice, pleaded 'Not guilty' to the murder of Nellie Trew.

Now he was represented. It is not clear whether the funds came from friends and relatives or from the primitive State legal aid scheme of the time. But he had a solicitor and barrister to defend him. Henry Slesser, Greenwood's thirty-five-year-old barrister – a different person from Sir Henry Slesser, in his eighties and a distinguished retired appeal judge – did all he could to probe the prosecution's case.

He underlined the varying recollections – in perfect good faith – of Greenwood's workmates as to what buttons, if any, had been missing from his overcoat during the weeks before the murder. He noted their different ideas as to whether he had been calm or agitated in the days following the killing. He challenged Carlin and Brown's evidence as to the 'I won't say it, then' conversation about the button. He tried – unsuccessfully – to persuade Crown pathologist Bernard Spilsbury to concede that a man, discharged from the Army on account of shell-shock, neurasthenia and a bad heart, would not have had the strength to overcome a healthy girl of sixteen.

When the prosecution case was over, and he rose to open the defence, he told the jury defiantly: 'I am confident that, having heard the accused and his witnesses, you will be convinced of my client's innocence.'

Greenwood and members of his family gave evidence. All said, in effect, that he was innocent. But defence counsel Slesser called on a witness who was in a different category. Not a relative – nor even a friend.

He was the young man, a stranger, with whom Greenwood had had supper at the Woolwich YMCA, on the night of the murder. He was an engineer's turner living in Plumstead. And he confirmed that Greenwood was in the YMCA at 10.10 that night, apparently undisturbed – and without any blood or mud on his clothes.

If his recollection was right it was a physical impossibility for Greenwood to have been some minutes before on Eltham Common, in the mud and the rain murdering Nellie Trew.

The jury stirred uneasily. Perhaps the Crown's case was not so watertight, after all? Perhaps the circumstantial evidence was misleading?

Then prosecuting counsel Travers Humphreys rose to cross-examine. And this vital alibi witness had to admit that on 26 February – much closer in time to the incident he was relating – he had told the police that he had definitely had tea at the YMCA that Saturday. But he could not remember whether he had also had supper.

Why did he remember it now? 'The incident has been more particularly recalled to my mind,' he said.

And here I give a word of warning: don't be too quick to give a knowing smile and say, 'Oh yes. I've heard that one before!' After all, we do not know how the police questioned him. We do not know if they merely asked in general terms where he had tea and supper on that particular day – or whether they asked him specifically, 'Did you have supper at the YMCA that night?'

If the first time he was asked that specific question was by David Greenwood's solicitor, preparing his defence for trial, might not then his answers have worked out in exactly the way they did? I am not saying whether the alibi was true or false. I am merely pleading for tolerance when assessing it.

Not that David Greenwood got much tolerance from his judge. Australian-born Mr Justice Atkin was to go on to become one of the greatest civil judges of this century. He died in 1944, honoured, distinguished, and undoubtedly the first great judicial law reformer of this century. But all that was in the realm of civil law. He had had very little experience, as a barrister, in criminal cases before his elevation to the Bench. And he was not a pre-eminent criminal judge.

His summing up was dignified, courteous to the accused – but biased in favour of the Crown.

'Circumstantial evidence may sometimes be, and very often is,' he told the jury, 'more conclusive than the direct evidence of someone who has witnessed a crime, who may be mistaken, or who may give misleading or even lying testimony. Facts and circumstances cannot lie.'

But he omitted to say that they can be misread.

The twelve men on the jury battled over their verdict. They were out for nearly three hours, before they returned to court – with a verdict of 'Guilty'. It may well have been a compromise decision. For they 'strongly recommended Greenwood to mercy, on account of his youth, his services to his country during three years of war, and his high character.'

Guilty or innocent, Greenwood was a remarkable lad. Throughout the trial, he had been outwardly calm. Almost unconcerned. Now, when asked if he had anything to say, he cried: 'I'm not guilty of this crime! I have never seen or spoken to Nellie Trew in my life.'

He pleaded with the judge to ignore the recommendation to mercy. 'Rather than have the disgrace of this crime on me, I would pay the full penalty,' he said.

Impressive: convicted men do not often beg their judge to sentence them to death.

Mr Justice Atkin responded coldly. 'Despite what you say, I shall forward the recommendation to the proper authorities,' he said. 'At the same time, it is not right that you should anticipate that the law will not take its course.'

He ordered him to be hanged by the neck until dead.

Greenwood was not executed. After an unsuccessful appeal, he was reprieved. The 'Button and Badge Murder' was officially closed, and those in authority congratulated themselves upon a brilliant piece of detective investigation. As Carlin wrote in his memoirs: 'It is a truism to say that in a detective's work nothing is too small to count.'

Some time afterwards – as prosecuting counsel Travers Humphreys relates in his memoirs – some junior members of his chambers were discussing the topic of circumstantial evidence. Greenwood's case cropped up, and Humphreys posed the problem: 'If Greenwood had used thread instead of wire to fasten the lowest but one of his overcoat buttons would there have been enough evidence to justify his conviction?'

'One impudent pupil' observed: 'It only shows how careful one ought to be in these small matters of dress.'

That is how the 'Button and Badge Murder' is left in most

accounts of this famous case – on a note of satisfaction for a police job well done, and with a quip by a young member of the Bar.

But what is not generally known is that David Greenwood served fifteen years in prison – throughout all of which time he never ceased to protest his innocence.

In 1929 a doctor who had become interested in the case sent a detailed memorandum to the Home Secretary, Mr J. R. Clynes, pleading for a review. Hundreds signed a petition organized by Greenwood's mother in 1930. But there was no official reaction.

In June 1930 a released fellow prisoner told the Press: 'Greenwood still talks of nothing else but his innocence.'

Finally, in April 1933, the gates of Parkhurst Jail swung open. And a thirty-five-year-old David Greenwood stepped back into freedom. 'I bear no ill-will to anybody,' he said quietly. He still maintained he was innocent.

He could still be alive today. He would be seventy-three this year. I have tried to trace him, but failed. Perhaps it is better that way. But he served fifteen hard years in jail and if you ask me 'Was he guilty?' I can only reply: 'I just do not know.'

9   *John Alexander Dickman*
A 'Triumph' of Circumstantial Evidence

As the train clattered along I watched the northern suburbs of Newcastle slip by: the narrow streets, the old houses opening out on to modern factory estates. Then bright modern houses, and finally, the green, open fields of Northumberland.

I was travelling on the mid-morning Newcastle to Ainmouth stopping train, and I was making this journey because on that very same line in the early years of this century occurred one of the few murders on a train in British Railway history.

On the morning of Friday, 18 March 1910 John Innes Nesbit, a forty-year-old cashier, sat in the equivalent mid-morning stopping train, clutching a black bag containing the wages he was taking to workers at the Stobswood Colliery, some distance along the line.

Unknowingly, he was within minutes of his death. For Nesbit was destined to be the victim of a famous 'train murder'.

Mr Nesbit was a small man, wax-moustached, bespectacled and wing-collared. He had been twenty-eight years with the same firm of colliery owners – ever since he was a boy – and had worked his way up to chief cashier. He was a senior, trusted official with a wife and two young daughters. His home was a three-storeyed terrace house in Heaton Road, a wide main artery leading out of the city.

One can picture him leaving his home that morning. Kissing his wife Cicely goodbye. Going to his firm's Newcastle office on Quayside to collect the wages cheque, then to the bank – where he cashed it for £370 9s 6d in gold sovereigns and silver – and then to the Central Station.

Nesbit was a popular man, well known in the locality. At 10.20 am, Charles Raven, a local commercial traveller, who knew him by sight, saw him walking through the gate towards Platform 4, to catch the 10.27 to Ainmouth. He was with another man. 'They were walking along together,' Raven afterwards told the police, 'although I did not actually see them talking.'

Percy Hall, a cashier at another colliery, was travelling on the same train, also to pay wages. He looked out of his window and saw Nesbit walk past and get into the next compartment. Nesbit was accompanied by a man.

'I had never seen the other man before,' Hall said later in court. 'I had a fairly good view of him for two or three seconds. He came quite close to me . . .'

Hall also had a companion, a colliery clerk called John Spinks. But he saw nothing. He was already sitting down on the other side of the compartment.

The train, which was non-corridor, started off on time. Its first stop was Heaton, the Newcastle suburb where Nesbit lived. There, his wife was waiting on the platform. It was her usual habit when he went to pay wages. Not – as she later insisted – to collect any money for herself, even though the bag he carried contained his own wages.

It was, she said, 'to have a little conversation'. Nesbit normally travelled in the rear of the train, but this time he was up front.

They had their 'little conversation'. Then: 'Don't be home later than six o'clock tonight. Auntie is coming!' she called. And the train pulled out of the station. His companion? 'I saw there was another man in the compartment,' she told the police next day. 'But I can give no description whatever of him, as I only had a momentary glance at him.' Those words were to prove of vital significance.

The train clattered on. At 11.6 am it reached Stannington, a small wayside halt where now only a level crossing and a few pieces of broken wall remain. Then it was a well-used little station: Hall and Spinks got out. As the train pulled past them on the platform, Nesbit bowed to them and they waved back. Although Hall did not notice whether Nesbit still had anyone with him, Spinks distinctly saw one other man sitting in the same compartment: 'But I did not know who he was. I had not seen him before.'

At 11.10 am the train pulled into Morpeth, the fair-sized country market town that was the next stop. Only four minutes had passed by. Yet a railway worker, John Grant, who joined the train as a passenger, walked past Nesbit's compartment and looking in saw no one there. Neither Nesbit – nor his companion.

At Widdrington, the small mining village three stops further down the line, Nesbit should have alighted. But he did not pass through the barrier. Only when the train reached its journey's end at Ainmouth, and a porter opened the compartment door, was Nesbit seen again. Dead. His head blasted by five shots from an automatic pistol. His body pushed tight under the seat.

His bag – and all its contents – were missing.

'Dreadful Tragedy in a Local Train' ran the headlines in the local newspaper. Within hours, witnesses came forward: Charles Raven the commercial traveller, Hall and Spinks the colliery employees, and railway worker John Grant.

The picture was clear: Nesbit had been shot in that brief four-minute journey between Stannington and Morpeth. It must have been split-second timing. The assailant had to kill the man, grab his bag, push the body deep under the seat – and then be ready to alight at Morpeth outwardly composed and calm.

Who had been Nesbit's companion? Was the man whom Hall and Spinks – and Mrs Nesbit – had seen with him on the train the same as the man whom Raven had seen 'walking along together' with him on to the platform? Where had he gone? What had happened to Nesbit's black bag?

The ticket collector at Morpeth said he remembered a man getting off the 11.10 from Newcastle and paying him the 2½d excess fare from Stannington. He had a third-class Newcastle-Stannington return ticket – and said he had travelled on in error. He carried his coat over his right arm: even though it was a brisk March day. Underneath it, he could have been carrying Nesbit's missing black bag.

The national newspapers picked up the story. It was headlines in practically every paper that weekend. Nesbit's photograph appeared in the Press. Cashier Percy Hall's detailed description of his mysterious companion was circulated to all police stations:

'About 35 to 40 years of age, about 5 ft 6 in high, about 11 st in weight, medium build; heavy, dark moustache, pale or sallow complexion; wore a light overcoat down to his knees; black, hard felt hat; well dressed and appeared to be fairly well-to-do.'

And on Sunday afternoon, the police got their first substantial clue: Wilson Hepple, an elderly artist, contacted the police at Morpeth. He lived at Acklington, a picturesque village further down the line. He said he too had travelled on that train. He recognized the murdered man from his photograph – and knew his companion.

'He is a man called John Alexander Dickman,' he told the police. 'I have known him for the last twenty years. As I was getting my ticket that day I saw him in the booking hall at the Central Station.' Then later, when he was pacing the platform waiting for the train to start, he saw him again. With Nesbit.

'They were walking up the platform past where I was standing.' A few moments later, he noticed them about to board the train. One had his hand upon the handle of a forward compartment. When he looked again, they had disappeared.

He had not actually seen them get into the compartment. But the implication was obvious! Dickman was the man who had travelled with Nesbit. He must be the murderer.

It sounded as if the case was almost over, even though Hepple was elderly, which might increase the possibility of mistaken identity. That factor is the greatest single cause of miscarriages of justice in our criminal courts . . .

'Question this man Dickman!' the Morpeth police telephoned their Newcastle colleagues that Sunday evening. Detective Inspector Andrew Tait of the city force had never heard of him. It took nearly twenty-four hours to locate him – and then Tait, at first, thought he must have got the wrong man.

For John Alexander Dickman was no low-life figure of the criminal fringe. He was a forty-five-year-old ex-company secretary, happily married with a young son and daughter. The boy went to a private fee-paying school. The family lived in a substantial corner house in Jesmond, a prosperous middle-class suburb of Newcastle.

The house still stands. 'To live there sixty years ago' – a local resident told me standing outside its solid brick walls – 'Dickman would have had to be quite comfortably off. Considerably more so than the murdered man, living down on Heaton Road.'

Detective Inspector Tait later frankly admitted in open court: 'I was not very sure that I had got the right man. He lived in a good residential district.' But he had discovered one significant fact about Dickman: 'In my inquiries, I found that all the people who knew him said that he was very hard up.'

This was true. Dickman was an early 'wheeler-dealer' – hard up on his luck. Having lost his job as secretary to a local colliery company when it had changed hands some four years before, he had been living on his wits, earning commission from introducing business men to his various contacts, arranging finance with local money-lenders, dreaming up marvellous sounding business deals – and gambling as a professional punter on the horses.

By March 1910, despite his apparent prosperity, his well-cut suits and superior manner of speaking, he was in serious financial difficulties. Only the day before Nesbit's murder, he had pawned a pair of expensive field glasses for 15s.

But many people desperately try to 'keep up appearances' in hard times without being murderers.

Dickman admitted at once that he had known Nesbit for many years. And he had seen him at the Central Station that Friday morning. 'I booked at the ticket window with him, and went by the same train. But I did not see him after the train left,' he told Detective Inspector Tait.

Why had he not come forward to tell the police what he knew? 'I would have done so if I thought it would have done any good.'

At the police station he gave a detailed account of his movements. It was a story he never afterwards substantially changed. He had left Nesbit, whom he only knew slightly, in the booking hall and travelled alone, in a rear compartment. His destination was Stannington where, although he did not have an appointment, he wanted to see a local colliery manager 'in connection with a new sinking operation there'.

It was Grand National day and he got so interested in his sporting newspaper that he went on beyond his stop – and got out at Morpeth, the next town down the line.

The new colliery he was visiting was about halfway between Morpeth and Stannington. So he decided to walk to it across the fields. But: 'I took ill of diarrhoea on the way and had to return to Morpeth to catch the train back to Newcastle. I have been very unwell since.'

He had travelled on the same train. He was the man whom the ticket collector had seen leave at Morpeth. But was he the man who travelled in Nesbit's compartment?

That same evening the police held an identification parade. Dickman was placed in line with eight other men – and, one after the other, the colliery clerks Hall and Spinks and Mrs Nesbit passed down the line.

The result was not very encouraging for the police; Spinks and Mrs Nesbit picked no one out. Hall walked once down the line, turned, walked past the men again, stopped at Dickman – and said: 'If I was assured that the murderer was in among these nine men I would have no hesitation in picking this man out.'

'An extremely weak so-called identification,' the Chief Constable of Northumberland later wrote in a special report to the Home Secretary. But the Newcastle police on the spot felt no such scruples. Although no gun had yet been found; although at that stage they had not even searched Dickman or his house; although they had not yet attempted to check his story, they arrested him.

'I do not understand the proceedings. It is absurd for me to deny the charge, because it is absurd to make it. I only say I absolutely deny it,' said Dickman.

The case against him all hung on identification. Some money, £17-odd, was found on him; but the police never traced the rest of the £370 9s 6d missing from Nesbit's black bag.

They never found the murder weapon – nor were able to prove that Dickman had ever owned a gun. They found slight blood stains inside his trouser pocket; but he claimed it was his own blood – he had cut himself while cutting his corns and must have put his blood-stained hand in his pocket.

They eventually found Nesbit's empty bag, flung down an air-shaft at a colliery near Morpeth. But in those days all provincial police were not yet using fingerprints in their murder investigations. They could not prove Dickman had ever touched the bag.

The police found a man whom Dickman told them he had spoken to at Morpeth after he had returned from – so he said – being ill in the fields, and before he got the train back to Newcastle.

But that proved nothing either way. Whether Dickman had used the intervening two hours in the way he claimed or – as the police said – to throw away the gun, rifle Nesbit's bag and throw it down the nearby air-shaft, he would still have been able afterwards to meet and chat with the man at Morpeth.

The case caused a national sensation. Letters appeared in the Press from people frightened to travel in non-corridor trains. There was great public sympathy for the murdered man and his bereaved widow and children. Popular feeling ran high against the man accused of 'this carefully planned and cold-blooded crime'.

The courtroom at Newcastle's Moot Hall was crowded throughout the two-day police court hearing in mid-April. Hundreds more waited outside. Even so, at the end of the hearing, Edward Clark, Dickman's solicitor, made a strong plea to the magistrates to throw out the charge.

'There is no case to answer,' he thundered. 'I do not ask you to give my client the benefit of the doubt. I ask you to give Dickman what every Englishman is entitled to until there is something against him – his liberty!'

But it was useless. A full Bench of seven local magistrates committed Dickman for trial to the next assizes.

Nowadays, when a man is arrested on a murder charge, the inquest is usually adjourned until after his trial. Not so, in 1910. On 28 April the local coroner's jury – having heard only the leading prosecution witnesses repeating their evidence – brought in a verdict of wilful murder against Dickman. And he had not even yet been tried!

With so much local feeling aroused, Dickman's trial should have been moved away from Newcastle, perhaps to the Old Bailey in London. The man responsible for not applying for a transfer to London was E. A. Mitchell-Innes, Dickman's dandified KC. He must have been blind or insensitive to a degree. But then he hardly seems to have had a very close grip on this case: 'Please will you not call me Mrs Dickman!' snapped Mrs Nesbit, the murdered man's widow, in the witness-box. 'You have called me Mrs Dickman all through!'

Mrs Nesbit, tight-lipped, anguish-faced, proved to be the trial's star witness. Remember her statement to the police on the day after her husband's death about his travelling companion: 'I can give no description whatever of him as I only had a momentary glance at him.'

Remember she failed to pick out Dickman at the identification parade. Now in the packed Crown Court on a warm July day, she said: 'I am now certain that the man I saw in that carriage is the man I now see in the dock, the man Dickman. I am perfectly certain of this.'

Mitchell-Innes – once he had got her name right – did his best to shake this catastrophic piece of evidence. Mrs Nesbit conceded that the man was sitting in the shadow, he had his hat on and his collar held up – but she remained 'perfectly sure' Dickman was the man.

Even so, Dickman gave his evidence well. He seemed assured and confident: 'I thought at the police station it was a most absurd charge to be made against me,' he told the jury. 'And I still think so.'

But Dickman reckoned without his judge. Lord Coleridge, son of a former Lord Chief Justice of England, gave the attentive middle-class jury a classic definition of circumstantial evidence:

A net of facts cast around the accused man...

It may be a mere gossamer thread. It may vanish at a touch. It may be that, strong as it is in part, it leaves great gaps and rents, through which the accused is entitled to pass in safety.

It may be so close, so stringent, so coherent in its texture that no efforts on the part of the accused can break through. It may come to nothing. On the other hand, it may be absolutely convincing.

The law does not demand that you should act upon certainties and certainties alone. In the passage of our lives, in our acts, in our thoughts, we do not deal with certainties... Summon to your aid your just and ordered reason.

If it tells you that the guilt of the prisoner is reasonably proved, then the law and the oath which you have taken alike demand that you should act with firmness and with courage.

It was deadly against the accused. At 2.30 pm on the third day of the trial, the jury returned with their verdict: Guilty.

'What have you to say why the court should not give you sentence of death according to law?' asked the bewigged clerk.

Dickman did not falter: 'I can only repeat that I am entirely innocent of this cruel deed. I have no complicity in this crime, and I have spoken the truth in my evidence, and in everything I have said.'

Only after Lord Coleridge had pronounced the words of the sentence and the chaplain had chanted, 'Amen!' did Dickman, at last, lose control. 'I declare to all men that I am innocent!' he cried, as they led him to the cells below.

The verdict was popular. Local feeling still ran high against the condemned man. When his wife visited him in prison – Newcastle's telephone exchange now stands upon the site – crowds booed as she passed.

But outside the city, a reaction set in. The national newspapers began to run articles and letters questioning the outcome of the trial. Was a man to be hanged because of the 'identification' of an unsure colliery clerk (Hall), an old man (Wilson Hepple), and an overwrought widow (Mrs Nesbit)?

It seems incredible, but in 1910 criminal appeals were only three years old. The Court of Criminal Appeal was only set up in 1907, largely because of the scandal caused by another disputed identity case: Adolf Beck, twice jailed on theft and petty fraud charges of which he was totally innocent.

Dickman appealed to this newly established court – one of the first men convicted of murder to do so. The main ground of his notice of appeal, drafted by his lawyers: misdirection by the judge.

The Home Secretary of the day was a new appointment, a rising young politician of thirty-five named Winston Churchill. He, too, was concerned with the growing anxieties about Dickman's guilt. He was not content that the appeal should be limited merely to legal arguments on Lord Coleridge's conduct of the trial.

On 18 July 1910 the Home Office announced that the Home Secretary, 'in view of the applications he has received questioning the justice of the conviction and of certain evidence brought to his attention, which may possibly be regarded as material', had taken the unprecedented step of officially referring the whole case to the Court of Criminal Appeal. This meant that its three judges should treat Dickman's case as an appeal on the facts as well as on the law.

In other words, Churchill was empowering the appeal judges to re-open the whole question of Dickman's guilt – or innocence.

The 'certain evidence' mentioned in the Home Office statement? Nothing less than that colliery clerk Percy Hall, one of the three vital identification witnesses, had admitted that before he 'identified' Dickman at the official parade at the police station before Dickman's arrest, an unnamed policeman had first shown him, through a half-open door, the accused man sitting down in another room.

What was his already 'extremely weak' identification – to quote again the Northumberland Chief Constable – worth after that?

On the other hand, Mrs Nesbit had also had second thoughts. She had now explained why she had not identified Dickman at the parade or when she first gave evidence in the police court:

'When speaking to my husband at Heaton station the view in profile I got of his companion did not enable me to identify him as anyone I knew. On giving evidence at the court I never saw the prisoner until I had finished my evidence, when I caught sight of him in the dock.

'He was in the same position, and I had the same view of his profile as I had in the train, and then I recognized him as being the same man. I then fainted, and was carried out of court.' She had fainted at the end of her evidence – but did that make her subsequent identification any more reliable?

One might have thought, with this fresh evidence, and with the fact that Home Secretary Churchill had officially freed their hands, Lord Chief Justice Lord Alverstone and his two fellow judges would have taken some time over the appeal. In fact, it was all over in one day. Without the prosecution even being called on to reply.

Hall's previous sight of Dickman before the official identification parade? 'We need hardly say that we deprecate it,' said Lord Alverstone. Yet: 'although Hall's identification might have been slightly influenced, it has so little bearing on the real merits of the case that it is quite impossible for us to interfere with the verdict on this ground.'

This was a witness who, if he was right, placed Dickman incontrovertibly as Nesbit's travelling companion – getting into a front compartment with him.

According to the Lord Chief Justice of England, that had 'little bearing on the real merits of the case'! Lord Alverstone was then sixty-eight, three years away from his retirement. His legal career had spanned nearly fifty years, but he had had very little time to gain experience as a criminal Appeal judge. Anyone can make their own assessment of how he was faring.

'Dickman received quietly the announcement that his appeal had been dismissed,' said a newspaper account. 'He continues to protest his innocence.'

So did others. Edward Clark, his solicitor, petitioned Home Secretary Churchill for a reprieve. Hundreds, if not thousands, signed petitions all over the country. His wife wrote pleading for mercy.

But Churchill did not reprieve. Why not? Many years later, when I was writing a book on the reprieve system, the late Sir Alexander Maxwell, then a young man at the Home Office and afterwards Permanent Under-Secretary of State, told me: 'Except in the rarest cases, the Home Secretary never sets himself up as a court of appeal from the Court of Appeal. Once the court had pronounced on the legal issues of guilt or innocence, he did not intervene on that ground.'

At eight o'clock on the morning of 9 August 1910, John Alexander Dickman was hanged at Newcastle Jail. Said an eyewitness: 'Dickman appeared to be the calmest man of the little company assembled in the cell. He walked to his execution as a soldier on parade.'

Was justice done? Was Dickman John Nesbit's killer? I really do not know. Even after over half a century, there are still little bits of evidence in the prosecution's case that make one pause before screaming that Dickman was innocent.

Why did he travel on to Morpeth if he had only bought a ticket as far as Stannington? Was his sporting newspaper really that engrossing? Why did he bother to make the journey at all if he did not have an appointment and the colliery manager was not expecting him? Could Wilson Hepple, the elderly artist who had known him for twenty years, be so hopelessly wrong to swear he saw him getting into a compartment with the murdered man – when he had not?

One thing is certain: guilty or innocent, Dickman would never be convicted in a modern court upon the evidence given at Newcastle Summer Assizes those far-off days in July 1910. And if, by some fluke, the prosecution gained a conviction, it is positive the modern Court of Appeal, Criminal Division, would sling it out.

The court can intervene where 'there is some lurking doubt

in our minds which makes us wonder whether injustice has been done', said present-day Lord Justice Widgery in a 1968 case. That is how many people may feel about the case of John Alexander Dickman.

10 *Herbert John Bennett*
Defender's Error

It was dark. There was no moon. The sea spray spattered my face as I walked along the sands at Great Yarmouth.

I climbed into a hollow in the dunes ringed with tough, free-growing marram grass. The surface of the sand was moist – this was near the spot where over seventy years before, almost to the night, a young woman was murdered.

In the morning her body was found. Her clothes in disarray, a black bootlace tied tightly round her neck, her hands still fixed in their final death agony in the sand. There was evidence of an attempt of sexual assault.

'She was a nice girl,' an old lady told me. 'Very nice. But didn't seem to want people to know too much about her.'

And they didn't. When they buried her 'on the parish' in the local churchyard the simple redwood coffin bore no name.

The story began three years earlier in July 1897, when pretty, twenty-year-old Mary Jane Clark – for that, in fact, was her name – married seventeen-year-old Herbert John Bennett. They were a good-looking couple. Mary Jane in a flighty way, with her dyed blonde hair, trim waist and smart clothes. Herbert, with his well-cut suits, sleekly groomed hair and handsome, if weak, face. But their virtues were only skin deep.

A petty theft, a small confidence trick, an insurance fraud – and in between, the occasional honest job as a shop assistant. That was the pattern of Herbert's existence for the first two and a half years of his marriage.

His wife's way of life was much better. Her speciality was selling cheap, new violins to the gullible working-class of a pre-television era as 'fine, old instruments'.

Neither did particularly well. Their homes were a succession of seedy, furnished rooms in South London. Then suddenly and mysteriously they went abroad. Depositing their two-year-old daughter with her grandparents, they sailed – on 17 March 1900 – for South Africa.

They were away for only seven weeks. The Boer War was then raging and it has been suggested that Herbert may have been trying to become a Boer spy.

Back again in their familiar round of furnished lodgings, Herbert – still not yet twenty-one – began to tire of Mary Jane and the child. He could not bring himself to sleep with his wife nor touch the child. 'Damn you and the baby too!' one of their landladies heard him shout. 'I'll follow you for the sake of the baby and, if you're not careful, I'll get you fifteen years!' screamed back Mary Jane.

In June 1900 they parted. Mary Jane and the child went to live in Bexley Heath. Herbert moved into 'digs' at Woolwich.

But they still saw each other. Despite the previous rows, Herbert visited Mary Jane frequently at her new home. Indeed, he found it for her, a furnished, semi-detached house at 1 Glencoe Villas. And wrote – typically – a false letter of reference to help her get a lease.

But these two were dab hands at falsity. Mary Jane told people that her name was 'Bartlett', 'Bennett', and 'Good'. She said miscellaneously that her husband was a commercial traveller, a sailor, a captain in the Marines and a private detective. This amiable, pretty little chatterbox seems to have been quite incapable by now of remembering which lie she told to whom. She was always getting mixed up.

What exactly was her husband doing? He had taken a job as a labourer at Woolwich Arsenal. A strange pursuit for a dandy who prided himself on his collection of suits and used to change his collar and cuffs three times a day.

The Boer War was still in progress. Rebels were active in Ireland. It is possible that Herbert was involved in clandestine activities. How else could a 'labourer' afford to maintain two homes: his 'digs' at Woolwich and Mary Jane's comfortable stucco villa at Bexley Heath? Not to mention smart new clothes and a liking for travelling first-class in trains?

But Herbert soon had other interests as well.

Three weeks after the split, he met Alice Meadows, a respectable young housemaid. She was everything Mary Jane was not: a natural brunette as against her dyed blonde, sober and discreet as against her chatter and flightiness, honest as against her waywardness.

She bowled Herbert over. 'I have never met anyone as good,

as pure as you,' he wrote to her. She, for her part, had never before been taken out by anyone so knowledgeable of the world, such a 'gentleman' – with so much money to spend.

In early August, he took her up to Great Yarmouth for the Bank Holiday weekend. On 28 August 1900, sitting in the first-class compartment of a train bound for a two weeks' holiday together in Ireland, he proposed marriage. And Alice accepted.

'That was to prove Mary Jane's death warrant,' later said prosecuting counsel.

Certain it is that the weekend after their return from Ireland, Herbert made some excuse for not seeing Alice as usual – and hared off to Bexley Heath. Where Mary Jane excitedly told a neighbour: 'My husband is taking me and the baby for a holiday!'

The next day – Saturday, 15 September 1900 – with the baby asleep on her shoulder, Mary Jane knocked at the door of Eliza Rudrum's home at No. 3, Row 104 at Great Yarmouth.

All that now remains of No. 3 is the door itself and the lower half of the front wall. Behind is an empty shell. But in 1900 it was a large, rambling house where Eliza Rudrum lived with her husband John, a respected local shoemaker, and their large family, and took in lodgers.

'I've been recommended by a friend's friend,' Mary Jane told Eliza.

Terms were quickly agreed (10s a week), the normal false name given (this time, 'Mrs Hood'), the baby put to bed and within minutes Mary Jane was out of the house again. 'My brother-in-law brought me up from London – I'm a widow, you see,' she explained. 'And he's waiting to take me out.'

Her 'brother-in-law' must have given her quite a good time. According to Eliza Rudrum later in the witness-box, Mary Jane tottered home slightly tipsy, hiccupping gently from 'three drops of brandy'. And claiming proudly, 'My brother-in-law is head over heels in love with me!'

Who was the mysterious 'brother-in-law'? He never materialized at the subsequent trial. But what did occur was that a waiter named William Reade at the Crown and Anchor Hotel identified Herbert Bennett as staying at his hotel that night. The same hotel as Alice Meadows was also to say she and Herbert had stayed at – with separate rooms – over the previous Bank Holiday weekend.

During the next week there was no more talk of her 'brother-in-law' from Mary Jane. She proved an exemplary lodger, taking the baby on the beach every day, returning home early at night.

Eighty-two-year-old Mrs Louisa Rudrum, who as a girl of sixteen was then living in the house – she later married one of the Rudrum sons – remembers them both very well. 'She was a lovely mother to that little girl,' she told me. 'The baby had beautiful, curly hair. You couldn't help loving her.'

But the following Friday evening something happened to make the Rudrums wonder if their lodger was perhaps quite so respectable after all.

At about 10.45 pm Alice Rudrum – one of the three Rudrum daughters – overheard 'Mrs Hood' talking to a man outside the house. 'You understand don't you?' he said. 'I am placed in an awkward position just now.'

The fascinated Alice heard the unmistakable sound of a kiss. Then footsteps as Mary Jane hurried indoors.

Who was this man?

It could not have been Herbert. He was in London: there was ample proof of that at the subsequent trial. And for once Mary Jane's chatter did not provide an answer.

Waiting for her inside the house was a letter from Woolwich. 'It's from my brother-in-law,' she told Eliza. 'He wants to meet me tomorrow night at nine o'clock under the big clock at the town hall.'

The following day Herbert Bennett made another trumped-up excuse for not seeing his 'fiancée', Alice Meadows. And shortly before nine, Mary Jane left the house to keep her appointment with her 'brother-in-law'.

But he was not the only man she saw that night. It never came out at the trial. But about seventy years later Mrs Louisa Rudrum told me categorically: 'She went out first of all at about half-past six, looking very nice. I was in the yard when she came back at about half-past eight.

'She went upstairs, came down again a little while later and said she was going out with someone else. She said she wouldn't be long.'

At 9.00 pm Alice Rudrum saw her waiting by the town hall. At 9.30 pm, William Borking, a burly local publican, served her and a man with two whiskies at his inn, the Mariner's Compass.

'The man was Herbert Bennett,' he later told the police.

At 10.30 pm occurred a macabre incident on the South Beach. A couple of youngsters were sitting in a sandy hollow when suddenly they heard a woman moaning, 'Mercy! Mercy!' They looked up. The sounds came from another couple not thirty yards away.

Then there was silence.

The wind howled. The sky was moonless. And the two youngsters were scared.

They got up to go. And as they passed the other couple, they could just about make out a woman lying inert on her back and a man crouching over her. Timidly, they hurried on.

They had witnessed the murder of Mary Jane Bennett.

Herbert Bennett was seen again in Great Yarmouth that night. Shortly before midnight he ran breathless into the Crown and Anchor hotel. 'I missed the last tram from Gorleston' (Great Yarmouth's sister town), he told the 'boots', young Edward Goodrum. 'I was worried in case you had locked up.'

The following morning, before leaving to catch the first train to London, he had early breakfast, and was served – and recognized – by William Reade, the same waiter who had seen him twice before at the hotel. He was also identified by a local newsagent at the railway station – waiting anxiously for the 7.20 to pull out.

Yet when six weeks later the police tracked him down as the dead woman's husband, and arrested him for her murder, he said blandly: 'I don't know what you are talking about. I have never been to Yarmouth. I haven't lived with my wife since January when I found a lot of letters from another man in her pocket.'

What about all the matters he had to explain?

The many witnesses who spoke of his living with Mary Jane for several months after January 1900? The false excuses to Alice Meadows to avoid seeing her those two vital weekends? His telling two friends after the murder that his wife and baby had 'died in South Africa'? His gifts to Alice of some of Mary Jane's more expensive belongings, taken from the house at Bexley Heath after her death?

And – most important of all – the fact that after his arrest the police found in his room a gold watch and chain last seen round Mary Jane's neck on the night she died?

Herbert knew when to hold his tongue. Recovering quickly from his initial panic, he put on a mask of coolness and detachment that later was much to be commented on. He refused to be rattled – or to proffer explanations that he might later regret.

'You had better not say anything now. If it is your intention to be represented by a solicitor later, I advise you to reserve anything you have to say,' the chairman of the magistrates told him on his first appearance at Great Yarmouth police court. And he followed the advice.

But there was one matter on which he could not remain silent. He had to answer, and as early as possible, the vital question: 'Where was he on the night of the murder?'

'I wish you would see my landlady at Woolwich,' he told the police. 'She can prove where I was on the night of 22 September.' But all she said was: 'Mr Bennett did not sleep at home that night. I saw him that afternoon in the street with a railway timetable in his hand.'

Not much joy there. So he tried again: 'There are two witnesses I would like to call,' he said. 'They can prove I was with them at Rose's Distillery, Woolwich, that night.' And he named two former workmates. But in the witness-box of the police court they both confirmed that they had seen him in that public house on a Saturday night in September – but it was the next one, Saturday, 29 September.

Herbert, it seemed, had run out of alibis. On 24 November 1900, the Great Yarmouth magistrates committed him for trial.

A few days later, however, there was a visitor to Norwich Jail, where Bennett was held in custody. He was a florid London business man named Douglas Sholto Douglas. He was taken along the corridor to Bennett's cell. He did not go in, but peered through the Judas window at the occupant.

Excitedly Douglas turned to Bennett's solicitor. 'That's the man I saw in London early in the evening of 22 September,' he exclaimed. And, of course, if he was right, Bennett could not possibly have been in Yarmouth at the time his wife was murdered.

The elation of those concerned with Bennett's defence was not quite as great as might be expected at this sensational development.

This was, after all, Bennett's third alibi. Would it be safe to put it to a jury? Would a jury believe it, bearing in mind that Bennett himself had not previously mentioned this incident which, if it could be proved, would clear him at once?

Herbert's trial opened at the Old Bailey on Monday 25 February 1901. Composed and calm he had a daunting effect upon the spectators as he sat expressionless in the dock, moving only to make the occasional note to hand down to his leading counsel, Edward Marshall Hall, KC.

'No one could be as magnificent as Marshall Hall looks,' F. E. Smith once said about Marshall Hall. A handsome giant of a man who for a quarter of a century dominated the courts of England, he was undoubtedly the most famous defender in the annals of our legal history.

But he was desperately tired when he undertook Herbert's defence. After a gruelling year in the courts, he had gone without a break into an exhausting election campaign which made him Conservative MP for Southport – and then straight into this major trial.

A solicitor who used to brief him in later years says: 'The man was brilliant – but erratic. You really briefed him for his final speech. That was always tremendous. But sometimes I wished I could have kept him out of court until he had to make it. He could be awfully bad with witnesses.'

And he was 'awfully bad' with the prosecution's witnesses in this case. Instead of accepting that Herbert must have been in Great Yarmouth on the night of the murder, Marshall Hall ranted and stormed throughout the whole of the trial's six arduous days.

He argued with the judge, reduced women witnesses to tears, made one of them faint in the witness-box, and had some of the men lose their temper with him. All in a hopeless cause: to try to prove that Herbert was not in Great Yarmouth that night.

The tragedy is that Marshall Hall himself was convinced that Herbert was there.

'My own theory is that he did go to Yarmouth and that he did take his wife out that night,' he wrote to a friend. 'But I do not believe he murdered her.'

He told Herbert, 'If you will only go into the witness-box and admit everything except the actual murder, I can get a verdict.' But the young prisoner – half his counsel's age and still only on the brink of manhood – was too frightened or too stupid to obey.

'I was not there,' he said dully.

'But that's hopeless!' said Marshall Hall.

'Very well, then, I won't give evidence!' said Herbert.

And now came the error that will for ever blacken Marshall Hall's record as an advocate, however illustrious the many victories that stand to his name.

It was a double error. Not only did he fail even to try to dissuade Herbert from his suicide-course of not giving evidence in his own defence, he thrust upon the lad the burden of deciding whether or not to call Sholto Douglas as a witness and produce the questionable third alibi – which we know he himself did not believe.

It was an error componded of omission, tiredness and resignation. It threw back on to this boy's shoulders the responsibility that he, as his counsel, should have borne.

Alone in the cell with his client – and we know this from an account Marshall Hall later wrote to a friend – he handed Herbert a piece of paper with two sentences written on it: 'I wish Douglas to be called,' and: 'I do not wish Douglas to be called.'

'In two hours' time I want you to send me back this piece of paper with one of these sentences deleted,' he told the boy. 'And remember, when you're making your decision, that you never said anything to anyone about this so-called alibi until Douglas himself came forward as a result of the publicity attending the police court hearing.'

Two hours later, a prison officer handed Marshall Hall the sheet of paper. 'I wish Douglas to be called' stood undeleted.

The rest of the trial was anti-climax. Sholto Douglas – whose motives till today remain mysterious – told a complicated and wildly incredible story about meeting Herbert, whom he had never seen before, while out walking in South London and, being unable to get rid of him, buying him a drink in a public house – 'to shake him off'. One would have thought it would have had the opposite effect! It sounded so preposterous it was met with open laughter.

If Herbert had given evidence in support of the alibi, it might perhaps – just – have put a doubt in one juror's mind. So that he might have scraped home with an acquittal. But standing on its own it was doomed to failure.

The jury took exactly thirty-five minutes to reject it.

'I say I am not guilty, sir,' said the prisoner firmly when asked if he had anything to say before sentence.

And even at the very end, on the morning of his execution, nineteen days later, he remained calm. 'No confession!' he said grimly before being led out.

The one who suffered was Marshall Hall. He endured a torment of remorse. 'I have done this case very badly,' he told the jury in his final speech. 'I made a mistake!' he always said in future years.

With passionate dedication – more than he had ever shown throughout the trial – he did all he could to get a reprieve, even going to see the Lord Chief Justice and the Home Secretary to plead Herbert's cause. 'I am convinced he did not murder his wife,' he wrote.

Many modern commentators on the case agree. Personally, I do not think we can go that far. But – because Marshall Hall never put his client in the witness-box – we can now never be sure.

Remember the man whom Alice Rudrum heard kissing Mary Jane on the night before she died – and who could not have been Herbert. Remember Mrs Louisa Rudrum's recollection of Mary Jane saying, in effect, that she was meeting two men that night.

Another possible version of the truth emerges.

Herbert was in Great Yarmouth that night. He took the gold watch chain from Mary Jane's body, something so personal that he could never afterwards bring himself to give it to Alice, his 'fiancée'. But he did not murder her.

What could have happened is that Herbert and his wife were in business together again. This time, playing the old 'con' trick of a pretty girl getting a married man into a compromising situation – so that her husband can appear and demand 'silence money'.

I believe that may well have happened on the night of 22 September.

Herbert arrived, by prior arrangement, on the sands of South Beach to 'surprise' Mary Jane in the arms of her respectable local lover – and instead found her still-warm body. The would-be blackmail victim had proved to be a sexual maniac.

This picture of the crime fits in with Marshall Hall's own

theory of the killing: 'I am confident that the murder was done by some erotic madman.'

And with the chilling fact that on another moonless night twelve years later another young woman was strangled with a bootlace in an identical way on the same stretch of lonely sand.

'Most local inhabitants – especially the older folk – believe they know who did it,' says a Yarmouth port official, Mr S. C. Sillis, who has lived and worked in the town most of his life. 'He was a local man all right, but the police couldn't prove it. Some also said there was a connection between that crime and the Bennett case.'

They may well be right.

In any event, for the later killing Bennett had, at last, the perfect alibi – mouldering in quicklime beneath Norwich jail. And he owed it, not a little, to his counsel.

11 *Charlotte Bryant*
A Mistake over Arsenic

Today the small farmworker's cottage in Dorset has been combined with its next-door neighbour to make one large, comfortable modern house. The old wash-house is almost derelict. Thirty years ago, however, the cottage was still a primitive dwelling and the wash-house with its old-fashioned copper was in constant use.

'Of course, we don't use this now,' said the present owner. But in the mid-nineteen-thirties Mrs Charlotte Bryant, the cowman's wife who then lived there with her husband and five children, had only this copper to do her washing in. And it seems macabre to recall that her life turned on what was once contained in the ashes beneath it.

Charlotte did not come from these parts. She was born in Londonderry, Northern Ireland, and did not arrive in England until she was nineteen, when – in October 1922 – she married Frederick John Bryant, a soldier in the Dorset Regiment. They had met while he was serving in Ireland during the 'Troubles'.

She was a pretty girl then: long brown hair, vivacious brown eyes, and the wide cheekbones of an attractive colleen. Fred Bryant was more dour: nine years older, born and bred in the country, a quiet, straightforward kind of man. Tall, powerful, reliable – and rather dull.

Near the Bryants lived Mrs Rose Curtis. She still lives in the same house. 'He was a good man, very quiet,' she told me. 'Then he picked up with this woman while he was in the Army.

'She was no good. I didn't have much to do with her. As a woman, I didn't care for her. I didn't want to associate with that kind of woman. She was a bad lot.'

Certainly, by the time the Bryants came to live at Coombe Farm, in March 1934, much of Charlotte's attraction had faded. The lustre had gone from her eyes, her hair was plaited into two tight buns on either side of her head and – at the age of thirty-one – she had only one tooth left.

Yet she had not lost her interest in men. With Charlotte came her husband – to take up a job on the farm – their four children, and the lodger, a wandering gipsy hawker called Leonard Parsons.

'She thought more of Parsons than she did of her family,' says Mrs Curtis. 'She used to go off with him for days in his car, leaving the children behind with Bryant. I have even seen her take the baby for a ride with Parsons – and Bryant tuck the baby's shawl around it as she got in the car. I couldn't understand a man behaving like that.'

The baby? A boy born to Charlotte after the move to the cottage.

Fred Bryant was a complaisant husband. He knew what his wife was doing; he knew also that, even while Parsons was living with them, she would go off to public houses, pick up men, bring them back to the house. She would then send the children out to play while she entertained her visitor.

But his wages were only £1 18s 6d a week and although Charlotte was a slut and the house was not well kept, at least they ate well. Not many farmworkers' wives in the mid-nineteen-thirties could buy their husbands fruit tarts or cream or tinned salmon. And Fred liked these dishes.

The household seemed content enough. It looked as if the situation could continue indefinitely.

Then in May 1935, for the first time in his life, Fred fell ill. 'Gastric trouble,' said Dr McCarthy. 'The symptoms were also consistent with an attempt at arsenical poisoning,' later said prosecuting counsel in court.

Thereafter, Fred was plagued with stomach trouble. There were two big attacks in August and early December. 'He was often ill,' says Mrs Curtis. 'He often used to complain about pains in his stomach. He was under the doctor from about August onwards in that year.'

About that time, Charlotte began to pester Parsons, the lodger: 'What would you do if I was a widow? Would you marry me?'

He already had a gipsy 'wife' and four children. But legally he was still unmarried. The comforts of the Bryant cottage began to pall. In November 1935, without any warning or explanation, he left for good. 'I had been there for a long time.

Trade was bad and I could hardly get a living,' he later said laconically in court.

Charlotte was distraught. Perhaps ominously, Fred had another of his 'bad turns'. He was doubled up with pain. But his wife did not stay home to nurse him. She was out scouring the countryside for her missing lover. She even twice hired a car – at 30s a time – to take her to the distant camp where Parsons's gipsy 'wife' lived, hoping to find him there.

'What about your husband? Haven't you got one?' she was asked. 'Yes,' she replied. 'But he is away in a nursing home. He is very ill and I do not think he will get better.' It was a strange remark.

She had one comfort in her distress: the friendship of a woman named Mrs Lucy Malvina Ostler. She had met Lucy, a widow with seven children (three of them at a Dr Barnado's Home), only a few weeks before. They had become constant companions.

According to Charlotte's later evidence, Lucy wanted to come and live in the Bryant cottage. Lucy denied this. Even so, they were obviously very close friends.

It was Lucy Ostler whom Charlotte sent for on Saturday, 21 December 1935, when Fred Bryant started his last illness. He was in great pain, lying on his stomach and groaning.

Dr McCarthy was called. He realized at once that this was the worst attack yet. He wanted Fred to go to the Yeatman Hospital in Sherborne. But the man was obstinate. 'This is my home and here I stay,' he said – a decision which probably cost him his life. Lucy agreed to stay the night, with her children, to help nurse Bryant.

The following morning his condition had deteriorated so greatly that the doctor insisted on his removal to hospital. Fred was past protesting. Shortly before three o'clock that afternoon, in the presence of Charlotte and Dr McCarthy, he died.

The doctor refused a death certificate. 'I was uneasy,' he later explained. 'I did not suspect arsenical poisoning until I saw him dying. But the moment I saw him die, the shock brought things home to me.'

With the possible murderess standing beside him at the bedside.

Unlike Lucy Ostler, Charlotte could neither read nor write. 'What is an inquest?' she asked Lucy. She told her. 'I suppose they'll go to all the chemists' shops to find out if anything has been bought,' said Charlotte. 'If they can't find anything, they won't be able to put a rope round my neck!'

And to an insurance agent giving her a lift home, she said: 'They cannot say I have poisoned him!'

But 'they' soon set out to prove exactly that.

The day after Fred Bryant's death, the first policeman called to see Charlotte. Lucy was with her, having moved into the cottage with her children. Both women denied knowing anything about Bryant's death. 'He had been ill a lot lately,' said Charlotte blankly.

Then for a week – it was, after all, Christmas – they were left alone. What happened during those bleak days in the isolated cottage was later to prove of vital importance in assessing the guilt or innocence of Charlotte Bryant.

One thing was clear: the post-mortem revealed beyond a shadow of doubt that Fred Bryant had been poisoned. Every organ analysed contained arsenic. But how had he come to take the poison? And how had it been brought into the house?

On 31 December 1935, both Charlotte and Lucy, together with their children, were taken into what can only be called 'protective custody' at the Public Assistance Institution at Sturminster Newton. The police wanted them out of the way so that they could ransack the cottage and search the garden – to try to find some remains of the arsenic with which Bryant was poisoned.

In fact, they found traces of arsenic almost everywhere. On the walls, the shelves, the floors, under the stairs, beneath the beds. But it proved nothing. Arsenic is a natural part of the soil in this part of Dorset.

Every time a member of the family came in from the surrounding fields they brought in traces of the poison on their boots. The police found nothing which could have been administered to Bryant.

Then they made a startling discovery. In nearby Yeovil a chemist remembered serving a woman with a tin of weedkiller containing arsenic on the afternoon of 21 December, the day before Bryant died. Because she could neither read nor write, the purchaser had signed the poison register with a cross.

At once, an identification parade was held at the Sturminster Newton Institution. Charlotte and Lucy took part along with other women of similar appearance. But the chemist was unable to recognize his customer.

The police were back to square one. So they appealed in the local Press for anyone who could help to come forward. Someone did. But it was not a new, surprise witness. It was Charlotte's friend, Lucy Ostler.

Five days after she had stood in the identification parade alongside Charlotte, she elected to make a fresh statement. It amounted to an accusation of murder.

She said that on the night before Bryant died, Charlotte shared a bed with her husband while she fell asleep on a cot in their room. 'The next thing I heard was Mrs Bryant's asking her husband if he wanted to take some Oxo. She tried to coax him to have it. I do not know if he took it, but I think so, because I heard him vomiting afterwards. That was about three o'clock.'

Twelve hours later, Fred Bryant was dead.

But that was not all. This woman – who admitted later in court that she was by now 'frightened' for her own position – went on to describe how on Christmas Eve, two days later, when they were alone in the cottage, Charlotte pointed to a small green tin in a cupboard and said: 'I must get rid of that!' Mrs Ostler described the tin. It coincided exactly with the weed-killer tin sold by the Yeovil chemist!

What had happened to it? She last saw Charlotte take it into the garden towards the wash-house. Then she came back, collected 'some rags and things' and returned to the wash-house – where later Lucy found the copper had been lit.

The story was still not over. Two days further ahead, on Boxing Day, Lucy said Charlotte wanted to do some washing in the copper. But she could not get the copper fire to burn. So Lucy raked out the grate for her – and discovered it was choked with old rubbish, partly burnt clothing.

And a burnt tin.

'I threw it on the rubbish tip in the garden,' she said. Immediately, a fresh search of the garden was made. And a burnt tin still bearing traces of arsenic was found among the scores that the sluttish Charlotte had thrown out. The weed-killer manufacturer confirmed that it could have been one of his.

A 9.30 am on Monday, 10 February 1936, a police car swept into the drive-way of the Sturminster Newton Institution. Charged with Bryant's murder, Charlotte said dully: 'I have never got any poison from anywhere, and that people know. I do not see how they can say I poisoned my husband.'

The Assize Court at Dorchester is an ancient courtroom. It has seen all manner of persons in the dock. From the leaders of the Monmouth Rebellion standing before the dread Judge Jeffreys in 1686 to the Tolpuddle Martyrs in 1834.

But few moments could have equalled in drama the scene on that Wednesday afternoon in May 1936 when the one-time friends Lucy Ostler and Charlotte Bryant faced each other across the court at Charlotte's trial.

Lucy was the principal witness for the Crown. Her evidence against Charlotte was deadly. If she was telling the truth, there could be no doubt of Charlotte's guilt.

Mr J. D. Casswell, Charlotte's leading counsel, suggested to Lucy that her recollections might have been mistaken. He invited her to 'reconsider' her testimony. It was a forlorn hope.

Lucy Ostler left the witness-box after over an hour's cross-examination with her evidence barely shaken.

How then was the defence to answer her damning testimony about the tin in the cupboard and its subsequent burning in the copper grate? Thirty years later, I put this question to Mr Christopher Arrow, Charlotte's solicitor. He remembers the case well: it was his first murder case.

'We called the two oldest children, a boy of ten and a girl of twelve,' he told me. 'It was an appalling decision to take. No one likes calling children into court. But we had to pull out all the stops!'

The children swore on oath that neither had seen any small green tin in the cupboard. That the copper fire was not lit at all on Christmas Eve and that it was the little girl (not Lucy Ostler) who lit the copper fire on Boxing Day – with no difficulty at all. And with no burnt tin among the ashes.

The children wanted to give evidence. Whatever Charlotte Bryant's failings, her children loved her. And they were adamant they were telling the truth.

Charlotte herself stuck firmly to her original statement to the police. She knew nothing of the murder. She had not given Oxo to her husband during the night and she did not have any weed-killer about the house.

Then came the expert witness. He was Dr Roche Lynch, the dapper, scholarly senior analyst to the Home Office. And he produced a piece of evidence that brought a stunned silence to the crowded courtroom. Grimly tapping his notes, he said: 'I submitted ashes taken from the grate beneath the copper to chemical analysis. I found that they contained 149 parts to the million of arsenic.'

The mention of arsenic was not surprising. One would expect to find some small amount of arsenic present in the ashes. Naturally. As a normal part of domestic coal. But Lynch went on: 'This is so abnormally large a proportion it indicates something containing arsenic must have been burnt in that grate.'

That clinched it! This was vital corroboration of Lucy Ostler's story of the burning of the weed-killer tin.

The trial lasted four days. But the jury took only an hour to return a verdict of guilty. 'I heard afterwards that it took them only ten minutes to reach their decision,' says Mr Arrow. 'The remaining fifty minutes were spent having lunch.'

Throughout the trial Charlotte had remained unmoved. But as Mr Justice MacKinnon's voice faltered on the words of the death sentence she suddenly gave a moan. Her head fell forward on to her chest, tears coursed down her cheeks, and she broke down uncontrollably.

There was precious little to complain of in MacKinnon's conduct of the trial. But an appeal was decided on, if only to gain time.

Then came the development which earned this case a unique place in the annals of our criminal history. It was discovered that Dr Roche Lynch had made a fantastic mistake.

He was one of the most famous expert witnesses in the land. A lecturer at not only one but two London teaching hospitals. It seemed unbelievable that he could have got his facts wrong. But he had.

After news of the verdict appeared in the papers, Professor William A. Bone of the Imperial College of Science and Technology got in touch with Charlotte's counsel.

The professor told him that Lynch's evidence about the normal proportion of arsenic in the ashes of domestic fires was hopelessly inaccurate. Lynch had said that 149 parts to the million – found in Charlotte's copper grate – was so abnormally high it proved something containing arsenic must have been burnt there. But, said Professor Bone, the normal arsenic content of house coal is never less than 140 parts to the million anyway;

and is usually as high as 1,000 parts to the milllion.

So that, far from the arsenic-content of the copper ashes being excessive, it was remarkably below what might have been expected. Not only did this not corroborate Lucy Ostler's story of the weedkiller tin being burnt in the copper grate. It directly refuted it!

Nothing was said to Charlotte Bryant. Her legal advisers did not want to build up her hopes. But Mr Arrow and Mr Casswell looked forward to the appeal with vastly increased confidence. They had Professor Bone waiting outside court to give evidence and it looked as if they would almost have a walk-over when Sir Terence O'Connor, KC, the leading prosecution counsel, told them outside the door of the court: 'Lynch has certainly made a dreadful blunder. He knew nothing about the contents of coal himself, but got his information over the telephone. He must have misheard what was said. It's obvious that he was wrong and you are right!'

But the three appeal judges, presided over by Lord Hewart, the Lord Chief Justice, threw out the appeal in less than an hour. Without even calling on the prosecution to state their views.

The judges scornfully refused to hear Professor Bone's evidence. Said the irascible Lord Hewart, a peppery little man renowned for his bad temper: 'This court will not listen to the opinions of scientific gentlemen bringing their minds to bear on evidence which they have not heard.' And he added, 'Moreover, it is clear that there has been no mistake!'

It was an amazing thing to say, when prosecuting counsel had privately admitted only minutes earlier that a vital mistake had been made.

Home Secretary Sir John Simon later explained to angry MPs that Lord Hewart meant that the appeal court assumed Lynch had, in fact, been mistaken. But that – even allowing for this factor – there had been no mistake in the jury's verdict: Charlotte was guilty of murder.

With respect, the logic is at fault. The true question that should have been asked – as twenty years later with Timothy John Evans – was: If the jury had known all the true facts, would they still have convicted? Today, Mr Arrow is still convinced that, despite the local prejudice against Charlotte, there is a chance they might not have done: 'If only Lynch had given accurate scientific testimony as to the arsenic-content of the copper ashes, the jury might have given Charlotte Bryant the benefit of the doubt. She might have been acquitted.'

As it was, she was hanged. Sir John Simon, a cool, steely lawyer-politician, refused Mr Arrow's petition for a reprieve.

I have read this illiterate countrywoman's letters from the condemned cell. They contain no whinings nor moans for mercy. Nor any sign of any confession or repentance. They are concerned solely with the future of her children.

In prison, she learned at last how to write – at least, her name. And, with pride, she scrawled her signature to a will in which she left all her fortune to be shared between her children. Its amount: 5s 8d.

'I've never known anyone so completely composed,' says Mr Arrow. 'I remember distinctly visiting her for the last time shortly before the day of her execution. "I am ready to meet my Maker," she said. She was quite ready to die. She was a lapsed Roman Catholic and I think her peace of mind was entirely due to the Roman Catholic prison chaplain. He must have been a wonderful man.'

Two days after she died, her children were adopted by the local Public Assistance authorities. Her family was split up. And the tragedy was complete.

12 *Steinie Morrison*
A Grievous Blunder

Now the restaurant no longer exists. On its site stands a modern warehouse and office-block. Clean and clinical.

But as I stood outside 32 Osborn Street, just off the noise and bustle of Whitechapel Road in London's East End, I pictured the building as it must have been over sixty years before. When Alex Snelwar's kosher Warsaw Restaurant offered food and hospitality to the struggling community of Jewish immigrants who had come to this country seeking refuge from the pogroms of Eastern Europe.

'I was only a child then. But I still remember the marvellous atmosphere there,' stocky greying-haired Mr Israel Snelwar told me in his North London flat. 'Alex Snelwar was my uncle. It was a wonderful place.

'People would come in out of the cold, to sit down and have a gossip. You could be there hours for the price of a lemon tea. It was like a village café on the Continent. All the locals used to come in and have a chat. It was very friendly.'

Among the 'locals' was short, bearded Leon Beron, a Russian Jew who had come here, by way of France, sixteen years before. He was treated with respect by the other customers. For he was a man of property. A landlord known to carry £20 to £30 on him: quite a sum in those days.

He was in the restaurant every day. Talking, eating, strolling from one table to another – from two o'clock in the afternoon until midnight, when the restaurant closed. But 31 December 1910 was the last time he said, 'Goodnight, Alex. See you tomorrow.'

For the following morning, his blood-stained body – battered and robbed – was found six miles away. Half-hidden under some bushes on Clapham Common. Slashed on each side of his face was a letter 'S'. Carved deliberately after death.

It was the bizarre beginning to one of the strangest murder cases of this century. A case which culminated in a trial which still serves as a talking-point when lawyers discuss the tactics of courtroom defence.

To us, 'anarchists' now seems a word of comedy... little fat men with black beards and rolling eyes, carrying bombs with sputtering fuses in some Whitehall Theatre farce. But in the winter of 1910-11 they were not figures of fun. Amid the thousands of immigrants packed into the narrow streets and congested dwellings of the East End were small groups of dangerous men who were dedicated to the cause of revolution and unrest.

Fifteen days before Beron's murder, the 'Houndsditch Murders' had taken place. Three policemen had been shot dead by burglars raiding a jeweller's shop in Houndsditch. The assailants were identified as a gang of anarchists led by a man known as 'Peter the Painter'. Some of the assassins had escaped and the police were scouring London for them, anxious for any clue. And now this fresh murder.

Although the police always denied that Beron's death was connected with the anarchists, he lived only a few doors away from the notorious 'Anarchists' Club'. And the word *'spic'* was Russian for 'false spy'. Could this be the significance of the 'S' slashed on Beron's cheeks?

Could it be that revenge – not robbery – was the prime motive for the killing?

The police lost little time in starting their inquiries. Within hours, they were talking to Alex Snelwar. 'Beron did not leave here alone last night,' he said. The police asked who was with him.

'A man called Steinie Morrison. He's been coming here the last two months. The funny thing is he put his head in this morning, took a look around, and went out again. Without a word. As if he were looking for someone.'

Who was this Steinie Morrison? Most of the regulars had noticed him in recent weeks. They could hardly have missed him. He was a 6 ft 3 in giant of a man, handsome, flashy, and powerful.

During the next twenty-four hours several people came forward to say they had seen Morrison with Beron. Not only had the two men talked together in the restaurant most of the evening. They were seen out together in the street afterwards as well.

'We were coming back – my husband Sam and me – from a

The author points to bullet-holes in a garden wall in Sainte Marie-aux-Mines, France. It was against this wall that Edward Slovik was shot for cowardice during the Second World War (see Chapter 18)

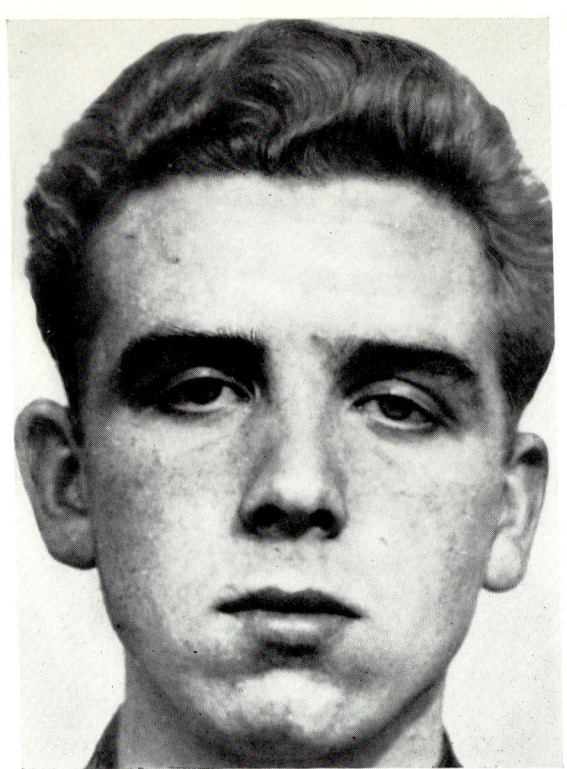

Left Alfred Burns, hanged with Edward Devlin for the brutal murder of widow Beatrice Rimmer (*see* Chapter 5)

Left Police Constable Jagger. His deathbed evidence convicted Alfred Moore (*see* Chapter 3)

Opposite Edward Devlin leaving the Manchester Police Headquarters for Liverpool where he was tried

Left Sir Edward Marshall Hall (*right*), the famous KC (*see* Chapter 10, 'Defender's Error')

Opposite Alexander 'Scottie' Mason arriving handcuffed at the Coroner's Court for the inquest on the murdered taxi-driver, Jacob Dickey (*see* Chapter 13)

Below The Bryants' house as it was at the time of the murder. They lived in the ivy-covered left-hand cottage (*see* Chapter 11)

Ivor Novello (*left*) in *The Dancing Years* during the most successful period of his career (*see* Chapter 16)

The Brains Trust at work, 1941. Professor C. E. M. Joad sits facing the camera between Quentin Reynolds (*left*) and Julian Huxley (*see* Chapter 14)

Alfred Moore, the farmer hanged for the murder of two policemen (*see* Chapter 3)

'Patsy' Cornwallis-West as she was at the height of her beauty, here attired for a fancy-dress ball (*see* Chapter 17)

New Year's party at my father-in-law's,' said a Mrs Nellie Deitch. 'And just as we were coming along Commercial Street between Philpot Street and Bedford Street I saw Mr Beron and this strange, tall man with a long overcoat coming towards me.'

The time? About 2.15 am. The estimated time of Beron's death: about 3.0 am.

The call went out: 'Find this "strange tall man". Find Steinie Morrison.' It seemed probable they would be the same person.

On 3 January the Houndsditch assassins were cornered by armed police and soldiers at the famous 'Siege of Sidney Street'. As the bullets spattered the wall behind them a detective reported to Detective Inspector Fred Wensley that they had traced Morrison to a baker's shop at Lavender Hill – close to Clapham Common. But he had left there nearly two months earlier. He had done so without reporting his change of address to the local police, as he should have done.

For Steinie Morrison – alias Morris Stein, alias Morris Tagger – had only recently come out of prison and was still under an obligation to report his whereabouts to the police. A professional thief and burglar, he had a string of previous convictions. And now he was missing.

The search was intensified. It was discovered he had moved to lodgings in the East End, at Newark Street – which he had left mysteriously a few hours after Beron's death. 'I'm going to Paris,' he had suddenly announced. He might be back sometime for his clean linen; he wasn't sure.

Then a cab-driver named Alf Castlin came forward. He had read about the murder in the newspapers. The report said the murdered man was a foreign Jew and he remembered that at about 3.30 on the night of the murder he had picked up two men from his cab rank near Kennington Church and had taken them to Finsbury Park station. They spoke in a foreign language.

He described the men: one was short, with a bowler hat and a dark moustache, the other was tall and dark – with a long overcoat; like the man seen with Beron near Alex Snelwar's cafe; the man who might be Steinie Morrison. Detective Inspector Wensley was all the more anxious to see Steinie Morrison.

On the morning of 8 January he got his chance. He had left plain-clothes men watching the Newark Street lodgings, just in case Morrison returned for his clean linen.

Surprisingly, Morrison did just that.

He was promptly followed to a nearby restaurant. And as he dunked his bread in his morning coffee, Wensley asked him to accompany him to Leman Street police station 'to assist us in our inquiries'. On their way, Morrison said grimly: 'This is the biggest mistake you ever made. I have no doubt you have made many. But this is the biggest!'

The next day, Morrison was put up for identification. Not only was he formally identified by the Warsaw Restaurant customers as the man who left with Beron on the night of the murder. Both Mrs Deitch and the cabman Castlin confirmed that he was the 'tall man with the long overcoat' they had seen much later.

Charged with Beron's murder, Morrison replied: 'All I can say is that it's a lie.' But the evidence against him was still building up.

In answer to a police appeal for help from cabmen who might have picked up two men in the East End or Clapham Common late on New Year's Night, two Cockney cab-drivers came forward.

One said that he had picked up two men in the East End at about 2 am and had driven them to Lavender Gardens, facing Clapham Common. The other said he had picked up a man on his own – tall, dark, wearing a long overcoat – at the Clapham Cross at about 3 am and had driven him to Kennington Church.

At a subsequent identification parade both drivers picked out Morrison as their man.

The evidence of these two men and Castlin, the earlier cab-driver, was to prove vital. If accepted, it carried Morrison – with the unsuspecting Beron – from the East End to Clapham Common. Then, after the murder, away from the scene of the crime: at first, on his own – from Clapham Common to Kennington Church – then with an accomplice (the 'short man with a bowler hat and black moustache' of Castlin's statement) from Kennington Church to Finsbury Park Station.

But what was Steinie Morrison's version? What was his account of that fateful winter's night?

He refused to say. This strong, flamboyant character was determined to keep the police guessing. They would have to wait for his trial to know his side of the story. Only then would his defence be revealed.

But by the time Morrison went into the witness-box on the fifth day of his trial at the Old Bailey in March 1911, much had happened.

His defence counsel was Edward Abinger: excitable, volatile and remarkably verbose. Although he had been in practice for twenty-five years, this was his first major murder trial at the world's No. 1 court.

I have discussed this case with Mr J. P. Eddy, QC, the former judge and magistrate. Now in his early nineties, Mr Eddy was present throughout the trial as a young law student. 'Abinger could not resist spreading himself,' he says.

The prosecutor was Richard Muir: ponderous, but deadly effective. The judge was Mr Justice Darling. Criticized as a lightweight upon his appointment to the Bench some years earlier, he had matured into a kindly impartial holder of the scales of justice. 'Both Muir and Darling did their best to save Abinger from himself,' says Mr Eddy, 'but he could not be saved.'

It was not simply his garrulousness: a cross-examination that should have taken 10 minutes took an hour. Nor his habit of arguing with witnesses instead of questioning them. Or his insistence on continually bringing the Houndsditch murders and anarchists into the case – even though by doing so he ran the risk of implanting in the jury's mind the notion that perhaps Morrison, born of Russian parents, was himself possibly an anarchist sympathizer.

His demerit to his client went further. On the second afternoon of the trial he was guilty of an error that all commentators on the case are agreed is fantastic in a counsel of so many years' experience.

It is an elementary rule of criminal defences that if your client has 'form' – underworld slang for previous convictions – you do your best to avoid giving the prosecution an opportunity to bring this fact out. Usually, they will only be able to do so if your client himself gives evidence of his own supposed good character in the witness-box or you attack the character of a prosecution witness.

In such cases, it is generally only fair that the jury should know the true record of a defendant making such a claim or launching such an attack.

A crucial witness against Morrison was Mrs Deitch, the

woman who said that she saw him with Beron at about 2.15 am in Commercial Street on the night Beron died. In the witness-box Steinie Morrison was to claim that he went to bed that night shortly after midnight and never went out again.

Her evidence had, therefore, to be impugned. It should have been easy enough – without attacking for one moment her good faith as an honest witness. This was the only time she had seen Morrison.

It was very late at night. She had been to a party. And her story conflicted with the cabman who said that he picked up Morrison and Beron to take them to Clapham at about 2 am – fifteen minutes earlier. They could not both be right.

It should have been not beyond the wit of competent counsel to shake this woman by a courteous, yet firm, cross-examination. Instead of this, Abinger did not even suggest to her that she might have been mistaken. Or use any other method to try to persuade her she was wrong. He simply launched a direct and vicious onslaught upon her – on the basis that she was running a brothel.

Even if that were true, it had little bearing on the case. She could still be giving accurate testimony. But she had never been convicted of this offence and to this day there is no proof whatsoever of Abinger's allegation.

In vain Darling, the judge, intervened to try to point out the dangers of this line of attack. All he got for his pains was the retort: 'Your Lordship might have given me credit, after practising in these courts for twenty-five years, for knowing a statute which every student of law must know.' Exactly! Even a student should have known that it was foolhardy, stupid and wrong.

Yet Abinger persisted. Even bringing into court a whole string of East End prostitutes each one of whom he pointed out to the witness with a stern, admonishing finger, crying: 'You know her, don't you? She's one of your girls!' It was almost farcical. At one point, when Abinger was asking Mrs Deitch where she had got her fur from, she rounded upon him and spat across the court: 'Why should I tell you? My husband bought it, what he worked for. I do not ask you where your wife got her fur from.'

The whole court laughed. But the giant in the dock remained

impassive. Was this pantomime worth throwing away the secret of his past record?

Eventually, he went into the witness-box and gave his long-awaited account of the final night. He admitted he had seen Beron – but only fleetingly. At the Warsaw Restaurant when he popped in for a cup of tea on his way home from a music-hall. And afterwards, just for a moment, in the street before he turned in to his Newark Street lodgings. That was all.

But it was only a matter of time before Muir, the prosecuting counsel, delivered the thrust that he would never have been able to make if Abinger had not so rashly attacked the character of a Crown witness. It came very quietly. The softly spoken question: 'When were you first convicted for felony?'

Abinger always claimed that he had cross-examined Mrs Deitch only after explaining the full consequences to Morrison – and obtaining his approval. Yet Morrison still seemed taken aback. He blanched, paused, then stammered: 'I cannot say – 1900, or something like that.'

Muir looked at the list of convictions in front of him. 'Was it 17 December 1898?'

Lamely came the reply: 'That might have been it.'

And so it started. Remorselessly, Muir took Morrison through the list. Two months' hard labour for stealing: six months' hard labour for burglary: fifteen months' imprisonment for receiving: five years' penal servitude for burglary: seven years' penal servitude for being a suspected person, possessing housebreaking implements, and burglary – all in the space of twelve years since his arrival in this country. He had come out of prison only fifteen weeks before Beron died.

The effect upon the jury was appalling. You could see it in their faces. For the only time in his trial Morrison lost his superb composure: tears welled in his eyes and he was close to breaking-point. For he was no fool. He knew the damage that was being done to his cause in the minds of the twelve solid householders who were his jury.

Abinger's final speech was impassioned – but erratic. 'Leon Beron was not murdered for his money,' he declaimed, 'but out of vengeance for what he knew in connection with the Houndsditch murders.' Mrs Deitch was 'a liar'. Most of the prosecution witnesses had committed perjury. An innocent man stood in the dock.

The judge summed up for an acquittal, openly regretting that the jury could not bring in the Scottish verdict of 'Not proven'.

A quarter of a century later, Darling explained to his biographer: 'I had myself no doubt in my own mind that Morrison was guilty of murder. But the view I took was that, had I been a juryman, the evidence that I had heard was not sufficient to prove to me beyond all reasonable doubt that Morrison had committed murder. Therefore, I summed up as I did.'

In particular, he queried the vital identifications – in the badly lit early morning streets – by the three cabmen. And the terribly narrow time margin left, on their evidence, for the actual commission of the murder.

But such impartial objectivity was too rarefied for the blunt, common sense of the Old Bailey jury. Morrison was a professional criminal: this time he had gone too far – that was all there was to it. The trial lasted nine days, but they took only thirty-five minutes to find Morrison guilty.

'May the Lord have mercy on your soul!' said Darling, pronouncing sentence of death.

'I decline such mercy!' cried Morrison. 'I do not believe there is a God.'

He was not hanged. After an unsuccessful appeal, Winston Churchill, then Home Secretary, reprieved him. Not only because there was too much doubt as to his guilt. But also because – on the evidence of cabman Castlin – even if he were guilty, he had an accomplice, who was never brought to justice.

It was seldom, if ever, the practice to hang one of two confederates in murder, if the other got away. It offended the sporting instincts of our law.

Not that Morrison was grateful for the clemency. Steadfastly maintaining his innocence, he petitioned the Home Office four times to be hanged – rather than suffer the dread of life imprisonment for a crime that he still averred he had not committed.

His petitions refused, he took the law into his own hands – and literally starved himself to death. In January 1921 he died in Parkhurst Prison Infirmary, aged 41.

Abinger always refused to accept that he had made a mistake.

He told Mr J. P. Eddy some time afterwards that the jury knew or suspected that his client had a criminal record. 'I cannot think how they could have got such an impression,' comments Mr Eddy. 'Along with others, I have always thought that the cross-examination was a profound mistake.'

While arguing his abortive appeal, Abinger said: 'The prisoner was convicted not in consequence of the facts proved against him, but in consequence of his character and his previous convictions.'

But whose fault was that?

13 *Scottie Mason*
The Lucky Thunderstorm

Though it was not quite dark, Shaftesbury Avenue glittered with lights.

Business was booming in London's theatreland. It was a magnet not only for those heading for the shows but the others who found simple pleasure in just being there, amid the gaiety and glamour – the office typists and their escorts who would say next day: 'We went up West last night.'

In the Globe theatre, Marie Lohr was playing in the first run of that delightful Lonsdale comedy *Aren't We All?* At the Apollo, the name in lights was that of Phyllis Neilson Terry.

The early evening theatre rush subsided. Now the dining hour moved to its peak. Around the Trocadero there was a subdued, well-ordered bustle of arrivals and departures.

The cabs in the rank near the Troc did not have to wait long for fares. One of them was hailed by a young man. The driver set off. His journey took him out of Central London. Away from the bright lights. Over the river.

To Brixton. And to his death.

Baytree Road is a quiet, suburban street in Brixton. No great traffic runs along it. It merely serves as a short cut from Brixton Hill down to the main road at Acre Lane. The houses on either side are gable-roofed, terraced, and two-storeyed, each with its small garden before and behind.

Now the houses are more gaily painted than they were in 1923, and the street lighting is better. But Baytree Road is still very much what it was then: a quiet, respectable road where the loudest noise you expect to hear is a car back-firing.

But forty minutes after the thirty-nine-year-old taxi driver Jacob Dickey had pulled away from the Trocadero rank on that May evening in 1923, his cab was standing in Baytree Road, both doors swinging open – and Dickey himself was struggling with a man in the middle of the road.

Shots were fired. Dickey slumped to the ground. People

appeared – and the assailant ran off round the bend in the road towards Brixton Hill.

Within minutes the police arrived. But Dickey was already dead: lying near his cab, a recently fired gun thrown down by his assailant as he ran.

But where was the assailant?

The police found a torch lying in the garage of 28 Baytree Road, just round the bend, and traces of flight in the adjoining back gardens. A path of footprints, broken trellis-work, and marks on walls led to the back garden of 15 Acre Lane.

And the two ladies who lived there told the police that after the shooting – which they had not heard – a man had jumped down from their garden wall. They thought he was a burglar. 'I want to get through to the street,' he said. Terrified, they had let him through their house and out into Acre Lane.

'Catch that man – and we've got our murderer!' Superintendent Francis Carlin told the detectives under his command.

They had some clues to help them. On the ground, near Dickey's empty cab, lay a jemmy wrapped in paper, a blood-stained suede glove and an ebony walking-stick with an unusual gold top.

A photograph of the stick appeared in the Friday newspapers and it soon brought results. Word came in that a small-time American crook named Eddie Vivian had been around Soho with a walking-stick just like it: in those days, a smart walking-stick was as much a part of 'sharp' dress as long hair and large, floral ties today. Vivian was a professional house-breaker known sometime to carry a gun. 'Bring him in!' said Carlin.

The police found him in bed. In the lodgings of his girl-friend, chorus girl Hettie Colquhoun, at Charlwood Street, Pimlico. Now it is a brightly painted, 'up-and-coming' street – then it was downright seedy.

'That's my walking-stick!' said Vivian promptly at Brixton police station. He also identified the torch found in the garage of 28 Baytree Road as 'looking like one that belongs to me'.

Where was he on the night of Wednesday, 9 May? 'I was in bed all day with stomach trouble. Hettie looked after me and got me my food. I never went out.'

Then how did his walking-stick and torch get to Baytree Road? 'There's a chum of mine, "Scottie" Mason,' said Vivian – and he proceeded to tell Superintendent Carlin a fascinating story. The same as he was later to give under oath at the Old Bailey.

According to Vivian, Scottie Mason – a twenty-two-year-old, fresh-faced youth from Lanarkshire – was an old workmate of his. They had 'done a job' together. And, although it had landed them both in jail, they had remained good friends.

Alexander Mason had been due to be released from prison the previous Saturday, four days before the murder, and Vivian had sent him some money in jail and told him to come straight to see him.

On Sunday morning Mason had turned up at their lodgings and – Vivian was amazingly matter-of-fact about this – they had at once planned to start up in burgling together again. On Monday and Tuesday they had made a reconnaissance of some likely looking houses in South London; and they were due to do a break-in on the Wednesday evening. But Vivian's stomach trouble had prevented his going out.

At about 7.30 Mason had set out on his own, taking Vivian's stick – 'to make him look posh' – and his gloves, the torch, and jemmy.

At 11.30 he had returned: bedraggled, covered with dust and dirt and bleeding. 'I've made a mess of things. I've shot a taxi-driver . . .' he said.

Thereafter, Vivian had given him shelter for the night, telling Hettie some wild story about Mason having got involved in a fight with some toughs.

And he had not seen him again.

It was quite a story. Understandably, it made Superintendent Carlin very anxious to see the missing Mason, but he still did not release Eddie Vivian. The little American was detained for further questioning.

The following day, Saturday, 12 May, Scottie Mason was recognized in the street by a detective sergeant and brought in for questioning. 'I suppose I am here in connection with Vivian,' he said.

At one o'clock the next day he was put on an identification parade together with Vivian. And the two ladies from 15 Acre Lane came in, to see if they could identify the man who had jumped down into their garden and walked through their house. They had no difficulty in doing so. 'That's the man!' each said, in turn.

SCOTTIE MASON

They were pointing to Scottie Mason.

Vivian was released and Mason charged with Dickey's murder. 'I cannot understand it,' he said. 'I was nowhere near Acre Lane that night. I know nothing whatever about the murder. You are making a mistake. I did not do it.'

Throughout the subsequent police court hearing, he had no counsel to defend him. As he told the police: 'I am down and out.' But the prosecution, even at this early stage, was already in the hands of one of the most able men at the English Bar: Sir Richard Muir, the Senior Treasury Counsel. ' "Dickie" Muir was a most formidable adversary,' a retired QC, who knew him well, has told me. 'He was an extremely competent prosecutor: courteous, thorough – and deadly!'

He always prepared his cases in depth and, in murder cases, always visited the scene of the crime. He did so on this occasion, being driven to Baytree Road by Superintendent Carlin. But a thunderstorm was raging and, contrary to his usual practice, Muir, portly and in his sixties, did not get out of the car to examine the area on foot. 'We'll have a scale plan at the trial,' he said. 'That will do.'

For the rest, he worked up the case in his usual methodical way. He wrote copious notes, then reduced the whole lot to a series of memos on small cards which he took into court in a little box. 'Muir's playing-cards', they were called.

Yet in this case one must have been blank: the card on which Muir would have written a summary of the defence.

For he did not know it. The one weakness in the prosecution's case – apart from having to rely on someone like Vivian as principal witness – was that Muir simply did not know what Mason was going to say.

Mason had made no written statement to the police and when, at the police court, he said he wanted to go into the witness-box and tell his story the magistrate stopped him. 'You might endanger your case by giving evidence without consulting a lawyer,' he said. 'You'll get legal aid at the Central Criminal Court. Wait till then!'

So when Mason's trial opened at the Central Criminal Court – the Old Bailey – on 11 July 1923, the prosecution had no inkling of what the defence would be.

Throughout the first day of the trial, Muir sat hoping to hear some indication from the questions that A. C. Fox-Davies, Mason's legal aid counsel, was asking in cross-examination. But there was not a glimmer. Fox-Davies played his cards close to his chest. He contented himself with polite, discreet queries which really took the case no further. Mason sat in the dock with a perpetual smile on his lips, an enigma with ice-cold eyes. Outside, Vivian paced nervously in the marble-walled hall waiting for what he knew would be his ordeal: his time in the witness-box.

Then surely the defence must be revealed! And it was – in the most startling way.

At about 11.30 on the second morning of the trial, Fox-Davies rose to cross-examine Eddie Vivian. Within seconds, the atmosphere in court was electric. Fox-Davies – tall, eagle-like and white-haired – picked up the weapon that had killed Jacob Dickey: 'I put it to you that revolver is your property?'

'And I put it to you that is a lie!' replied Vivian.

When had he eaten the sardines which had made him ill on the Wednesday? As far back as the previous Sunday.

'Now, Vivian, I put it to you that you were not ill on Wednesday. That was a pure fake invented by arrangement with Mason to allay Hettie Colquhoun's suspicions?'

'Nothing of the sort.'

He admitted buying the jemmy found at Baytree Road. He agreed Hettie had never seen it. He admitted she knew he had been convicted of burglary.

'And she tried to persuade you not to go on with it, didn't she?'

'She did, yes.'

'It was to allay Hettie's suspicions that you concocted the story about being ill?'

'Nothing of the sort.'

'At any rate you did allay her suspicions, didn't you?'

'I am not going to tell her I am going to do a burglary, am I?'

He denied having told Mason that he sometimes used a 'shady' taxi-driver to drive him around when house-breaking or burgling. Denied that he had ever told Mason he knew where to find one. Denied that he knew such a driver called 'Jackie' or 'Jakey' – or that he had ever met Jacob Dickey in his life.

Incidentally, the veiled suggestion that Dickey was a 'shady' taxi-driver, was expressly withdrawn by Fox-Davies in his final speech. It is regrettable that it was ever made. Mrs Annie Cohen, the dead man's sister, has told me: 'He was a highly respected, honest man. He was never called "Jackie" or "Jakey" in his life. "Jack" was the name everybody knew him by.'

Then Fox-Davies came to the crime itself. In a court in which all eyes were turned towards the man in the witness-box, he put it to Vivian that Mason had left their lodgings at 7.30 on the Wednesday evening, as he said. But that after Hettie had also left at 8.30, Vivian had dressed, gone out, met Mason and arranged to meet him later that evening at the corner of Baytree Road where they were going to do some burgling.

He put it to Vivian that he had then gone to the Trocadero cab rank. That he had hailed Dickey's cab. That he had asked him to take him to Baytree Road. That he had there had a dispute with Dickey.

'And that you fired the revolver and you murdered Dickey?'

'It is a deliberate lie!'

It was one of the most dramatic cross-examinations ever heard in a British court of law. Not to be equalled until thirty-six years later, when across a crowded courtroom Timothy John Evans's counsel accused chief prosecution witness Christie of murdering Evans's child.

Crook against crook. Which one would the jury believe?

When he went into the witness-box later that day, Mason denied that he had ever had a gun. He said that two days before the killing Vivian had produced a revolver and he – Mason – had told him to put it away: 'I told him I wouldn't work with anyone who had a gun.'

On the evening of the murder they told Hettie that Vivian was ill to stop her worrying about their 'pulling a job' that night.

He went to Baytree Road to wait for Vivian to arrive with the 'shady' taxi-driver. But something went wrong. As he saw the cab approach he heard quarrelling. The cab stopped. Vivian jumped out and the driver grabbed him. Then there were gun shots. And this, according to Mason, was what happened next: without waiting, Mason took to his heels – 'frightened to death'. He climbed over the front wall of 28 Baytree Road, and dropped down into the garage yard. Within seconds Vivian clambered over the wall after him. 'My God, Scottie, help me. I can't walk!' he gasped. 'My legs are gone. I can't move!'

But Mason believed in the survival of the fittest. He jumped over another wall and eventually made his way out into Acre Lane through No. 15.

By the time he got back to their lodgings Vivian was already there. How had he got away? 'He told me that after I had left him he climbed over some walls, went into the street, mingled with the crowd and went home by Kennington Road.'

It was a good story. It placed Vivian in Dickey's taxi. It corroborated the presence of Vivian's possessions in the roadway. It explained away the yarn about food poisoning to Hettie.

And – most important of all – it accepted the evidence of the two ladies at No. 15 that it was indeed Mason who had walked through their house.

By not challenging these two highly respectable witnesses, Mason highlighted that the prosecution case to a very large extent stood or fell by the evidence of Eddie Vivian, a self-confessed villain.

Yet the jury still convicted. It took them only seventeen minutes after a four-day trial to bring in a verdict of Guilty against Scottie Mason.

They simply did not believe him – and they probably did not like the mud thrown at the dead taxi-driver, Dickey. Attack, especially upon someone who cannot answer back, is not always the best form of defence in an English court.

But this story abounds in twists. The Home Secretary at the time was William Bridgeman, a gentle, kindly man. Although Mason's appeal was dismissed, he remained unhappy with the verdict.

Five days before Mason was due to be executed, Bridgeman reprieved him.

Forty-three years later, I asked his son, the present Lord Bridgeman, why. 'He was not utterly convinced in his own mind that Mason was guilty. He could not be wholly sure that the real culprit was not that witness for the prosecution, Vivian. There was a doubt.'

A laudable sentiment – but, in fact, there was no doubt. Mason was the murderer: of that, most modern commentators are convinced. Not only because his defence was linked with the obviously false story of Jacob Dickey being a crooked taxi-driver. But also because there was, in this case, the most fantastic error in court. An error compounded of police negligence and, for once, slipshod preparatory work by the usually impregnable prosecutor, Sir Richard Muir.

Think back to Mason's account of the scene a few moments after Dickey fell mortally wounded in Baytree Road. Mason has climbed over the wall into the garage yard of No. 28. With difficulty Vivian has followed him – and appeals for help because his legs have gone. He cannot move.

How on earth, then, did he possibly escape? How did he arrive back at their lodgings even before Mason did?

There was no evidence by any other householder of an intruder getting through their house to Acre Lane, as Mason did. How did Vivian manage it? The question was never asked at the trial. Prosecutor Muir did not even know it should have been posed.

For the scale plan of Baytree Road and Acre Lane used in court was inaccurate and out of date.

A careless police constable had taken a tracing from the last Ordnance Survey without checking if there had been any subsequent changes. Accordingly, he showed on his plan an opening between the houses fronting Acre Lane at the back of the garage yard – through which Vivian could easily have escaped.

But this opening did not exist! It had since been fully blocked by a newly erected building.

If Vivian had been in that enclosed garage yard with an injured leg, he could not possibly have got out! But Muir, not having examined the area properly because of the pre-trial thunderstorm, did not realize this.

After the trial – while Home Secretary Bridgeman was still considering the question of reprieve – Muir went back to the scene of the crime. This time, no thunderstorm was raging and he got out of his car to investigate the spot. He wandered all over the area.

'Good Lord!' he said, on his return. 'If only I had seen this earlier, I could have proved that Vivian never got away in the way Mason said he did. If the Home Secretary reprieves Mason, the fellow will get away with his life because of a thunderstorm!

And so it was: this callous young killer 'got away with it'.

But the last word remains with Mr Philip Dickey, the

murdered man's nephew. 'Mason was saved by water – but he died by water,' he says. Released from prison in 1937, Scottie Mason was serving as a merchant seaman when – during the Second World War – his ship was torpedoed. And he was drowned.

14 Professor Joad
All Because of a Train Ticket

'Here it is!' called out my wife. 'I've found it!' We were in Hampstead Churchyard on a lowering, overcast evening. We had been searching for one particular grave.

The rain was falling in a slight drizzle. The atmosphere was sombre and touched with sadness. All around us were the graves of people who had lived or died in that celebrated 'village' in North London: the actor Anton Walbrook, Kay Kendall, Rex Harrison's young attractive third wife, dead so tragically of leukaemia at thirty-two, Labour Party leader Hugh Gaitskell.

And many others, lesser known. Most of the graves are well tended and with headstones bearing clearly their names, picked out in black or sharp relief against the stone. 'In loving memory of...' or 'In grateful memory of...'.

But the gravestone by which my wife now stood was austerely bare. It stated merely date of birth and date of death. There was no contrasting colour to pick out sharply the name. More than twenty years after the man's death, his name was already fading into the stone.

Yet at one time this name was known in almost every household in Britain: Joad. Professor Joad of the BBC's famous wartime Brains Trust.

He was a celebrity of vast consequence, a man respected and admired. Then came scandal – almost trivial in its nature – but practically overnight he lost his fame and his reputation.

Instant oblivion overcame him. And now it seems sadly appropriate that his name has lost its sharp imprint upon the wearing stone which marks his grave.

Cyril Edwin Mitchinson Joad was born at Durham on 12 August 1891. He was the son of a Victorian schoolteacher, and was brought up in a normal late-Victorian professional background. He went to Blundell's, a public school in the West

Country, and then to Oxford to one of the most conventional and traditional colleges, Balliol.

But he soon showed that he was neither conventional nor traditional. He reacted violently against his upbringing and his class-background. He was a Socialist. And though, on coming down from Oxford, he joined the Civil Service, he spent the least possible time at his desk actually working on official business.

A flood of books, articles, pamphlets on philosophy and morals – his two pet subjects – flowed from his pen. Agnostic and pacifist, he would boast in later life that he used the office hours in his sixteen years as a civil servant solely to write his articles and books. He combined a brilliant flair for expounding the ideas of others, with a delight in expressing his own strongly iconoclastic views.

In 1930, when he was thirty-nine, he threw up his Civil Service job and became what he really wanted to be: a full-time teacher of philosophy. He took an appointment as Head of the Department of Philosophy at Birkbeck College, University of London. Six years later, he was made a Doctor of Literature.

He was undoubtedly one of the most gifted university teachers of his generation. And his influence went far beyond the confines of any one university. His popular books on philosophy and the great thinkers of the past, written lucidly and in 'ordinary English' that everyone could understand, earned him substantial royalties. Rightly, too, they brought him considerable renown.

I asked recently for some of his books in two leading London lending libraries, and in both of them, not only were they still in stock, but many were out on loan, still being read in the early 'seventies by young minds anxious to learn.

When, in November 1940, the idea of a Brains Trust – 'serious in intention, light in character' – was first approved by the BBC, it was only natural that one of the first 'brains' to be thought of should be Dr Cyril Joad.

The Brains Trust was one of those beautifully simple ideas that was so perfect and so 'right' for its time that it seems difficult to believe that anyone actually thought of it. In fact, the notion of inviting listeners to send in questions to a resident team of well-known experts for them to discuss in a breezy, off-the-cuff way in a weekly radio programme, was no single person's idea.

The programme first went out on the air in January 1941 as a modest little feature for serious-minded members of the Forces. But it was soon being repeated on the Home Service and, its producer Howard Thomas later proudly wrote, it 'rose from the early obscurity of Wednesday afternoon half-hours to peak-time broadcasts of forty-five minutes each on the two best days of the week.'

The programme's format was simple. Ten or a dozen questions were put each week to its three resident members and one visitor. The subjects ranged from: 'Who made God?' or 'What is Beauty?' to 'What is a sneeze?' or 'What is Love?' As Norman Longmate writes in his recently published *How We Lived Then*, a history of everyday life in World War Two: 'Whatever the topic, millions of people accepted what the speakers told them. The Brains Trust had only to mention a book for it to go out of print, as happened to *War and Peace*. When the Brains Trust denounced advertising or over-protective parents, they provoked splendid public storms that boosted the listening figures still further.'

There was no television during those war years. A visit to the cinema could mean a tiresome, possibly hazardous journey through blacked-out streets and with inadequate public transport. The radio was the number one method of enjoyment and relaxation of the British public. Its stars soon became the public's idols.

And so it proved with the carefully chosen trio that formed the original resident team of Brains Trust experts. Joad, with his squeaky, high-pitched voice – sharp, lucid and quick. Professor Julian Huxley, famous scientist and secretary of the London Zoological Society – urbane, matter-of-fact, always controlled. And Commander A. B. ('Archie') Campbell – burly, jovial, well-travelled: a 'man of the people' against the two academics.

'The combination proved unexpectedly effective,' wrote Joad later. 'The public liked to hear the scrapping which Huxley and I brought to the discussion of such questions as the relation between the brain and the mind. It liked still more to hear Campbell keeping up his end with both of us.'

Huxley was always the most serious and the most deliberate. Campbell prided himself on his tall stories, and used to like to trot out what happened to him 'when I was in Patagonia'.

Joad too was not above coining a catch-phrase. The expression

'It all depends on what you mean' became a popular by-word. Punch published a cartoon showing him saying to a waiter, wanting to serve him some soup: 'It all depends on what you mean by (a) thick and (b) clear.'

When he spoke at public meetings, mounted police had to escort him through the crowds. A 'Professor Woad' appeared in a West End revue. The wartime Ministry of Food launched a dish known as 'Joad-in-the-Hole'.

When he quoted, during the programme, 'an old Confucian saying' – 'What be the economy to go to bed early to save light if the result be twins?' an angry Tory MP asked questions about him in the House of Commons.

Donald McCullough was the sole permanent question-master of *The Brains Trust* in its early days. Later, he alternated in the chair with others. But for most people who remember the programme he is the most closely identified with it.

I had lunch with him in Norfolk, near the lovely country house overlooking the sea where now he lives in retirement. The slow, slightly hesitant voice is still the same – although he is now over seventy.

'I can't stand pompous bores, even if they are brilliant,' he told me. 'But Joad was never a bore. Nor pompous. He was a great popularizer of his chosen subject, philosophy. Ours was strictly a working relationship. We were never close personal friends. But he was a superb technician, and I admired his technique immensely.'

When the war ended, *The Brains Trust* continued to flourish. The original formula was varied. There was no longer a resident team of three whom you could count on hearing every week. But Joad, Huxley and Campbell still 'appeared' regularly. All three continued very much in the public eye.

Joad, in particular, remained a public name. Active in work for the Labour Party and the Fabian Society, speaking at innumerable dinners and meetings, writing a regular weekly column in a popular Sunday newspaper, still teaching at Birkbeck College and producing books and essays. He fully justified the claim at the head of his newspaper column: 'Britain's Foremost Philosopher'.

His private life was not without its blemishes. 'You are doubtless aware that Joad's private (sexual) life was somewhat complicated,' Professor (now Sir) Julian Huxley, in his mid-eighties, has written to me.

The late Kingsley Martin, one-time editor of the Left-wing *New Statesman* and intimate friend of Joad, was more blunt:

> Love affairs, of course, were among his constant activities [he wrote in the second volume of his autobiography] and he made no secret of them. His friends often compared him to a faun. His stiff, bristly beard and bright, roving eyes suggested an immense physical vitality and insatiable appetite.
>
> He made no secret of his success with women and said he was not interested in talking to any woman who wouldn't go to bed with him. He found a surprising number who would.

Joad was married – although there seems doubt whether it was once or twice. *The Times*, in its obituary, said he was married twice. The *Dictionary of National Biography* in its latest supplement published in the year 1971 mentions only one wife. Joad himself, in his *Who's Who* entry, ignored all mention of any!

Sex was not his only weakness. Even more was vanity his sin. 'He was an immensely vain individual,' a present-day BBC producer who worked with him as a young man told me.

Although billed as 'Professor' Joad, he never really was a professor. His highest academic title was 'doctor'. 'I once took this up with him,' remembers Donald McCullough. 'But he claimed that he had been a professor for a short while at some American university.

'Once he wrote to me that I was not giving him a fair crack of the whip and was continually shutting him up. He said that if I didn't mend my ways, he would have to "take it further".

'I wrote back saying that I considered his was one of the most eminent minds in Europe at that time and that, in justice to himself, I had to contain his "talented brilliance". He so liked my soft words that he wrote back a charming letter, and all was forgiven.

'Yes, he was a vain man! But full of good will for the human race and with no malice in his character.'

Others were not so understanding of his foibles. Commander Campbell – and others – used to complain that he never paid for his round of drinks. And one senior BBC official wrote in an internal memo: 'We recently built up Mr J. B. Priestley as a radio personality, but I do not think I detect in Priestley the exhibitionism which I personally detect in the relish with which Joad trots out slick answers to profound questions.'

Professor Asa Briggs in his *History of Broadcasting in the United Kingdom* relates how a producer rejected a possible question – 'Would the Brains Trust advocate a moral philosopher in the Cabinet?' – on the simple, one-word ground: 'Joad'.

This background of distrust perhaps explains why, when the crunch came, Joad found he had surprisingly few friends in the power-structure at the BBC.

The scandal that blasted Joad's life has nothing to do with sex. Nor with vanity. It was petty and small-minded – and all the sadder for that.

At 10.50 on the morning of 5 January 1948, the Atlantic Coast Express pulled out of London's Waterloo Station, bound for Exeter. On board the train were Dr Joad and his secretary. They booked two places for the second sitting at lunch.

And it was as their lunch was being served some hours later that a ticket inspector came along. Joad's secretary presented her ticket. But – 'I haven't got one,' said Joad. 'I was late and the collector let me through. I got on at Salisbury. Can I have a return from Salisbury to Exeter, please?'

He duly paid 24s. And the inspector gave him a Salisbury-Exeter return ticket.

But the dining-car attendant later told the inspector that something was wrong. How could the famous, bearded 'professor' – whom there is little doubt they had recognized – possibly have got on at Salisbury, when both he and his secretary had come along to book two places for lunch before the train had ever stopped at Salisbury?

The inspector went back to Joad, and queried his story. No fewer than four times, Joad repeated that he had got on at Salisbury.

Only when the train arrived at Exeter did Joad admit to the inspector: 'I am sorry I made a mistake. I did come from Waterloo, but rather than have any fuss or bother I will pay the fare.'

It was an asinine remark for 'one of the most eminent minds in Europe' to make. It was quite clearly a confession of guilt.

And quite clearly it could not have been 'a mistake'.

Worse floundering was to follow. Joad wrote to the railway authorities that there had been 'a misunderstanding', and enclosed a postal order to cover the Waterloo-Salisbury part of the journey. But in a separate letter to the superintendent of the railway police he told a different story.

He claimed that he had a Waterloo-Salisbury return ticket on him when he went through the barrier at Waterloo Station – but that he was 'dismayed' to find he had lost it when the inspector asked him for his ticket on the train.

Either way, it was a mess. The eminent philosopher and teacher of morals had been caught out in what prosecuting counsel called at Tower Bridge Police Court on Monday, 12 April 1948 'an ordinary common ticket fraud'.

Joad did not personally attend court to answer a charge of 'Unlawfully travelling on the railway without having previously paid his fare and with intent to avoid payment'. Counsel on his behalf pleaded guilty. Mr H. H. Maddocks, the Tower Bridge stipendiary magistrate, did not waste time in excessive words. 'For a man in his position, there can be only one penalty – the maximum,' he said.

With due solemnity he fined Dr Joad £2 – the maximum fine now for the same offence is £25! – and ordered him to pay 25 guineas costs. 'Dr Joad Fined for "Common Ticket Fraud" ' was one newspaper headline that evening.

He had tried to save himself 17s 1d.

On that same evening, there was a *Brains Trust*. Dr Joad took part in the programme as usual. No one referred to the unfortunate incident in court. His voice appeared as confident and self-assertive as ever.

He had already been booked for four more programmes. But the following Friday, during a Commons debate on the Criminal Justice Bill, Captain Marsden, then Tory MP for Chertsey, said: 'In the last week a public figure was convicted for telling lies and defrauding the public, and he was hired the same evening by the BBC to entertain millions of people.

'In my earlier days such a man would have had to hide his face in shame for a long period before he appeared again.'

Public attitudes, of course, have changed greatly since then. Nowadays a young, unmarried woman MP can conceive an illegitimate child and claim her private morals are her own affair. If Joad were alive today, and committed the same ticket offence, it would probably not even rate front-page news.

But the nineteen-forties were not the nineteen-seventies.

On Sunday evening, 18 April 1948, the eve of Joad's next scheduled *Brains Trust* appearance, the BBC sent out a brief two-line programme alteration: 'Home Service 8.30 pm. *The Brains Trust*. Please delete C. E. M. Joad and insert Commander Stephen King-Hall.'

Donald McCullough was on a visit to New Zealand at that time. 'It was the most awful fall of an idol,' he says. 'I regretted the decision. I was deeply saddened by the whole thing – but I thought it was right.'

It really was a fall. *The Brains Trust* continued on radio for several years. It even transferred to television and ran on, in one form or another, until the early 1960s. But Joad was never asked to take part in it again.

Apart from one short talk several years later, he never broadcast again. He continued with his teaching, and books and articles, and newspaper column and his writing – but he had lost his largest audience. More than that, he had lost public respect.

There was now no hope of a professorship. 'It has taken me down a peg or two, disinflated me, and reduced me to my proper proportions,' he wrote. Donald McCullough recalls: 'I continued seeing him from time to time. He was a much-subdued character.'

Why had the authorities chosen to prosecute him? Was it all that serious? Surely they must have realized that the effect upon Joad and his career – in the climate of thought of the late 1940s – would have been catastrophic? Did they not feel that for a public and highly vulnerable figure such as Joad the penalty would be out of all proportion to the offence?

Kingsley Martin put those very questions to Field-Marshal Lord Slim, who was then deputy chairman of British Railways. 'He said he had prosecuted with great reluctance,' records Kingsley Martin, 'and would not have destroyed a man's reputation for a single offence.

'But the railway authorities had convinced him that Joad made a habit of defrauding them and that he had no alternative but to make an example of him.'

My own recent inquiries bear this out. Last year 21,089 cases of ticket fraud were reported to the British Transport Police Force – but there were only 8,800 prosecutions. 'We do not prosecute blindly or lightly,' an official spokesman has told me. 'We normally only charge people we have had our eye on for a considerable time. We are very selective in this.'

Joad was prosecuted not just for one error. The great philosopher was an habitual ticket-defrauder. On a petty but persistent scale.

Why did he do it? Donald McCullough once asked him in later years the reason for the Waterloo-Exeter incident, and got a cryptic reply: *'Hubris'*. *Hubris* is a Greek word for 'pride'. Perhaps Joad was ruefully admitting that his conceit was so great he thought he could get away with it.

McCullough's own idea is that Joad must have a strange feud with the railway companies, which had been nationalized only four days before his offence. It must have been a violent reaction to some slight where he thought himself wronged.

I regret that I am more cynical. I never knew Joad. I saw him a couple of times, once addressing a meeting at Brighton and the other time drinking rather too much wine in a Soho restaurant. I can claim no personal knowledge. But I rather think the mainspring of his cheating of the railways was more mundane.

It was the same as with most people who do this kind of minor fraud: meanness or greed. Money – the desire to spend it or the desire to avoid spending it – is a great leveller. It makes philosophers walk with pick-pockets and professors with common thieves.

The rest was anti-climax. In his new quieter frame of mind, the one-time pugnacious agnostic turned to religion. He became a believing Christian and a church-going member of the Church of England. He wrote a book which many believe to be his greatest – *The Recovery of Belief* – to communicate his joy at rediscovering God.

He was to need that rediscovery. In 1952, four years after the ticket incident, cancer of the base of the spine was diagnosed. He died an agonizing but brave death, spread over several months.

When finally they buried him in April 1953, the swelling majesty of a Bach anthem accompanied the ex-agnostic to his last rest. But no official representative of the BBC was present at the funeral.

15 *Sir Leo Money*
Influence and the Law

The tattered notice on the green notice-board is hardly legible in parts. At the top it says 'The Hyde Park Regulations 19' – then the rest of the date is missing.

Halfway down on the left among a list of 'prohibited acts' one can just make out: 'Behaving or being clothed in any manner reasonably likely to offend against public decency'.

What a contrast between those grim words outside the redbrick police station in the heart of London's Hyde Park and the informal scene all around on any warm summer's day. Couples lying on the grass linked in embrace; youths strolling past stripped to the waist; pretty girls sunbathing in bikinis. All is casual, relaxed, at ease. Very much a scene of the 'seventies.

It had all been very different soon after ten o'clock on the evening of 23 April 1928. On that evening two plain-clothes policemen had escorted, to the spot where now I stood, an excitable, greying-haired little man who was spluttering with rage. Behind him followed a girl. 'I am not the usual riff-raff,' shouted the angry little man. 'I'm a man of substance. For God's sake, let me go!'

Next day, the newspapers carried the headline: 'Famous politician and girl on Hyde Park indecency charge.' A scandal had broken whose repercussions resound even to this day.

Sir Leo Chiozza Money was a man of brilliant talent. Born in Genoa as Leo Chiozza, he came to this country in his early teens and before long achieved success as a financial journalist. He had a gigantic knowledge of trade statistics. He seemed to know literally everything about tariffs – German, French and US.

He married an English girl and assumed the English surname of 'Money'. He wrote books, pamphlets and articles. Finally, he went into politics. For twelve years he was a Liberal MP. He was knighted, a friend of Cabinet Ministers, ex-Parliamentary Private Secretary to Britain's First World

War Prime Minister, David Lloyd George.

But by April 1928, Sir Leo had eased off a little. He was no longer in Parliament. He was still eminent, very much respected – but already living in semi-retirement with Lady Money and their only daughter in their large, comfortable Hampstead house in Bishop's Avenue – a road that nowadays is still called 'Millionaires' Row'.

Sir Leo was fifty-seven, an age when, perhaps, some men find the company of young girls less than half their age rather tiresome, with their chatter and their stupidities. But, despite all his engrafted Britishness, he was still very much an Italian – swarthy, voluble and passionate.

On the evening of 23 April 1928, he took a young companion for dinner to a discreet but fashionable Soho restaurant. She was a pert, twenty-two-year-old factory worker from North London. Her first name was Irene. It is unnecessary, after all these years, to give her surname.

There were differences not only of age, but of class and background. But Sir Leo and Irene had been out to dinner or the theatre several times before. Irene had a fiancé and she knew that Sir Leo was married, with a child. 'I suppose it was vanity ... that she was sufficiently interesting to attract a man who was a public figure and a gentleman,' her father, a clerk in an accountant's office was to comment later.

Sir Leo and Irene always insisted that there was no financial link between them. No expensive presents or chic clothes. To quote her father again: 'She always said that Sir Leo was a perfect gentleman, and that he always treated her as a gentleman should treat a lady.'

She was a virgin. Subsequent medical evidence left no doubt as to that. But did sex play no part at all in their relationship? She may well have been flattered by his attentions; and that could have been sufficient for her.

But what of Sir Leo – was he merely trying to keep youthful in spirit by seeking the company of youth? Or was his interest more basic?

On that spring evening, after dinner, and with the warming taste of wine on their lips, they strolled arm in arm in the dark, beneath the stars. The sound of traffic was distant on the evening air.

Suddenly, an intruder burst upon them. He caught hold

grimly of Sir Leo's hands. 'I've been watching you two,' he said gruffly. 'I'm a police officer. You've been behaving indecently. Come along to the police station. I'm going to charge you.'

Another plainclothes policeman appeared. Sir Leo was hustled down the dimly lit path to the Hyde Park Police Station. He struggled continually. 'You've made a mistake. She is a respectable girl,' he said.

A man came up. He had been sitting near by. 'Is this your umbrella?' he asked. Without waiting for a reply, he handed it over. 'Stop him. Get his name and address. He can tell you we were doing nothing wrong,' shouted Sir Leo.

But the policemen did not call the man back. The stranger turned away into the darkness. 'Did it not occur to you that it would be the correct thing to get that man's name and address, or get him to the police station?' the leading policeman was afterwards asked in court. He replied: 'I was too busily engaged with the prisoner to think much about the man.'

At the police station, the two policemen told Station Sergeant Thompson what they said they had seen: the couple kissing. Sir Leo with his hand on the girl. His clothing disarrayed.

Sir Leo paced up and down in indignant fury. 'Why didn't they get the name of that man with the umbrella? I want to telephone my friend, the Home Secretary. It is disgraceful the way I am being treated!'

Sergeant Thompson was an astute, experienced officer. He sent one of the policemen back into the park to try to find the missing witness, but the search failed. The sergeant allowed Sir Leo to telephone the Home Secretary's home.

Thompson would have been less than human if he had not heaved a sigh of relief that the Home Secretary – austere solicitor William ('Jix') Joynson Hicks – was out when Sir Leo put through his call.

As quickly as possible, he released Sir Leo and Irene – who at first refused to give her name and address – on bail on condition that they attended Marlborough Street Court at 10.30 the next morning to answer a charge of 'being concerned together in behaving in a manner reasonably likely to offend against public decency', contrary to Regulation 24 of the General Regulations for Hyde Park.

'I am sure that today the police turn a blind eye to practically everything but the ultimate in the Park at night,' a solicitor practising in the modern Great Marlborough Street magistrates' court has told me. But in the 'twenties almost anything beyond a kiss could land a couple in court.'

Often kissing is all that a couple would say they were doing. Unfortunately, cynical magistrates – used to hearing the same defence time and again – seldom believed them. Convictions were frequent. The police evidence was nearly always accepted. Only if a man had money and the determination to make a fight of it, was there much hope of getting an acquittal.

Mr Robert Jackson, biographer of solemn-faced Sir Archibald Bodkin, then Director of Public Prosecutions, admits: 'For a long time there had been recurrent and disquieting rumours circulating in London about the activities after dark of the police in Hyde Park.'

Yet knowing this, and realizing the danger, why on earth did worldly, successful Sir Leo take this girl in the Park – even if his intention was merely to sit quietly under the stars and talk amiably about life? Even if completely innocent, he must have known the risk he was running.

It does not make sense – unless the answer is to be found in the pleasant dinner and delightful wine they had enjoyed earlier.

As it was, Sir Leo and Irene stood side by side in the dock at Marlborough Street Court on the morning of 24 April 1928. Formal evidence of arrest was given. They were remanded on bail for a week.

Lady Money, who was present in court, stood surety for her husband and his friend. It was a bold step. But, then, a wife's position in such circumstances is always delicate – and often sad.

A week later, on 1 May, Marlborough Street Court was crowded. There were more crowds outside. Reporters and Press photographers jostled on the pavement. The courtroom itself was tense – as if it were the Old Bailey and a man was on trial for murder. For, although the maximum penalty was a £5 fine, the dapper man in the dock beside the anxious-faced girl was, in one sense, as much on trial for his life as if he faced a capital charge.

Nowadays a conviction for park indecency would probably earn a well-known public figure a profitable television appearance on a 'progressive' late-night discussion programme. But in 1928 it would have meant complete social ruin. Sir Leo Money, the brilliant outsider who had scaled society's most impenetrable citadels, would have had to withdraw utterly from normal life.

The counsel who rose and told the magistrate, Mr H. L. Chancellor, that the plea on behalf of both his clients was 'Not guilty,' was portly, highly successful Sir Henry Curtis Bennett, KC. I knew, slightly, his son Derek, later also a QC. I remember his telling me once: 'Anyone who briefed my father knew that they could always count on a first-class court performance.'

And so it was here. The two police officers gave their evidence clearly and without hesitation. They told the magistrate on oath what they had seen. But 'Curtis' as he was known at the Bar, mauled them in cross-examination.

Almost everything they said was challenged. They claimed they had approached from the front – no, it was from the back. They said the couple were sitting on a bench near a path – no, it was some two hundred-odd feet from the path. They said he was struggling to get away – no, he was struggling to go after the vital, missing witness, who had disappeared after handing over Sir Leo's umbrella.

At the end of the prosecution evidence, on the second day of the hearing, Curtis made a strong plea to the magistrate to throw out the case. He conceded: 'Most stupidly, in my opinion, these policemen have given evidence that an offence has been committed.'

But – and this is a point that other commentators on the case seem to have missed – the magistrate did not at that stage accept that there was, in legal jargon, 'no case to answer'.

'No, Sir Henry,' he said. 'I think there is a prima facie case. Please call your evidence.'

Sir Leo went into the witness-box. His voice was firm. His manner defiant. Several times he repeated that there was no truth whatever in the suggestions made. His clothing was not disarrayed. They had been doing nothing improper. He did not struggle. 'I was behaving as any innocent man would who was resisting an assault.'

'Is there any truth in the suggestion that you were guilty of any indecent conduct on that night or, indeed, at any time with this young lady?' asked Curtis.

'No truth whatever,' said Sir Leo. He denied emphatically

that he had ever kissed her. Note this last fact. It was to prove of crucial significance.

Forest Fulton, the able prosecuting counsel and later a judge, could not ruffle Sir Leo in cross-examination. He put it to Sir Leo: 'Obviously, if your story be true, the policeman must have invented what he said.' The witness replied calmly: 'I suggest he was making a mistake. I say he was cruelly mistaken.'

Sir Leo returned to the dock. Irene was already walking towards the witness-box. Then 'That will not be necessary,' said the magistrate. 'After hearing the case so far and the positive denial Sir Leo has given, I have heard enough and have come to the conclusion that both defendants are not guilty.'

He ordered Sir Leo and the girl to be discharged – and awarded the defence ten guineas costs out of public funds. It was a slap in the face for authority. Not only a complete vindication of the defendants, but an attack on the propriety of their ever having been charged in the first place.

It was a popular verdict. Irene's father rushed to the dock. Both her parents kissed and caressed her. Friends crowded round and – in the words of one reporter – 'showered upon them congratulations which will be re-echoed by the public'.

The Hyde Park police had got their come-uppance. A famous man's honour had survived untarnished. A girl's good name had been preserved. The affair was over with a triumphant outcome – or so it seemed.

No one likes having their nose tweaked. Especially if you hold a position of power and importance. 'Jix' Joynson Hicks, the Home Secretary whom Sir Leo had unavailingly tried to telephone on the night of his arrest, felt almost a personal responsibility for what he considered 'his' police force, the 20,000 men of London's Metropolitan Police. He was most unhappy with the courtroom result.

Where stood the authority of the London police if, once their evidence was challenged by a leading KC and an eminent person in public life, a legally qualified magistrate was prepared to say – virtually – that the case should never have been brought?

If the two police officers were lying, then they should pay the price for their deceit, for only in such a way could public confidence in the integrity of the Force be maintained. And, if they were not lying, then the truth should be established.

The day after the acquittal, Joynson Hicks sent the papers in the case to Director of Public Prosecutions, Sir Archibald Bodkin – with an urgent request for an investigation as to whether the two police officers should be charged with perjury.

Bodkin, son of a judge, steeped in a tradition of authoritarian respect for the law, gladly undertook the assignment. He viewed the whole incident as a disaster for the forces of law and order and he mistrusted the foreign-born Sir Leo and his young girl friend.

He had no investigating staff of his own. So he asked the Metropolitan Police Commissioner Brigadier-General Sir William Horwood, to depute 'one of your most experienced CID officers'.

'My dear Bodkin,' wrote back Horwood. 'I think the best man we have for the work is Chief Inspector Collins.'

Chief Inspector Alfred Catteral Collins, a white-haired police officer with thirty-two years' experience and no fewer than ninety-two recommendations from judges for his zeal, was a typical, old-style Scotland Yard detective. Heavy, thorough – and deadly.

Sir Archibald Bodkin obviously took a strong interest in the case. For two hours on Monday, 14 May 1928, he personally briefed Collins as to the lines of his inquiry: 'This is a peculiar case, and I want you to get to the bottom of it,' he said as Collins settled his ample form into an armchair in his office. 'The first thing that strikes me as strange is that Sir Leo Money should be associating with a young woman in a very different station of life. We must probe carefully into that.'

As the diligent chief inspector took notes Bodkin detailed the order in which the witnesses should be interviewed. First, the two policemen who made the arrest. Then Irene. Then the girl who had introduced her to Sir Leo. 'Finally, you must see Sir Leo himself.'

Collins was quick off the mark. That evening he interviewed the two Hyde Park policemen. They stood by their evidence.

At 1.50 the following afternoon Irene was called into the welfare officer's room at the factory where she worked. Two plain-clothes detective sergeants were waiting for her. She had never seen them before.

They said they wanted her to go with them to Scotland Yard. 'We should like you to accompany us concerning the Leo Money case,' one said.

'I thought that was all over,' said the girl.

'So it is,' replied the detective sergeant, 'but we should just like you to come with us and clear up a few matters at Scotland Yard.'

So Irene went with them, after being assured: 'You will be quite all right. There is a lady outside to chaperon you in the car.'

But at Scotland Yard the policewoman 'chaperon' was soon dismissed. For nearly five hours Irene was interrogated by Chief Inspector Collins – with just one other policeman in the room.

By the time Irene left the Yard that evening Collins was in possession of a seven-page typewritten statement, signed by the girl, and initialled by her on every page. It contained the vital phrase:

'We were quite often close to one another and I was inclining towards Sir Leo. So far as I remember, his right hand was closed over my left.... *He had kissed me several times before the policeman came up.*'

Those are my italics. For remember Sir Leo's denial in the witness-box of any 'indecent' behaviour with this young girl. Remember his emphatic statement that they had never even kissed.

As Bodkin read Collins's report the next day, he must have known that, with that statement in his hand, there was not the slightest chance of getting any court to convict the two Hyde Park policemen of perjury.

Once the girl was admitting that she and her older friend had gone as far as kissing in a public place, no jury would sustain a perjury charge against policemen who swore that they had in fact gone rather further.

At this stage, it might be thought that Bodkin would have been content. Now was the time to leave well alone. To drop any further investigation. Merely report back to Home Secretary Joynson Hicks that, in his view, there was insufficient evidence to ground a perjury prosecution.

But he didn't. He told Collins that he should carry on and interview Sir Leo Money.

Sir Leo – and his solicitor, the highly experienced Mr Herbert S. Syrett – were less amenable than the young factory girl from North London. Syrett angrily refused to allow Collins to interview his client without his being present, or first approving the questions. Collins – for the time being – was blocked.

Next morning Collins reported back to Bodkin the lack of co-operation from the solicitor, Mr Syrett. It was too much for Bodkin. He had just read in his morning newspaper that a Labour MP – primed by Sir Leo – had tabled a question in the House of Commons asking if the Home Secretary was aware of the 'third degree methods' used by Collins in his interview with Irene.

And now this! Someone was actually having the temerity to obstruct a chief inspector in an investigation that he personally was directing! Bodkin dictated angrily a letter to this impertinent solicitor: 'I beg to inform you that where I am inquiring into a matter of public concern, there is no necessity for me to obtain your consent or indeed to consult you on any matter whatsoever.'

The suggestion that Syrett should first approve the questions to be submitted to his client was 'a wholly impossible proposition'. Bodkin stated that he must 'insist' that Sir Leo spare a little of his time to give Collins 'a full and frank and detailed narrative upon the matters on which I have instructed Chief Inspector Collins to question him.' And he threatened: 'If you decline, I must take other steps to procure what is essential for me to have before me.'

The letter was near-hysterical. Undoubtedly, it went beyond Bodkin's legal rights. Even the Director of Public Prosecutions cannot demand that a subject of the realm submits himself to untrammelled questioning by an investigating police officer – least of all, when he has been successfully acquitted of any criminal charge brought against him!

But the letter proved abortive. It was overtaken by events.

For that very night in the House of Commons there was such a storm about the allegedly improper methods of Chief Inspector Collins in his five-hour session at Scotland Yard with Irene that Home Secretary Joynson Hicks had to concede 'the fullest and most impartial public inquiry'.

Even so passionless an upholder of the Establishment as Sir John Simon, later Lord Chancellor, said, during the Commons debate: 'I say to myself, if that had happened to my daughter – how would I feel?'

The affair had now gone far beyond merely a dubious incident one night in a darkened park. Sir Leo, and his problems, were pushed aside. Now the issue that dominated public discussion was the rights of the police when questioning witnesses in a supposedly free country.

A tribunal was set up under the same Act as that used for the 'V & G' insurance affair. A recently retired Appeal Court judge, Sir Eldon Bankes, was the chairman. His two colleagues were a Tory lawyer-MP and a Labour non-lawyer-MP.

For six days, the tribunal heard evidence at the Law Courts. Top-ranking counsel were involved: Sir Patrick Hastings, KC, was brought in to lead Sir Henry Curtis Bennett for Irene – paid for, of course, by Sir Leo. Norman Birkett, KC, was briefed for the police.

Irene and her family were witnesses. So were Chief Inspector Collins and his sergeants; the two Hyde Park policemen; the Metropolitan Police Commissioner; Sir Archibald Bodkin; and Herbert S. Syrett.

But – although he sat in court throughout – Sir Leo Money did not go into the witness-box.

The main allegations against Chief Inspector Collins were that:

1. It was wrong to interview Irene at all without first informing her solicitor or telling her of her legal right to refuse to answer questions.
2. She should have been given prior warning of the police visit.
3. The policewoman 'chaperon' should not have been dismissed.
4. Collins himself had acted improperly during the interview. He called Irene by her first name. He said things like: 'We have all been young in our time. We have all had a bit of fun. Have you ever had a man?' and 'Irene will spoon with me' when tea was brought. He had asked her to give a practical demonstration of how she and Sir Leo had been sitting in the park.

The sole matter for the tribunal was the propriety of the police interview with Irene. It was not their function to inquire into whether Sir Leo and Irene had been properly acquitted at the earlier court case.

This led to an Alice in Wonderland situation. For the tribunal was hamstrung from pronouncing on the one vital piece in Irene's statement: that she and Sir Leo had been kissing. Now she swore that it was untrue. She claimed that she had signed the final page and initialled the others only at the end of the interview, when she 'was feeling awful' and 'would have signed anything to be able to get away'.

For his part, Collins doggedly maintained that he had exerted no improper pressure. And that his conduct had been fair and honourable.

In the end, the tribunal split on party and professional lines. Bankes, the retired judge, and his Tory lawyer-MP colleague said in their Majority Report that they preferred the evidence of Chief Inspector Collins, 'a man beyond middle age, married and with family', to that of Irene. They described her as 'intelligent, of quick perception' and 'quite capable of taking care of herself'.

The Labour non-lawyer-MP said he preferred the evidence of Irene – 'frank, simple, and childlike'. 'Certain of her replies were forced into a form that misrepresented what she wished to say,' he wrote in his Minority Report.

In any event, police practice was changed. For the Majority Report recommended that in future all witnesses asked to make a voluntary statement should be warned of the possible consequences. That the police should, if at all possible, visit witnesses at home and not their place of work. That whenever a woman was to be questioned on 'matters intimately affecting her morals' another woman should be present – unless the witness expressly asked her to leave.

Home Secretary Joynson Hicks at once accepted those recommendations. They still remain in effect today – a living reminder of the Sir Leo Money Scandal.

But what of Sir Leo and Irene? What was the truth of the matter, so far as they were concerned? I have discussed this matter with a retired barrister who knew Sir Patrick Hastings and remembers having been present himself briefly at the Bankes Inquiry. 'I recollect that Pat Hastings formed the view that the Inquiry was too kind to the police,' he says, 'and that the Minority Report of the Labour MP was the correct finding. Pat thought that Eldon Bankes, a devout Churchman, was too upright and unworldly a man to preside over such an inquiry!'

So that would mean that Irene really did not admit that she and Sir Leo had been kissing before they were arrested. That the two Hyde Park policemen really did commit perjury and swear that they saw what they had not seen.

Perhaps. On looking back over more than forty years, I have

a further possible solution. That Irene was innocent, but Sir Leo was not! That she went in the Park, perhaps stupidly or naively, to talk or hold hands or possibly exchange a slight brush of the lips.

But, that as those two police officers came along, Sir Leo – his passion fired by the night and the wine – grabbed her and behaved, in the words of the regulations, 'in a manner reasonably likely to offend against public decency'.

The inquiry was not quite the end of the Leo Money affair.

Five years later, on 11 September 1933, Sir Leo Chiozza Money was charged on two summonses at Epsom Court for 'wilfully interfering with the comfort' of a thirty-year-old woman passenger in a train compartment and unlawfully assaulting her. As with Irene, he pleaded 'Not guilty' and gave evidence in support of his denial. But the five JPs on the Bench, one of them a woman, preferred the evidence of the shop assistant passenger who described how Sir Leo had grabbed her and smothered her with kisses against her will. 'My life is centred among the ladies. I could not live without them,' she claimed he said.

The Epsom court believed her. They fined Sir Leo. And he did not appeal: an infallible acceptance of guilt. That was the end of his public reputation.

He lived on – a sad, discredited figure – until finally, in September 1944, quietly he died. A near-genius flawed by Mediterranean passion.

16   *Ivor Novello –*
The Tragedy of a Rolls

I can still remember the only time I saw Ivor Novello – the great matinee idol of the nineteen-thirties and forties – on the stage. It was at the London Hippodrome in the summer of 1945. The war in Europe was over. Japan had yet to be crushed.

I was a schoolboy of sixteen, and I sat with my mother in the dress circle to see the famous Novello in his most appropriate setting: a matinee performance of his lush musical play *Perchance to Dream*. It was a romantic story of true love triumphing over the generations. It was not to my taste. But I was in a very small male minority in that crowded house.

For 'Ivor' – as he was known to everyone in show business – was the classic 'man with the perfect profile' for unmarried and middle-aged ladies. In his early fifties, but with his beautifully waved white hair dyed a youthful dark shade, he held women enthralled with the gentle warmth of his melodies, the escapism of his plots – and the boyish charm of his smile.

Yet it was through the adoration of one of his most devoted women fans, that – a year before I saw him – he was involved in one of the saddest Home Front scandals of the Second World War.

'Ivor Novello' was not his real name. He was born David Ivor Davies, the son of a corporation rate-collector and a music-teacher mother, Madame Clara Novello Davies, in a terraced Cardiff house on 15 January 1893. A handsome child, talented, with all the Welsh genius for music, he always remained devoted to his mother – who herself attained fame as a teacher.

He wrote his first musical play at the age of nineteen. It was still-born: he could find no one to put it on. But at twenty-one he smashed through to immediate success – and a fortune – with 'Keep The Home Fires Burning', one of the most famous songs of the First World War.

In the inter-war years, his name now changed by deed poll to

'Ivor Novello', his smouldering good looks made him a Hollywood silent screen star.

In 1935 one of his greatest hits, *Glamorous Night*, was put on in London. It was a stupendous success. It made Novello king of the theatre world. It was the first of a series of Novello hits. One was appropriately called *The Crest of the Wave*.

The outbreak of war in September 1939 temporarily killed off Ivor's *Dancing Years* – along with many other West End shows – then playing at Drury Lane. But after an eighteen-month tour of the provinces, it returned in March 1942 to the West End, to the Adelphi Theatre, and continued playing to capacity audiences.

People wanted escape. Ivor gave it to them. He still lived a life of luxury at the Aldwych flat, with delightful weekends at 'Red Roofs', his country home at Littlewick Green near Maidenhead, Berkshire. He still lived exactly the sort of Technicolor life he had known for nearly thirty years.

For instance: 'He adored tea,' someone who worked with him a great deal and knew him intimately has told me. 'Fans got to know this, and some of them used to give him their tea ration. They were happy to do so, and he was happy to receive it.

'If you had suggested to him that possibly he was taking an unfair advantage with all the wartime restrictions going on, he would not have understood what you were talking about.

' "I'm not cheating anyone," he would have said. He was so patriotic, so royalist, so pro-everything to do with his country that he would never have touched anything that was in any way unlawful – or what he considered against the war effort.'

That may be so. But there were not many civilians who by the late summer of 1942 were still driving around in their own chauffeur-driven Rolls-Royce with their initials picked out black against the deep red of the bodywork.

Ivor's Rolls-Royce used no petrol. It was driven by a strange looking, gas-propulsion unit attached to the back – 'It looked terrible. Like a sort of mobile immersion heater,' says one of Novello's acquaintances of those days.

As from 1 July 1942, the basic petrol ration – a pitiful amount of non-branded 'pool' petrol – had ceased to exist. 'The Government want all unnecessary cars taken off the road,' said the official announcement.

Soon this was followed by the news that even the rich men who had had their cars converted to gas propulsion would also feel the pinch. These were the months of the build-up of all available materials and men for General Montgomery's historic break-through at El Alamein in October 1942. The belt on the home population was really being drawn tight.

As from 1 September 1942, even gas-driven vehicles were no longer allowed to be driven on the road without a licence from the Ministry of War Transport. But Ivor adored his weekends at 'Red Roofs' – for which he needed a car. He loved the quiet and the rest, and the good country air.

Fred Allen, his secretary, wrote off for a licence to the nearest Regional Transport Commissioner's office at Reading – although I doubt if anyone bothered to tell Ivor such a mundane detail!

Allen wrote that the show ended too late for Ivor to catch a train to nearby Maidenhead. It was necessary for him to go home every weekend to continue his work, play-writing and producing, which was recognized by the 'Government as of national importance'. And it was 'essential to his health' because – as was the case – he was still recovering from a serious attack of pneumonia.

But the civil servants at Reading were unimpressed. They refused the application. They seem to have thought that Ivor should have stayed in town on Saturday night and gone down to the country next morning by train. The application was renewed to the Regional Commission's head office in London. Again it was turned down. The date: 22 December 1942.

By now someone had to tell Ivor. A chink of reality, at last, filtered through into his life. He came into his dressing room at the Adelphi Theatre on Christmas Eve: despondent – and petulant.

It was crowded, as always. 'Anybody here want a Rolls?' asked Ivor. 'Mine's no good to me because I can't get a licence. I think I'll give it to the Red Cross!'

He was clearly distressed.

A middle-aged, dumpy woman in glasses sitting in the corner saw her chance. She was one of Ivor's most devoted fans. Completely infatuated with her idol, she had managed to get herself – over the years – unobtrusively accepted into his outer circle. One of his many dressing room hangers-on.

'She was one of those middle aged spinsters who fasten their love on one glamorous man in the theatre,' says his official biographer Peter Noble. 'You can still see her type outside many a stage door.'

I do not propose to give her name. She has disappeared into obscurity. She could be still alive. There is no point in causing her renewed suffering.

She spoke up: 'My firm can use your car,' she said. 'We've got an office at Reading. That's not far past Littlewick Green. We might still be able to take you down there on a Saturday night and bring you back on a Tuesday morning.' Ivor's understudy, Barry Sinclair, usually gave the Monday performance.

Ivor was overjoyed. This woman, who usually passed unnoticed, was now the centre of attention. The star poured out his gratitude – with many a 'darling' interposed.

A few days later, she visited him again. The details were worked out. On 6 January 1943, Fred Allen formally transferred the car into her firm's name. The firm also took over the insurance policy. On 8 January the fan wrote on her firm's headed notepaper asking for a licence 'to facilitate speedier transport by the managing director and staff between our many works and factories.' On 6 March she duly collected the permit – and handed it to Ivor.

He was so delighted that he gave her a cherished pair of earrings belonging to his beloved mother who had just recently died.

In fact, the whole transaction was a fraud. The fan's firm knew nothing about the car or her relationship with Ivor Novello. She was not the managing director's secretary – as she told both Ivor and the Regional Transport Commission – but a £3 17s 6d a week filing clerk. She even lied to them about her true name.

Ivor continued to use the car at weekends. But the firm never had it during the week. In fact it has not been satisfactorily explained to this very day exactly who did have it during the weekdays!

'I am convinced,' says Peter Noble, 'that there was no real sinister motive on Ivor's part. He was not that sort of person. He lived like a nobleman. He accepted special treatment naturally as part of his way of life.

'I don't think for one moment that he deliberately set out to see who could get him some petrol or a permit or whatever it was. When he got it, he would say: "Oh, thank you, darling – how sweet of you!" And that was it!'

But the authorities did not share the same casual attitude to wartime rationing offences. The Black Market was a problem. Says social historian E. S. Turner in his book on wartime Britain 'Very few citizens had the moral strength to resist the offer of something tasty offered with a wink.'

In August 1943 – right in the middle of the period when Ivor was happily travelling back and forth from 'Red Roofs' in the luxurious comfort of his Rolls-Royce – show business was electrified by the news that famous bandleader and theatrical impresario Jack Hylton had been fined £155 and sentenced to prison for a fortnight for a petrol rationing offence.

Given an official petrol allowance for a van on his Oxfordshire farm, he had used it to ferry actors and himself from West End theatres to the Savoy Hotel, the Ambassadors Club and various restaurants.

Heavy fines were usual for rationing offences. But: 'I impose a sentence of imprisonment as an example to you, Hylton, and others that a petrol allowance is not lightly granted and is a privilege not to be abused,' said magistrate Mr Harold McKenna at Bow Street Police Court. Note that name.

On appeal, the prison sentence was quashed. An additional fine was imposed instead. Mr Eustace Fulton – again, note the name – the Chairman of London Sessions Appeals Committee and his fellow magistrates took into account that Hylton was the first celebrity to be given a jail sentence for such an offence. But the warning was clear: next time a famous name came before them, he could not expect to be so lucky.

Meanwhile, Ivor continued to float blissfully between the Aldwych and 'Red Roofs'.

On 8 October 1943, Ivor Novello received a mysterious telephone call. The managing director of a large firm asked him to visit his office. It was important.

Somehow the truth about Ivor's Rolls-Royce had been discovered. For the first time, Ivor learned his fan's real name, her true position in the firm – and that her bosses knew nothing whatever at the time about her dealings with his car.

It was clear that there had been a rigorous examination within the firm about the use of the car. The fan had been questioned and made three signed statements. Two were concerned with her position inside the firm. The third was addressed to Ivor.

The managing director now handed this third statement to Novello. In it the fan admitted: 'I did not get my employer's permission to obtain the permit for your motor-car. This was done entirely without his knowledge.' Then oddly she added: 'I undertake not to approach you as long as I live.'

What to do? Even Ivor was now made to realize the grim situation in which he found himself.

But – and this never appeared in subsequent Press reports of his case – he decided against any attempt at a cover-up. Through their respective solicitors both the firm and Ivor himself immediately informed the authorities. 'He was not a deceitful person. It was not in his nature,' I have been told.

But he was frightened. The thought of a court case. Being hauled in front of a magistrate. The unpleasant publicity. All conspired to make him tremble.

When a Fuel Ministry inspector came to see him, he panicked. He told him that it was all the fan's fault. It was all her idea. He did not know he was doing anything illegal. He would not have wanted to break the law. All perfectly true, perhaps – but not very gallant.

When his remarks were repeated back to the fan, she very quickly became an ex-fan. 'That is grossly unfair,' she said, 'He was willing to do anything crooked as long as he had the use of the car. Why, he knew every move, plan and suggestion the whole way through! He agreed to everything and knew the company had never used the car.'

With such a statement in the authorities' hands, there could be only one outcome. On the morning of 24 March 1944, a plain-clothes detective sergeant rang the front doorbell of Ivor's London flat. He handed Ivor a summons to appear at Bow Street Court to answer a charge that he 'did unlawfully conspire' with his woman fan 'to commit offences against Paragraph 1 of the Motor Vehicles (Registration of Use) Order 1942 Contrary to Regulations 70, 90 and 92 of the Defence (General) Regulations 1939.'

It was signed 'Harold McKenna' – the magistrate who had been thwarted in his desire to send Jack Hylton to jail!

Ivor tried to put a brave face on it. 'Probably persons in my profession overrate their importance,' he told the detective sergeant. 'But really I am engaged on important war work for morale, and my licence should not have been refused. The suggestion of my conspiring with a person of this woman's type is repugnant.

'Oh, the publicity it will mean! I don't mind myself, but I detest causing a stain on the theatrical profession.'

Each of us can form our own judgment on those words. Personally, while making every allowance for his distress, I do wish he had not gone so abjectly – and snobbishly – to pieces.

On Monday, 24 April 1944, Ivor Novello stood alongside his one-time fan in the dock at Bow Street Police Court. Later, his friend and noted theatrical historian W. Macqueen Pope was to write: 'Never before had a famous actor-manager, a man whose music was known to everyone, a man whose success was phenomenal, a man who had sent armies marching and sent them into battle with his song on their lips, lightening their weariness and their staring at death by his gift of melody, never before had such a man stood there.

'This hardly seemed real. It seemed like a scene in a play.'

But it was deadly real. Prosecuting counsel opened his case. Evidence was called. Ivor's stupid – and damaging – remarks were recounted to the impassive magistrate.

Then the managing director went into the witness-box. He told how his firm was completely innocent in the matter. But he also said: 'Quite obviously, Novello was deceived as completely as I was.'

That might be all right so far as it went: about the fan's real name, about her real position in the firm – and about the firm's knowing nothing of the transaction. But what about the vital point of the case: the charge that he conspired with her knowingly to break the law?

She chose not to give evidence. There could, therefore, only be one witness as to that essential central fact: Ivor himself.

He made a complete hash of it.

W. Macqueen Pope is now dead. But he was present in court throughout the hearing. He has left us this account of Ivor in the witness-box: 'I have seldom, if ever, seen a worse witness than Ivor. He was an actor and he never gave a worse performance.

'He was not so bad, naturally, when answering his own KC' – the famous courtroom advocate 'Khaki' Roberts – 'but when cross-examination began, he was really terrible. He was in a panic. He kept turning to his own counsel as if for help. Every answer he gave was muddled. One felt cold and sweaty with fear.'

The trouble was that he gave all too clearly the impression that he was trying to shelter behind his woman fan. And, in fairness to Ivor, I must admit that 'Khaki' Roberts – whom one would have expected to know better – did not try to restrain him.

Indeed, he positively encouraged him. At one point Roberts told the magistrate that he must represent his client's co-defendant 'in the strongest permissible language', as a liar.

'Do you agree with that?' asked McKenna. 'I am afraid I do,' replied Ivor. 'I think she has been all her life stage-struck, and has a great gift for self-dramatization.'

Harold McKenna was an old-fashioned gentleman. A product of Winchester and Christ Church College, Oxford. He was the last person to respect a man trying to hide behind a woman's skirts. Even if she were really to blame, a magistrate like McKenna – and there are still many who exist today – would have expected Ivor not to have been quite so hysterically anxious to put all the dross on to her shoulders.

His judgment was terse: 'I have no doubt,' he told the woman standing beside Ivor in the dock, 'that you have been very untruthful. You will be fined £50 with £25 costs.'

He turned to the star: 'I have no doubt that you, Novello, knew what was going on. The maximum fine is £100. That would be no punishment to you – and so I sentence you to eight weeks' imprisonment and order you to pay £25 costs.'

W. Macqueen Pope 'hardly dared look at Ivor. He was turned to stone.' He was granted bail, pending an appeal. His friends took him away. Next morning the nation's newspapers carried the story in thick headlines across the land.

Ivor steeled himself to go on working. His next performance was a matinee. Somehow he got through the ordeal. 'I was deeply touched by the reception I was given,' he afterwards told a reporter. 'The sympathy seemed to come over the foot-lights in waves.' It was estimated that, at least, 1,500 of the 2,000 in the audience were women.

'We had to go on doing the show – being gay – for practically a month, not knowing whether our star was going to end up in prison,' a member of the cast has told me. 'It was terrible. For him – and for us.'

On the morning of 16 May 1944, Novello arrived by taxi at the London Sessions courthouse in Newington Causeway for the hearing of his appeal. He was wearing a belted camel-hair overcoat and a brown felt hat pulled down over his eyes. Photographers and women thronged the court entrance as he entered the building to face the London Sessions Appeal Committee, which was headed by Mr Eustace Fulton, its full-time lawyer chairman.

Fulton – son of a judge: stern and rigid – soon showed that Ivor was unlikely to be treated as leniently as Jack Hylton – less than a year earlier. When Fred Allen said, in the witness-box, that he had not the faintest suspicion there was anything wrong about the car transaction – 'otherwise I would not have touched the damn thing' – Fulton pulled him up for his use of the word 'damn'.

Fred Allen apologized. He stammered and spluttered, and said he was not used to giving evidence, etc. 'Oh, get on!' said the judge.

'I am sorry to hear your Lordship show signs of impatience,' interposed 'Khaki' Roberts.

'I have shown every patience!' retorted the angry judge.

Ivor again gave evidence in his own defence. 'He was not quite so bad as before but he was not a good witness at all,' records W. Macqueen Pope.

But this time he had distinguished friends present in court to speak for him: Dame Sybil Thorndike, her husband Sir Lewis Casson, and Sir Edward Marsh, retired civil servant and secretary to many past Prime Ministers. All spoke of his honourable character.

His co-defendant did not appear. She had not appealed against Mr McKenna's judgment. No one has ever heard her side of the story, given under oath in the witness-box.

'Khaki' Roberts made an impassioned hour-long speech for his client. He urged the Bench to uphold Novello's plea of Not guilty. But even if he were guilty, magistrate McKenna's sentence had been passed 'in a moment of absolute savagery'.

'If Mr Novello had been foolish or trusting,' said his counsel, 'in the words of the poet, "Lord God, he has paid in full".'

Many people in court were moved – except Mr Eustace

Fulton and his five fellow magistrates. After a ten-minute retirement, they returned to court with their judgment: 'The appeal against conviction will be dismissed. The appellant was rightly convicted of the crime with which he was charged,' said Mr Fulton.

The only concession was that his prison sentence was halved. He would have to serve four weeks in jail – instead of eight. Ivor seemed stunned. He stood for a moment – silent as a statue, his head bowed. A court official touched his arm and, like a man in a trance, he moved slowly towards the door to the cells.

Suddenly, as he reached the door, he turned, confronted the crowded courtroom – all faces looking anxiously towards him – and flung open wide his arms in a gesture of infinite despair. It was magnificent theatre – played out against a background of life.

Ivor's four weeks at Wormwood Scrubs Prison almost killed him. 'He was an extraordinary person,' a friend has told me. 'He never liked being alone. Even when he went to the theatre to see a play or show, he would never go on his own – or with just one companion. He would always have to be with at least four other people. He once told me: "If I see they are enjoying it, it makes my own enjoyment four times as much!"

'You put such a man in prison, when he is alone from six in the evening to six in the morning – and you don't know what damage you are doing to him as a person.'

The authorities at Wormwood Scrubs treated Ivor kindly. They let him conduct the prison choir. But he nearly went out of his mind. Halfway through his four-week sentence, he wrote: 'I've got fourteen more days and nights. Oh, Christ Jesus help me to get through this and come out sane...'

Soon after midnight struck on Monday morning 13 June 1944, the green-painted door of Wormwood Scrubs opened – and a pale, much thinner Ivor Novello walked back into freedom.

Just over a week later, he made his return to *Dancing Years*. 'For the first time, one saw him nervous before the curtain went up,' a member of the cast has told me. 'We didn't know what was going to happen. Neither did he. Just one voice out of those two thousand people had to yell out "Jailbird!" – and I don't know what would have happened.'

It turned out a triumph. When Ivor walked on the stage, the applause was like a thunderclap. People stood. People cheered.

'It was ages before we could start the show. It was like a salute to theatrical royalty,' recalls the member of the cast. 'It was a magical night. Ivor was in tears – and so were many of us!'

That is right. One must accept it. The night of Ivor Novello's return to the theatre is one of the most famous occasions in stage history. It is even mentioned in a recently published history of life in the Second World War.

It is also true that Ivor went on to write several more famous – and highly successful—musical shows. But a part of him died during his four weeks in Wormwood Scrubs.

Says Peter Noble: 'I have no doubt that it shortened his life. He died only seven years later – in March 1951 – of a heart attack. I am convinced the anxiety of his case and his weeks in prison weakened his heart.' He never liked to talk about the experience. It was as if he were eternally trying to forget.

One thing is certain: it cost him the knighthood that otherwise he would assuredly have obtained. John Gielgud, Laurence Olivier, Ralph Richardson – the other three great names of the Second World War Theatre – were all honoured in this way. But not Ivor. The Establishment has a long memory – it would never forget that he spent four weeks in jail, alongside murderers and villains, for conspiring to break the law.

But was he really guilty? Can one pass judgment on a person like Ivor Novello in terms that the law uses and understands? I leave it for 'Khaki' Roberts, his counsel, writing his memoirs in 1964, shortly before his own death, to give the reply: 'I have always regarded Ivor as a completely innocent man; he always so assured me, and there seemed absolutely no evidence to the contrary.... I personally never had any doubt at all as to the innocence of Ivor Novello.'

Innocent or guilty, he paid a terrible price for the comfort of a Rolls-Royce.

17 Mrs Cornwallis-West
An Ageing Beauty

Ruthin Castle is now a comfortable, elegant hotel looking out upon the green-banked valley of the River Clywyd in North Wales. It was once genuinely a castle and a private home – the seat of the Cornwallis-West family, the most powerful in the area.

On the wall of one of the ground floor rooms there is a large framed painting of a beautiful woman, her face on her left hand leaning on the parapet of a balcony. Flowing dress. Soft brown hair. Large plumed hat. Wasp-waist. The pose of the knowing enchantress.

Staring at her coldly, from a corner across the room, is another portrait, that of Edward VII in the glorious, bemedalled uniform of a field-marshal. But in the flesh there was nothing cold about his regard for the adorable 'Patsy' Cornwallis-West, wife of Colonel William Cornwallis-West, Lord Lieutenant of Denbighshire.

'When he was Prince of Wales, the King was often down here at weekends,' an elderly resident had told me in the nearby town of Ruthin. 'He used to stay with Mrs Cornwallis-West and her husband.'

'She was his mistress,' said Mr Terry Warburton, a director of the family company that owns the present-day Ruthin Castle. And he showed me the secret staircase which Edward VII used to climb to meet his love. 'She was only sixteen-and-a-half when she married. Her husband was twenty years older than she was. They say he didn't mind.'

But youth does not endure. And beauty is of the hour. By the summer of 1915 Edward VII was dead. Colonel Cornwallis-West was eighty. Patsy was sixty – and dyed hair, heavy cosmetics, and a too-young taste in clothes proclaimed all too vividly the tragedy of the one-time beauty who could not adjust to losing her charms.

Her appearance may have become just a little absurd. But she still had the passions of a young woman. She was still avid for love – and the attentions of young men.

It was this avidity which took her over the edge of permissible conduct, and produced the scandal which ruined her public life.

Mary Adelaide Virginia Eupatoria – 'Patsy' – Cornwallis-West was of impeccable family background. Granddaughter of a marquis she had married one of the wealthiest men in Wales, himself the grandson of an earl.

Kaiser Wilhelm II of Germany was a personal friend. A flowering chestnut tree planted by Edward VII still stands in the grounds of Ruthin Castle. Her three children all married well – Daisy, the elder daughter, married a German prince; Constance, the second daughter, became Duchess of Westminster; George, the son, married the widowed Lady Randolph Churchill, Sir Winston Churchill's mother.

'Patsy' was in fact, Sir Winston's step-grandmother. Half-forgotten on the shelves of Ruthin Public Library, I found a book of reminiscences written in 1908 by Sir Winston's mother. It contains this account of 'Patsy' in the full glory of her powers: 'It was difficult to find a fault in her bright, sparkling face, as full of animation as her brown eyes were of Irish wit and fun. She had a lovely complexion, curly brown hair, and a perfect figure.'

Such a woman, aided by her husband's prestige in the county, wielded almost autocratic power over Ruthin and the surrounding countryside. Even today, as you descend into the town, the high clock-tower of Ruthin Castle out-tops every other building on the scene – including the ancient parish church of St Peter.

There was scarcely a public activity in North Wales with which she was not associated. The Denbighshire County Comforts Association; the Nursing Association for Ruthin and District; the Discharged Prisoners' Aid Society; the Belgian and Serbian Relief Funds.

But there was none in which she took a closer interest than her work for the wounded soldiers of the First World War in the Army convalescent homes, set up in that quiet, remote corner of the country.

That was how she came to meet – one day in the summer of 1915 – twenty-eight-year-old Sergeant Patrick Barrett. He was a handsome, straightforward kind of man – with dark, good looks and a charming kind of simple country honesty. He had been badly wounded in the lungs at the Battle of the Aisne in Northern France. He lay weak and still grievously ill in a bed at 'Bryncelin', a convalescent home at St Asaph – twelve miles from Ruthin.

Picture the scene. The great lady enters the ward, attended by doctors and nurses. Those soldiers who can, struggle to their feet and stand in a pathetic attempt at attention. Others – including young Patrick – can only lie back in bed, their faces wan against the pillow-slips.

Patsy Cornwallis-West passes down the beds. She pauses to talk to this man, then the other.

Finally, she arrives at Patrick.

We will never know what words were said. What sudden magic made that woman's heart tremble. But one thing we do know: from that first meeting, Sergeant Barrett had a new and powerful protectress.

The ageing ex-mistress of a King fell in love. Patrick was not her age – nor her class. He had joined the Royal Welch Fusiliers, of which her husband was an honorary colonel, as a boy private direct from school. He had little education. He was of humble background.

She set out to improve his status. As his health slowly bettered, she campaigned on his behalf. General Sir William Mackinnon, GOC Western Command, was an old friend of hers. So was Lieutenant-General Sir John Cowans, Quartermaster-General of the Forces and member of the Army Council. So also was Lieutenant-Colonel Delme-Radcliffe, Commanding Officer of the 12th Battalion Royal Welch Fusiliers.

Delme-Radcliffe applied formally to the War Office for a commission for the wounded Sergeant Barrett – and for him to be attached to his battalion. The application was warmly supported by the two generals, and by Honorary Colonel Cornwallis-West.

With such backing, there could be little doubt of the outcome. On 24 December 1915, Patrick Barrett was gazetted Second Lieutenant. Henceforth, he would be more socially acceptable as a friend of the Colonel's lady.

But Patsy was not the only woman who took an interest in the war-wounded Patrick Barrett. The convalescent home where he was staying was part of the large private house of a Major and Mrs R. E. Birch.

Major Birch had been for years agent for the Ruthin Castle estate, and his wife was an old friend of Patsy's. Though not quite in the same social top-bracket as the Cornwallis-Wests, they were, in their own small city of St Asaph, roughly equivalent to Patsy and her husband in Ruthin. They came from a fine family – with the major's brother a serving general and his nephew later to be Tory politician Nigel Birch, now Lord Rhyl.

'She was a fine woman, Mrs Birch,' an elderly male resident of St Asaph told me. 'She was always doing good for people. She paid for my singing lessons – and she dropped dead in the cathedral here listening to me singing in the choir!'

It was suggested at the time that the middle-aged Mrs Birch had herself more than a motherly interest in the handsome young officer, in fact that she was jealous of his increasingly warm friendship with Patsy, a woman older – but richer – than she.

But my St Asaph acquaintance would have none of that: 'She and the major had no children of their own,' he told me. 'She genuinely took an interest in the young.'

In any event, there seems little doubt that she viewed Patsy's developing obsession with Patrick as undesirable. Almost certainly she must have been most unhappy when Patsy announced her intention – early in February 1916 – of coming to spend a few days at 'Bryncelin'. But what could she do? Her husband was, after all, in the Cornwallis-Wests' service and Patsy was the Lord Lieutenant's wife.

During her stay, Patsy seems gradually to have thrown away all restraint. Now, at last, she was under the same roof as her beloved! She wanted to be near him, to touch him, to find again her lost youth and her departed beauty in his arms.

But 'Bryncelin' was no ideal lovers' trysting-place. It was a wartime convalescent home and she was the local grand lady on an official visit. On the first day, she wrote Patrick an impassioned note that, on some pretext, she managed to get handed to him:

Boy, dear, I am just thinking of you and your happiness. I see you are chafing against the tight hand over you [meaning Mrs Birch]. I would so love just to have you quite to myself at Ruthin, and I will arrange either for this Saturday or next.

She proposed to come too, but please, I want you alone... God bless you darling... Boy, I trust you so; believe every word you say, feel as if you could not tell me a lie; and yet! Well dear, I must have a few words somehow alone today. Patsy.

And 'somehow' they did find a privacy in that convalescent home. How or where cannot be stated with certainty. Perhaps in a small ward temporarily free of other occupants. Perhaps in a rest or recreation room.

It is clear, however, from a letter which Barrett later wrote, that while they were alone Mrs Cornwallis-West kissed the young officer. How long they were alone, what declarations of passion were made – these must remain matters of surmise.

Youth has no monopoly on romance. For some women, age is an irrelevance.

But Patsy's snatched encounter seems to have been discovered. Or at least, suspected. Next day, Patrick received a second clandestine note:

Boy, she has said some cruel hard things to me today. I think, dear, I shall go tomorrow morning—she has been very rude—but I will tell you all. When we can sit in peace in my flower boudoir I will teach you to love really beautiful poetry... write to me often ... just write as you feel, express it—spell it as you like. I shall understand. Patsy.

They were not alone again. It must have proved impossible for Patsy to contrive a meeting. All the more, she clung to her hopes of Patrick visiting her at Ruthin the following Saturday. Yet Mrs Birch was steadfastly in the way. Patsy would have to dissemble; to be cold to Patrick in public – so that his self-appointed watch-dog would be put off the scent.

She wrote a third note to explain:

Boy dear, I may be wrong, but I don't think I am. Mrs Birch does not, I feel sure, want you to come to me next Saturday, and will stop it somehow by saying you are not strong enough... But I want you so much to come, dear. Don't mind how I treat you today; you will know the real me, Patsy, all the time, and understand.

The letters make sad reading. Any human heart crying out to another in anguish commands pity – even though the spectacle of the painted, faded beauty scribbling such fevered notes contains something of the ridiculous.

To the perplexed Patrick Barrett, there was nothing funny about the situation. He decided once and for all to call a halt.

Dear Mrs Cornwallis-West [he wrote in his firm, almost schoolboy hand], I expect this letter will surprise you very much. I have been awake most of the night thinking over all you have said and wrote to me.

I must speak my mind on paper, which I don't seem able to do when I am with you. So I must tell you I don't like the way you have wrote about Mrs Birch. I came to Bryncelin a very sick man, and she nursed me back to life, and she and Mr Birch gave me a home life for which I had always prayed.

She does not have tight rein on me... It will be a great sorrow when I have to leave the only home I ever had, and her wonderful motherly care for me.

... I don't think I could look Colonel Cornwallis-West in the face because you kissed me: he was very good to me. I don't want to understand poetry. I only want to live a good life and serve my God and King.

I don't understand why you called me 'darling'. The other ladies never do, and they do not want to teach me poetry.

I honour and respect you very much, and some day I hope to do something for you. Your notes frighten me very much; you see my religion, as you know, compels me to go to confession, and it is the first time in my life I shall not be able to confess properly.

Will you please make some excuse for not asking me to Ruthin. Patrick Barrett.

Even after all these years, the simple, almost childlike, honesty hits out at you from the written page. Can you imagine the effect it had on Patsy Cornwallis-West? The resentment, the anger – and the shame.

She stormed out of the house, and hastened back to Ruthin Castle. She was determined to make this young ingrate pay for his impertinence.

She summoned up the full command of her power and influence. Angry letters went off to General Sir William Mackinnon, to Lieutenant-General Sir John Cowans and to Lieutenant-Colonel Delme-Radcliffe. Naturally, she did not disclose that she had been rebuffed in her attempt to seduce a young officer. She resorted to the classic weapon of a woman spurned: a malicious lie – but with Freudian undertones. She accused Patrick Barrett of having pursued her, of breaking into her bedroom at 'Bryncelin' – and attempting physically to assault her. She demanded that he be transferred to another battalion.

The allegations were laughable. But neither the two generals nor Lieutenant-Colonel Delme-Radcliffe burst into laughter. Either they believed her – which seems pretty incredible – or else they determined cynically to humour another of 'dear Patsy's' caprices.

The colonel personally rebuked Barrett in front of his fellow officers without giving him a chance to reply – and formally applied for his transfer to the 3rd Battalion. General Mackinnon supported the application.

And, at the War Office, Lieutenant-General Cowans wrote to Patsy:

> Orders have gone by wire for B. to be transferred at once to the 3rd Battalion. It is really all we can do ... I think all has been done that can be done by us officially—as it would never do for us to mix ourselves up in private quarrels and misunderstandings. I am very sorry, but I am sure you will understand this—I would fight for you if I had time.

But Barrett did not change battalions. His health – still not fully recovered from his wounds – broke. He could not be moved from 'Bryncelin'. And now he too found powerful supporters. Major Birch and his wife were appalled at Patsy's conduct. The major resigned as agent on the Ruthin Castle estate. They wrote letters of angry protest to the War Office – but were ignored.

They looked elsewhere for support, and contacted wealthy mine-owner-MP Sir Arthur Markham. He was perhaps the most famous backbencher of the day, and a vigorous critic of the Asquith Government's feeble handling of the nation's war effort. While hundreds of thousands died on the muddy fields of France, he was vitriolic and persisted in his attacks upon the incompetence of the War Office under its prestigious but woefully inefficient leader, Lord Kitchener, who was famous as a general, but hopeless as a Minister for War.

Kitchener ignored Markham's attempts to earn justice for Patrick Barrett.

But at about 7.40 pm on the evening of 5 June 1916, a German mine brushed against the bows of the battleship Hampshire, which was taking Kitchener to a war meeting in Russia.

The ship heeled over to starboard, settled down by the head, and sank within a quarter of an hour. Kitchener disappeared for ever into the chill waters of the North Sea.

His successor at the War Office was a very different sort of a man: David Lloyd George. A Welshman like Patrick Barrett. A 'man of the people' from humble origins like Patrick Barrett.

He was just the sort of man to welcome an opportunity to 'put the generals in their place' and to have a swipe at the traditional feudal sources of power in his native Wales – both at the same time!

On 7 August 1916, War Minister Lloyd George told the Commons that the Government was to bring in a special wartime Bill which would set up a court of inquiry to investigate not only the conduct of serving soldiers – as with an ordinary court martial – but also that of civilians.

Even before Lloyd George's statement, the House had been buzzing with speculation and rumour. Now it learned of this unprecedented action. But the situation too was without precedent. For this was no longer a minor clacking of tongues in a remote part of North Wales.

The scandal had reached Whitehall, overspilled into the corridors of Parliament – into the soft comfort of many a St James's club.

It was said that, not only had Patsy used her influence to get her reluctant lover transferred to another battalion, but that she had done so for a specific purpose: so that he should be sent back to the front line in Northern France.

The allegation was monstrous. It amounted almost to a charge of murder – with two generals as accessories before the fact.

Lloyd George chose carefully the words with which he introduced his Bill: 'There is one reason why I am exceedingly anxious that it should get through at the earliest possible moment,' he told the Commons. 'There are circumstances which involve imputations upon officers and upon others. It is not in the public interest that a matter of this kind should go uninvestigated for a moment more than is absolutely necessary.'

Three days later, the Royal Assent was given to the Army (Courts of Inquiry) Act. By the end of the month, the names of the court were announced: a distinguished field-marshal, a general, a High Court judge and an MP. But a World War was raging. The need to maintain public morale was paramount.

The amount of dirty linen to be washed in public must be limited. 'The proceedings throughout will be conducted in private,' said the official War Office announcement.

At 10.30 am on 6 September 1916, the court sat for the first time at the Middlesex Guildhall, facing Parliament Square. Patsy was summoned to give evidence. So was Patrick Barrett. And Major and Mrs Birch, and Generals Mackinnon and Cowans, and Lieutenant-Colonel Delme-Radcliffe.

All went into the witness-box. All were examined – and cross-examined – by counsel, and the members of the court.

The hearings dragged on through most of the month. But no details leaked to the Press. Even the names of witnesses were not disclosed.

On 29 September 1916, the court submitted an Interim Report to War Minister Lloyd George. No public announcement was made. But a few days later, Second Lieutenant Patrick Barrett – still convalescing at 'Bryncelin' – received a secret official letter from the War Office: he had been completely vindicated. He 'entirely merited the grant of his commission and there has been nothing in his conduct since which has been in any way unbecoming an officer and a gentleman.'

What of the others? What were the court's findings on the two generals, Lieutenant-Colonel Delme-Radcliffe – and the illustrious Mrs Cornwallis-West? The War Officer letter was silent.

The court submitted its final report to War Minister Lloyd George on 16 November 1916. Still, there was no public announcement. But the court's findings were nothing less than sensational: General Mackinnon had shown 'a want of judgment and discretion', Lieutenant-General Cowans was guilty of 'not merely indiscretion, but a departure from official propriety'; Lieutenant-Colonel Delme-Radcliffe had 'acted hastily, harshly, and improperly. We regret to think that, under the influence of a lady of position in the county, he allowed himself to deny justice to one of his junior officers.'

Their worst strictures were kept for Mrs Cornwallis-West:

We feel obliged to record our opinion that this lady's conduct, as revealed in this case, has been highly discreditable, both in her behaviour towards Second-Lieutenant Barrett before his letter of 14 February, in her vindictive attempts to injure him afterwards, and in the untruthful evidence she gave before us.

Not only did they brand her a liar. They added:

It appeared in evidence that this lady holds positions of some importance in the county of Denbighshire in various associations of a public character for assisting in war work. In our opinion it is to be regretted that she should hold such positions.

It was not until 22 December that a statement was made in the Commons. By then, Lloyd George had become Prime Minister, and Lord Derby was War Minister. The Under-Secretary of State for War, Mr Ian MacPherson, told the House that Lord Derby had decided as follows:

General Sir Henry Mackinnon: This 'old and distinguished soldier has now retired under the age clause and no action, even if it were asked for, in his case is either possible or desirable.'

Lieutenant-General Sir John Cowans: Lord Derby did 'not wish to protect any officer from the consequence of any action simply because of his high position, but he feels that this is not the moment, after he himself has just taken office, when the best interests of the country would be served by not continuing to avail himself of his services . . .

'Under the circumstances, the best interests of the Army and of the nation will be served by informing Sir John Cowans of the displeasure of the Government at his action, while at the same time retaining him for the present in the position of quartermaster-general.'

Lieutenant-Colonel Delme-Radcliffe: his conduct was 'very seriously impugned'. He had been 'removed from command of his battalion'.

'The lady implicated in the case': 'She is outside the jurisdiction of military control, and Lord Derby feels he cannot do better than leave the verdict of the Court to stand for itself.'

The pattern was clear: the two generals got off scot-free – in fact, Cowans remained as quartermaster-general through to the end of the War and beyond. The colonel and the county lady were thrown to the dogs.

Patsy at once gave up all positions of public office in Denbighshire, and retired into private life. By the rigorous standards of her time she had no alternative. The cardinal offence was to be found out.

What about the allegation that Patrick Barrett had been transferred to the 3rd Battalion – to be sent back to France?

Lieutenant-Colonel Delme-Radcliffe had told the Court of Inquiry that it was merely 'to remove him from the district'. Mrs Birch – although her husband did not go so far in his evidence – maintained firmly in the witness-box that the motive was more sinister: Patrick Barrett was being sent back to possible death.

In the result, the Court praised Major and Mrs Birch, in general terms, for their 'defence of a friendless young officer' – but rejected this specific charge as 'without justification'.

For my part, I am not so sure the charge was not well made out. I have checked the official history of the Royal Welch Fusiliers – written several years afterwards. I cannot help thinking that it cannot just be pure coincidence that the 3rd Battalion was the 'Special Reserve Battalion' and 'sent drafts of officers and men to the battalions serving on all fronts.'

'Heaven has no rage like love to hatred turned Nor hell a fury like a woman scorned,' wrote seventeenth-century playwright William Congreve. His words would seem to fit Patsy Cornwallis-West.

She did not long survive the case. In July 1920, she died in seclusion after a painful illness: aged sixty-five. The two generals lived on, to die contentedly in retirement, Second-Lieutenant Patrick Barrett settled in the St Asaph district, and, so I am told, died sometime in the 1930s.

The scandal is now completely forgotten – except in that distant corner of Wales. 'It almost stopped the War, didn't it?' said a cheery old gentleman to me in St Asaph. To the locals, the tale of the Lady of the Castle and the Young Soldier who rebuffed her advances has entered into folk-lore.

18 Edward Slovik
Shot for Cowardice

They would not let me see his grave. 'It is completely out of bounds,' said the cemetery official. 'If the President of the United States of America himself arrived, I would not let him see the grave without that little white permit card from the Pentagon in Washington – and you've almost got to be the President to get one!'

I was standing at the entrance to a beautifully maintained American Military Cemetery in the hills above the small town of Fere-en-Tardenois, 70 miles from Paris. In front of me was the terrible whiteness of more than 6,000 marble crosses.

But it was not a hero's grave I had come to see. Behind the superintendent's house, shielded from outside eyes by high walls and tall trees, lie the graves of ninety-six men – killed not by the Germans or any foreign enemy. But by the American military authorities themselves.

Ninety-five of them were villains: murderers and rapists. The ninety-sixth, lying in his grave without a cross, was a twenty-four-year-old boy called Eddie Slovik, Private Eddie Slovik, 36896415, Company G, 109th Infantry, 28th Division, United States Army. Date of death: 31 January 1945.

He has a unique niche in history. For he is the only American soldier since the American Civil War to be shot for desertion before the enemy. He is the American Army's only executed coward in the last hundred years.

'Three years ago, a man turned up here from Eddie's mother with flowers for the grave,' the cemetery official told me. 'He had a letter from her. I am sure he was genuine. But I could not let him put the flowers on the grave himself. I could not let him in. I took the flowers – and put them on the grave!'

Why – of all the 40,000 American soldiers believed to have deserted before the enemy in the Second World War – was Eddie Slovik the only one to die?

Eddie was no clean-cut, all-American college boy. Born in 1920, the son of a Polish-born Detroit car factory worker, he was one of the under-privileged. His father was often out of work. Money was tight. There were four other children to look after. The home environment was unhappy. Eddie ran wild, was easily led, got mixed up with local street gangs.

At the age of twelve, he had his first conviction – for breaking into a brass foundry with other youngsters. He was put on probation.

These were the years of the Great Depression. It needed more than the ministrations of a hard-pressed and under-staffed probation service to keep Eddie out of trouble. Petty theft, breaking and entering, disturbing the peace – always with associates – that was the pattern of his youthful existence.

In October 1937, Eddie, still only seventeen, pleaded guilty to embezzlement. He always pleaded guilty. He never tried to bluster his way out. That was later to prove a significant factor in his conflict with the US Army.

He served nearly a year in the Michigan State Reformatory (equivalent to our Borstal) and was then paroled. But four months after he was back, having pleaded guilty – again – to stealing a car with two pals 'just to go for a ride'.

He spent the next three years of his life in reformatory or jail. Finally, in April 1942, he walked out to freedom: to start work with a plumbing firm in Detroit. There were plenty of jobs for healthy, well set-up young Americans. Five months earlier, Japanese planes had dive bombed Pearl Harbour. The United States was at war. The cream of her able-bodied young men were being called to the colours. Eddie, though physically fit, was automatically in the low 4-F grade because of his record. The Draft Board told him that Uncle Sam did not need his services.

Now twenty-two, Eddie at last had a chance to make something of his life. He had money in his pocket. He met a girl, Antoinette Wisniewski, also born of Polish parents. She was five years older than he, a cripple with one leg shorter than the other and dogged by the ever-present fear of epilepsy. Yet she was a strong, dominant character. They fell in love. She provided him with the strength and backbone he needed. He adored her.

For the first time Eddie began to expand and develop as a human being. On 7 November 1942, the young ex-convict and the crippled potential epileptic were married. And for a few months Eddie and his bride were ideally happy.

They both worked. They saved and bought a car. Eddie got a better job. Antoinette became pregnant. The one-time 'dead end kid' was becoming a decent citizen.

But this was 1943. American battle casualties were mounting. More men were needed. 'Replacement men' the army called them. The draft boards could no longer be so choosy about their material. They began to scrape the barrel of available manpower. And they came up with Eddie Slovik.

7 November 1943 was Eddie and Antoinette Slovik's first wedding anniversary. On that day, after a year in furnished lodgings, at last they moved into a home of their own. It was a flat equipped with furniture they had almost beggared themselves to buy outright or on hire purchase. That moment was the culmination of a long struggle.

But that same evening Eddie's sister brought round a letter that had been sent to their old address. It was from the army. It said that they were considering changing his classification from 4-F to 1-A, and he could expect soon to be drafted.

As Antoinette later told American author and researcher William Bradford Hule, she and Eddie both burst into tears. 'Wouldn't you know they'd wait until a time like this!' exclaimed Eddie. 'Eighteen months ago, when I got out of jail and had nothing, they wanted no part of me! Now, when I'm a married man with a pregnant wife, and all this – now they want me to go to the army! Wouldn't you know it!'

One can sympathize. It was tough luck. But millions of other young men in America and Britain received similar summonses and made the best of it. Eddie Slovik was not very good at making the best of things.

On 24 January 1944, Eddie Slovik left home for the US Army. There had seldom been a more reluctant soldier. Why had 'they' done this to him? Why didn't 'they' leave him alone? He did not go out drinking with the boys. In three or four letters a day to Antoinette he poured out his anguish.

She lost their baby. The miscarriage brought on her dormant epilepsy. She could not work. Money was short. She only had her army allowance of fifty-five dollars a month. What would happen to their home? Their furniture?

They both tried – unsuccessfully – for Eddie to get out of the army on compassionate grounds.

They were miserable, bitter and sad. Why did this have to happen to them? Why couldn't they just have been allowed to carry on as they were – building a decent life for themselves?

These two people of European stock – but born thousands of miles away in the safe heart of America – never once seem to have considered the reason for Eddie's call-up. Hitler, Nazi Germany, the concentration camps, occupied Europe, Pearl Harbour, Japan – these did not come into their reckoning.

And so, still complaining, still deeply worried about how Antoinette could cope without him, Eddie – together with 7,000 other GIs (mostly replacement men) – set sail for Europe in the troopship *Aquitania*. The date: 7 August 1944.

Eighteen days later, on 25 August 1944, Eddie had his first taste of action. The Second Front had been launched ten weeks previously. Slowly and with much heavy fighting, by British and American troops, the German grip on the French countryside was being prised open.

When Eddie had arrived in France on 20 August he had, with other replacement men, waited for assignment. Then came the command: he was to join up with G Company, 109th Infantry Regiment, 28th Division. The company was at Elbeuf, a small town on the south bank of the River Seine about eighty miles north-west of Paris.

Eddie and eleven other replacements arrived to find a charnel house of blood and destruction. But Eddie did not report to the 109th, a crack rifle regiment. He did not put finger to trigger. Shells blasted overhead, guns spat death, buildings crumbled in ruin – and Eddie spent the whole of that first night in the battle area cowering in a fox-hole.

The following morning, he still made no effort to join up with his company. Instead he wandered bewilderedly through the shattered streets with another newly arrived young American until they found a small Canadian Army unit – with whom they stayed for the next six weeks. The two American lads made themselves useful. They foraged for food. They helped in back-of-the-line activities. They moved forward with the Canadians across Northern France – but never in actual combat with the enemy.

Eddie Slovik and his young companion could not remain indefinitely with the friendly Canadian soldiers. Eddie could have done what quite a few American deserters did: simply melt into the countryside, pinch a bit, scavenge a bit, dabble in the black market – and make a war-free, nameless life for himself. But that way, the 'little boy lost' from Detroit would never get back home. Going on the run and changing his identity, would effectively destroy any real hope of ever seeing Antoinette again.

It seems almost certain that Eddie, during those agreeable weeks with the Canadians, decided on a bold course of action that would be bound – so he reasoned – to get himself sent back to the States. Not at once to the comfort of his home or the warmth of his wife's embrace. But, at least, back to safety and away from vicious steel that could tear the flesh to pieces.

On 5 October 1944, Eddie and his companion caught up with the 28th US Division at Elsenborn in Belgium. They were not put under arrest. No charges were laid against them. Astonishingly, it was accepted that they had genuinely lost contact with their company.

Eddie's companion was redetailed. A month later, he was wounded in battle. He survived the war to return with honour to his native land.

And Eddie? On 8 October 1944, he deliberately and coolly refused to go into action against the enemy. He told his Company commander that he would not serve with a front line company. He was 'too nervous'. Unless he could be kept behind the lines, he would run away. 'Don't talk nonsense!' said the commander, and assigned him to a forward platoon.

Eddie did not join the platoon. He walked quietly out of the company office, threw away his rifle and walked purposefully up the street. Away from the company, away from the army, away from the war.

But only for one night.

Next morning, he presented himself at a nearby regimental headquarters – and handed to an astonished young army captain a written slip of paper. Remember his simple straightforward pleas of guilty in time of peace, with the inevitable jail or reformatory sentence to follow. Now he was hoping to achieve the same result in war.

The slip of paper began: 'I Private Eddie D. Slovik 36896415 confess to the desertion of the United States Army.' It is an amazing document. It is a signed admission of desertion before the enemy. An offence punishable under US Army law by death.

I am quite sure that Eddie did not think for one moment that he would be shot. I believe that he expected to be tried and court martialled and sentenced to death. Nothing less could happen to him with such a confession in the hands of the authorities.

But confessing to desertion was not unknown as a way of getting out of active service in the US Army of the Second World War. No fewer than 2,864 American soldiers were tried by wartime general courts martial. Sentences ranging from twenty years to death were imposed. Forty-nine of the death sentences were approved by the superior military authorities – but, so far, not one of those sentences had been carried out.

All that happened was that the deserting Serviceman was shipped back to the States – which is just what Eddie wanted! He would then spend the rest of the war in a home jail, knowing full well that, once peace came, he would within a few years almost certainly be paroled. It was the coward's established escape route from the battlefield and Eddie Slovik saw no reason why he should not take it.

The US Army, at that time, had a procedure for trying to save deserters from the shame they had brought on themselves. If the man agreed to go back into the line charges would often be dropped. An army colonel offered such a deal to Eddie Slovik. But Eddie refused. He was determined to get back into that safe prison cell thousands of miles on the other side of the Atlantic.

Eddie Slovik's court martial took place on a cold autumn morning in November 1944. The scene was a converted courtroom in a public building in Rotgen, Germany, only a few miles from the Belgian frontier.

Eddie had no lawyer to speak for him – merely a young, untrained army captain from Philadelphia. But there was nothing this officer – or anyone else – could do for Eddie. That slip of paper: 'I Private Eddie D. Slovik ... confess to the desertion of the United States Army,' spoke for itself.

Eddie declined to give evidence. He 'stood mute', in army legal terms. There was only one possible verdict that the nine staff officers comprising the court could return: Guilty. Eddie Slovik was sentenced to "be shot to death with musketry". The entire proceedings had taken a little over an hour and a half.

But Eddie was not despondent. He knew that his get-home-safe plan had to go through this stage. The presiding officer of the court martial had subsequently stated that neither he nor his eight fellow judges believed the sentence could be carried out. For Eddie, all was going according to plan.

But now appeared on the scene a grizzle-haired, tough American general named Norman B. Cota, commanding officer of the US 28th Division. The actor Robert Mitchum played General Cota in the film *The Longest Day*. Cota – who died in retirement of a heart attack last year – was no coward-lover. He was himself a man of the highest bravery. He was proud of the traditions of his division, one of the oldest in the US Army. He saw no reason why he should be as soft as most other division commanders. He confirmed the death sentence.

For the first time Eddie, now removed to an iron-spike walled prison on the Boulevard-Mortier, in the north-west outskirts of Paris, began to fear that something might go wrong. According to his calculations, General Cota should have commuted his sentence to one of long imprisonment. Why hadn't he done so? What was going to happen?

It was frightening to sit in his cell, and wait.

But Eddie Slovik still could not bring himself to believe that General Cota had spoken the last word on his case.

After all, dozens of other death sentences had been approved by the divisional commanders – only to be quashed by the Commanding General, European Theatre of Operations, General Eisenhower himself. Surely 'nice-guy' Ike would not let him down?

And possibly Ike would have intervened – had not, on the morning of 16 December 1944, the Germans began their last desperate throw – the arrowed lunge in the Ardennes which rolled the American front back fifty miles. Never had the morale and discipline of the American Army been so severely tested.

General Eisenhower himself in these guarded words in his post-war book *Crusade in Europe*, admits some of the effect of Rundstedt's unexpected lunge: 'It would be idle and false to pretend that the Allied forces, in all echelons, did not suffer strain and worry throughout the first week of the Ardennes attack.'

On 22 December, still within that first week, he issued an Order of the Day to his troops. One of the few that he actually wrote himself: 'I call upon every man, of all the Allies, to rise now to new heights of courage, of resolution and of effort. Let everyone hold before him a single thought – to destroy the enemy on the ground, in the air, everywhere – destroy him!'

The next day, 23 December, sitting in his office in the Hotel Majestic near the Arc de Triomphe where only months before the German Military Command had had their Paris headquarters, Eisenhower signed the confirmation of Eddie Slovik's execution. As American law then stood, there was no right of appeal to the President. No redress to any civilian court. Eisenhower's was the last word.

The military legal authorities decided that Eddie should be executed by the men of his own division. Perhaps because that distinguished unit's honour had been slurred by their new recruit's cowardice. Perhaps because the division was conveniently remote from Paris, deep in the Vosges Mountains where the last grim scene could be enacted in some privacy.

No public anger was aroused by Eddie's impending death. There was nothing in the papers. Nothing in any official war communiqué. Antoinette Slovik, back in Detroit, was told nothing. Eddie's letters dried up – that was all.

In January 1945, 28th Divisional headquarters were in the small Vosges town of Ste Marie-aux-Mines, snuggling up to the German frontier. A suitable place would have to be found. And that required a wall.

They chose a wall in the garden of No. 86 rue général Bourgeois, on the northern outskirts of the town. One can see the reason for the US Army's choice. It is remote. Not looked upon by neighbours. You reach it by crossing a bridge over a stream, and down one side of the large rear garden there is the seven-foot-high, thick stone wall.

'I remember when the American soldiers came and told my family and myself to leave the house for thirty-six hours,' Mlle Bethe Roth told me. 'We were not told why. But when I came back I found two bullet holes in the wall.' They are still there.

It was on the evening of 30 January 1945 that the gates of Eddie's prison in Paris swung open, and a US Army weapons carrier drove out. In it sat five men – four military policemen and a handcuffed Eddie Slovik.

Blizzards blew across central France. The roads were treacherous. The five men huddled in the vehicle had a long way to go. Two hundred and eighty miles, in fact.

To Eddie, in the snow and the dark, it must have seemed as if they were taking him to the end of the world. The journey ended at 7.30 on a bitterly cold, snow-swept January morning.

He was given a short time with an Army priest. Then at 10 am, before General Cota and forty-five other assembled witnesses, he was marched out into the garden, strapped to a post in front of the wall, a hood put over his head – and a detail of twelve men, all expert marksmen, given the order to fire.

One bullet was a blank, two bullets thudded into the wall to give silent testimony that remains to this day – and nine smashed into his body. But he did not die at once.

Every man in that garden saw him slump forward, then struggle up at least twice. No bullet had found his heart, to bring instant death. US Army doctor Robert E. Rougelot stepped forward. His heavy footsteps cracked on the snow. He put his stethoscope to Eddie's chest: the heart was still beating.

The order was given to recharge the rifles. Still, they waited – watching twenty-four-year-old Eddie D. Slovik die. Finally, just as the squad was about to fire again, Dr Rougelot turned and said: 'He's dead!'

'Today I had the most regrettable experience I have had since the war began,' wrote the colonel commanding the 109th Regiment in a message to his soldiers on 31 January 1945. 'I saw a former soldier of the 109th Infantry, Private Eddie D. Slovik, shot to death by musketry, by soldiers of this regiment. I pray that this man's death will be a lesson to each of us ...'

Antoinette Slovik was told merely that her husband had 'died in the European Theatre of Operations'. There is no mention of the case in Eisenhower's *Crusade in Europe* nor in the official *History of the US Army in World War II*. The official US Army historian of the European Theatre of Operations, General S. L. A. Marshall, has admitted in an American magazine article that he knew nothing of the affair.

The people of the United States would have remained totally ignorant of what had been done in their name but for a book by an American journalist, William Bradford Huie, published in 1954.

Looking back on the disturbing affair after more than a quarter of a century, what judgment should be passed on Eddie Slovik and on those who participated in his death?

Recently, I have been in touch with Dr Rougelot, the man who pronounced Eddie Slovik dead and who has studied the full background of the case.

Writing from his home in New Orleans, Dr Rougelot tells me:

It has always bothered me that Slovik allowed all this to happen. He was given ample opportunity again and again to recant or to back away from his original position. I spoke to the psychiatrist who examined him and it was his impression that Slovik was a kind of 'dead-end-kid'; a product of socio-economic, ghetto-like environment and possibly a-social.

I believe that in the beginning he thought he could 'beat-the-rap', but as the inexorable process of military law became eventually inescapable he probably succumbed to some deep death wish, which we so frequently encounter when life fails us or we fail life.

That is probably true. Most people, even those without any streak of heroism, would be protected from the fate of Eddie Slovik by a sense of shame. Slovik felt no shame. But was it still necessary to shoot him?

By the time those rifle shots rang out in the Vosges, the Battle of the Bulge was past its crisis. The Germans had started to retreat. Their maximum point of penetration had been reached. The Americans were already once again on the advance.

So why shoot Private Slovik – unless, of course, at that stage of the battle no one could be sure the Germans were not really falling back to recoup and surge forward again? The need to preserve discipline was still as high as ever.

A French newspaper has called the unhallowed plot where Eddie Slovik's body lies *'Le Plot de la Honte'* – 'The Plot of Shame'. But whose is the shame?

Each must give his own answer.

19 *Victors' Court Martial*
The Sequel to the 'Great Escape'

'They had a fair trial,' said Carl Stirling, QC, retired Deputy Judge Advocate General of the Forces. 'They all had lawyers to defend them. I was the Judge Advocate, and the impression I got was that everybody was impressed by British military justice and the common sense of it.'

Mr Stirling, now in his eighties, was talking to me about the little-known military trial that was the sequel to the famous 'Great Escape' of March 1944, when British, Commonwealth and Allied officers staged a mass break-out from a prisoner-of-war camp in Germany. Never had the German security services been so humiliated and infuriated. They reacted with appalling savagery. And as a result, three years after the great break-out, eighteen Germans stood trial before a British military court at Hamburg.

But this court had been assembled to do justice, not to seek blind revenge. Carl Stirling told me: 'The same strict rules of evidence applied, the same rules of law prevailed as if it was a trial for murder at the Old Bailey. The Crown had to prove that each of the accused had committed a war crime.

'It was not for the accused to prove that they had not. In my summing up to the military and air force officers comprising the court I said that if there was a reasonable doubt, they should give the benefit of that doubt to the accused.'

Millions have seen the film about the Great Escape, starring Steve McQueen.

But the film was a glamorization. One of its characters was a handsome, lovable baseball-playing American. There was no American involved in the Great Escape.

The reality was a story of bravery by officers from Britain, the Commonwealth and some European countries. And the aftermath was a tragedy of blood and bitterness.

The story begins in the spring of 1942. Hermann Goering, No. 2 Nazi and head of the German Air Force, was getting tired of captured RAF officers' constant and determined efforts to escape. RAF prisoner-of-war camps were his particular responsibility as Luftwaffe chief, and he was being made to look ridiculous. The building of tunnels in the camps seemed to be going on all the time.

So he had a special new prison camp built: the notorious Stalag Luft III. It was near Sagan, a small, remote town about a hundred miles south-east of Berlin in the heart of the Silesian pine forests. Goering boasted it was 'escape-proof'.

'They simply cut a huge square out of the thick pine forest,' fighter-ace Wing Commander R. R. Stanford Tuck, DSO, DFC, and former prisoner of war, has told me. 'They built this huge, hemmed-in camp literally almost in the middle of nowhere. The ground was sand, to make it more difficult for tunnelling. And the temperature varied from sub-zero in winter to the hundreds in summer. It was not a very pleasant place.'

That is a massive understatement. Yet the special problems of Stalag III did not deter Tuck and nearly six hundred selected fellow RAF and Allied Air Force officers from plotting the 'Great Escape'. It was the most daring mass breakout ever planned.

The man in overall charge of the scheme was a debonair, twenty-nine-year-old South African called Roger Bushell. 'He shared a room with me,' Tuck, now a slim, dark haired fifty-six-year-old, told me at his Kent farmhouse. 'He was a marvellous fellow. He was a pre-war barrister at the Old Bailey and was a great friend of mine. I'd seen him shot down over Dunkirk in May 1940. I'd taken over command of his flight. And now I joined with him in planning this escape.

'It was our duty as officers to escape, if we possibly could. It is always a prisoner's duty, if captured, to try to escape.'

The Sagan idea was grandiose. No fewer than two hundred men were to get away on a moonless night and disperse into Germany.

'Roger would have liked to get the whole camp out!' says Tuck. 'He wanted our escape to be the biggest and best ever done – and cause the biggest possible mess-up of German internal security.'

The escape took a year to plan. Tunnels were started, but soon discovered. Documents were forged. Civilian clothes fashioned out of Air Force uniforms and parcels from home. A complicated system of trolleys was built to haul escapers along the 360 ft underground path to freedom.

The escape tunnel grew near completion. With only weeks to go, the intending escapers began to team up in pairs (they were to go in groups of two). Bob Tuck paired up with Roger Bushell.

'I spoke fluent Russian, and he had perfect French and German. We would have been quite a good team.'

Then the prison camp authorities struck. They must have had an inkling that something was going on – but did not know exactly what. Twenty of the most prominent prisoners – including Tuck – were called out on parade, and summarily ordered to be ready to leave within thirty minutes. 'They marched us out, into Sagan, right out the other side and up a hill. There they locked us in a small high-up camp called Belaria, where we didn't have a chance of getting out.'

Tuck and his nineteen companions were out of the 'Great Escape'. But it made no difference. Roger Bushell – 'I'm sure he would have been a judge by now,' says a barrister who knew him – carried on with his arrangements.

On the bleak, moonless night of Friday, 24 March 1944, the escape took place. But from the start it went grievously wrong. A massive air raid on Berlin made the lights fail throughout the camp – and in the tunnel.

The tunnel itself broke surface ten feet short of the protective cover of the pine forest. There were delays and doubts. In the end only seventy-six men – including Roger Bushell – got away instead of the proposed two hundred.

Group Captain 'Wings' Day, AM, DSO, MC, was one of those seventy-six. Now a bluff, tough white-haired man, he takes up the narrative: 'They were brave chaps,' he says. 'The tunnel turned out short, but that made no difference to these fellows.

'The important thing is that it came up outside the camp's perimeter. The sentries concentrated on looking inside the camp for possible escapers – not outside!'

Day still remembers what it was like waiting in civilian clothes in a crowded room at Sagan railway station for the next Berlin train – with a sprinkling of escaping prisoners, in various civilian disguises, standing around the place, being jostled unknowingly by German soldiers and civilians.

'I saw a fellow named Tom Kirby-Green. He was a good-looking, tall chap. He was supposed to be a Spanish worker, and I suppose he looked Spanish enough – he was dark enough. But to me, he looked very much like Tom Kirby-Green! To anyone who knew him, he stood out like a sore thumb.'

The small booking-hall of Sagan station was packed with a tight wedge of German servicemen, civilians, women and children – all waiting for trains badly disorganized and thrown off schedule by the massive air-raid on Berlin. The air was warm and fetid. Thick blackout curtaining smothered the windows. From the adjoining station bar came sounds of song.

And in the middle of it, desperate men, who, hours earlier had been penned behind barbed wire together, avoided each other's eyes.

All the prisoners waiting for trains managed to get safely away. But, by daybreak, nineteen of the escapers had been picked up.

Fifty-seven were still at liberty. German internal security forces were thrown into a hopeless panic. 'Despite all the talk of Teutonic efficiency, the Germans can get into the most awful flap!' comments Wing Commander Tuck laconically.

At six o'clock the following morning, Saturday, 25 March 1944, the telephone rang at the home of sixty-three-year-old Max Wielen, head of the Criminal Police for the Breslau region (Sagan was within his area). Wielen was not a member of the Gestapo, Hitler's secret police of dedicated hard-core Nazis, but of the civilian police organization Kripo. He was an ordinary policeman, head of the local CID. But his duties included co-operating with the camp authorities over security.

Wielen had been dreading a major break-out from Sagan.

For months he had been urging Colonel Von Lindeiner, the courteous elderly Luftwaffe officer in command at the camp, to take stronger measures to deter escapers – but to no avail. The colonel had tiresomely old-fashioned ideas about respecting prisoners' rights under the 1929 Geneva Convention.

Now, as he hurriedly dressed, Wielen knew that a storm of abuse from Berlin would burst on all concerned with security at Sagan. He realized at once that only the sternest measures could even partially attempt to redress the damage to German – and his own – prestige.

He ordered a *Grossfahndung*, a nationwide hue and cry, the

highest search order in Nazi Germany.

The German radio broadcast the news, and thousands of troops and auxillaries at once turned out to search. The ordinary police, the security, railway, and frontier police, the army and air force, SS men and Gestapo, Home Guard, Hitler Youth – everyone was called out on to the streets and into the fields to track down the escaping men. An estimated five million men were involved in the hunt.

So huge an operation was bound to produce results.

'It was inevitable that most, if not all, the prisoners would be recaptured,' says Wing Commander Tuck. 'My admiration for those brave men is untold.

'But the very size of the escape was against it. The Germans had to throw everything they had into getting back those prisoners.'

On Sunday morning, 26 March 1944, Adolf Hitler, in his Bavarian mountain retreat at Berchtesgaden, read a special Gestapo report on the escape. Goering, security police chief Heinrich Himmler and Nazi field-marshal Wilhelm Keitel were present. They waited anxiously while the Führer completed his reading.

He screamed. He ranted. He flew into a rage. 'All prisoners are to be shot on recapture!' he shouted.

Discreetly, the multi-medalled Goering protested. Not on humanitarian grounds, or because he was worried that the Geneva Convention forbade reprisals on escaping prisoners. He suggested tactfully that to shoot all the prisoners would too obviously be cold-blooded murder. No propaganda about shooting men who resisted arrest would be able to cover up such wholesale slaughter. Besides, he was worried about what might happen to his own air force prisoners in Allied hands.

'Very well,' said Hitler. 'More than half are to be shot!' And with that he closed the subject – leaving it to his underlings to sort out the finer details of mass murder.

The responsibility for carrying out Hitler's decree was Heinrich Himmler's. The prospect seems to have caused him no scruple.

That Sunday evening he called in Ernst Kaltenbrunner, his hatchet-faced second-in-command.

The result was the infamous 'Sagan Order' teleprinted by Kaltenbrunner to all regional Gestapo and Kripo (CID) headquarters the next morning. It is one of the most disgraceful documents in military history:

> The frequent mass escapes of officer prisoners constitute a real danger to the security of the State. I am disappointed by the inefficient security measures in various prisoner-of-war camps. The Führer has ordered that as a deterrent, more than half of the escaped officers will be shot.
> The recaptured officers will be handed over to the Gestapo for interrogation. After interrogation the officers will be transferred to their original camps and will be shot on the way. The reason for the shooting will be given as 'shot whilst trying to escape' or 'shot whilst resisting' so that nothing can be proved at a future date.

Only three men – two Norwegians and a Dutchman – who escaped from Sagan ever finally reached England. Within less than a fortnight, all seventy-three others were recaptured. And fifty of them were shot.

How were these fifty chosen?

Sitting in his office at Kripo headquarters in Berlin, a Kripo general named Arthur Nebe went through a list of all the escapers – supplied by the diligent local police chief Max Wielen – and, after consulting their files, marked with a red cross the names of those who were to be shot.

Later, at the Hamburg Military Trial, a Kripo clerk gave a vivid word-picture of Nebe at work. He would look at one card and say, 'Der muss dran glauben' ('He is for it') and put the card on the bigger pile in front of him. Then he would look at another and say, 'He is so young. No!' And put it on a smaller pile.

At Belaria prison camp a German staff sergeant who knew that Wing Commander Stanford Tuck and Roger Bushell had been friends at Sagan entered Tuck's room. He hung his head: 'Don't let anyone know I've told you Herr Oberst (Colonel),' he said, 'but Herr Major Bushell has been shot!'

Tuck at first did not believe him. He thought the German might be playing some kind of malicious joke.

He put the German on his honour as a soldier to tell the truth. The man said: 'Herr Oberst it is perfectly true. I am as upset as I am sure his friends will be.'

Roger Bushell and his companions were taken in small groups of two or three from the various places where they had been recaptured throughout Germany. Then they were gunned down. The official Law Report of the 1947 Hamburg Trial says:

In every case the officer commanding received orders from the Central Security Office in Berlin. He then made the necessary arrangements for their execution.

The party carrying out the shooting usually consisted of either the Commanding Officer himself or another officer detailed by the Commanding Officer to be in charge of the party, one or more Gestapo officials as escort and a driver.

Those detailed were briefed by the Commanding Officer as to their duties and pledged to absolute secrecy by handshakes and by a reminder of the SS oath to the Führer.

They then set out at night in one or more cars to fetch the prisoners from the local jail where they were handed over by the Kripo. After a short drive the car stopped by the roadside, the excuse being always that the prisoners wanted to relieve nature.

The place selected was always near a crematorium. The driver or another man remained by the car to see that no cars or passers-by would stop in the vicinity. The other Gestapo officials would take out the prisoners and kill them by shooting them in the back, usually only a short distance from the road.

The bodies were inspected by the nearest doctor, who issued a death certificate. The bodies were then cremated and the urns sent to the Kripo regional headquarters at Breslau for onward transmission to Stalag Luft III.

The man responsible for 'onward transmission' was Breslau Kripo chief Max Wielen. But it was no longer gentle Colonel von Lindeiner who received them at Sagan. He had, early on, been released from his command and replaced by a new and sterner commandant.

The Nazis tried to keep secret the true fate of the Sagan Fifty. 'Orders carried out, prisoners shot while trying to escape,' read the official report in every case.

But the truth leaked out. On 17 April 1944, a Swiss inspector, as representative of Switzerland, the 'Protecting Power' under the Geneva Convention, paid a routine visit to Sagan Camp. And Group Captain Massey, senior British officer, told him the disturbing news that all the officers shot 'while trying to escape' had been killed. Not one had merely been injured. Strange that every Nazi bullet had found a fatal mark!

Suspicion of murder soon gave way to shocked realization of the tragic actuality. On 23 June 1944, Anthony Eden, then

Foreign Secretary, rose in the House of Commons and told hushed MPs of 'an odious crime against the laws and conventions of war'.

He gave a solemn pledge in the name of His Majesty's Government: 'They will never cease in their effort to collect the evidence to identify all those responsible. They are firmly resolved that these foul criminals shall be tracked down to the last man wherever they may take refuge. When the war is over they will be brought to exemplary justice.'

The chain of command – and of responsibility – for the Sagan murders ran down from Hitler himself, through the three present at that fateful Sunday morning conference at Berchtesgaden – Goering, Himmler and Keitel – to Kaltenbrunner, Himmler's second-in-command, then to Nebe, the Kripo general who sorted out the cards of those who would live and who would die, then to Max Wielen, the Breslau police chief, and finally on to an unknown number of faceless, nameless Gestapo men who actually did the killings.

By the time of Germany's surrender, both Hitler and Nebe were beyond human justice. Hitler had committed suicide in a Berlin bunker in late April 1945 and Nebe had been strangled by Hitler's own orders for his part in the ill-fated 'Generals' Plot' against the Führer in June 1944.

Within three weeks of Germany's surrender, Heinrich Himmler also put himself beyond mankind's justice. A prisoner in British military hands, he bit upon a small phial of cyanide secreted between his teeth. Within minutes, he was dead.

Goering, Keitel, and Kaltenbrunner stood trial with eighteen other top Nazis at Nuremberg from November 1945 to October 1946.

All three were sentenced to death on indictments covering many matters. All three died: Keitel and Kaltenbrunner by judicial hanging, Goering by suicide – like Himmler, he swallowed cyanide.

That left Max Wielen and the actual men who had physically committed the murders. Where were they? Who were they? They had to be found if the pledge given to the Commons was to be fulfilled.

Colonel Alexander Scotland, a mild man in his mid-sixties, was chief of the War Crimes Investigation Unit. Now he is dead. But in his book, *The London Cage*, he sets out the full story of how his men and dedicated RAF investigators probed and questioned and travelled thousands of miles, all over Germany and even deep into Russia, searching out the guilty. Their labours took just over two years.

Finally, on the morning of 1 July 1947, Max Wielen and seventeen fellow Germans stood in the No. 1 Courtroom of the Curio Haus, a converted concert hall in Hamburg, Germany. 'Many more should have been in the dock beside them; but at least we had eighteen,' Colonel Scotland has written.

It was a British Military Court, set up under a Royal Warrant signed by King George VI. The president of the court was a red-tabbed major-general. His fellow judges were three Army colonels and three senior RAF officers. The Judge Advocate, wigged and gowned as if for an ordinary court martial, was Carl Stirling, KC.

The German lawyers defending the eighteen accused had a thankless task. That their clients had physically done the acts with which they were charged could, in most cases, hardly be denied.

The documentary evidence of captured German files was against them. Plus the self-criminatory statements that many of these hard-core Nazis, bound to Hitler by their SS oath of loyalty, had already made to their interrogators.

For instance, Otto Preiss, of the Karlsruhe Gestapo: 'I do not consider myself guilty. I only acted in accordance with orders.'

Or Erich Zacharias, of the Border Police: 'I carried out the task first because it was an order, secondly because I was assured that nothing could happen to me later, and also because I justified myself there was a war on and that the airmen might have killed hundreds of civilians by bombing.'

Or Eduard Geith, of the Munich Gestapo: 'I could have refused this order, but I am convinced that a refusal would have had the severest consequences.'

The main defence was that used by most Nazi – and Japanese – defendants in war crimes trials, that of 'superior orders'. The accused claimed they were only obeying orders that it would have been suicide to disobey.

Carl Stirling showed what he thought of this defence fairly early in the proceedings.

A Kripo clerk had just given evidence about General Nebe sorting out the cards of those who were to die or live. 'I am convinced that all who carried out the shooting order were deeply ashamed of themselves,' he said.

At once, Mr Stirling pounced: 'Did nobody in the police disobey the illegal order?' The witness replied: 'Murder orders such as the Sagan order were not daily occurrences.'

'Even in the Third Reich,' came back Mr Stirling, 'was it not unusual to take an Englishman with his hands manacled and shoot him like a dog in a field?'

'Yes,' was the quiet reply.

In the end, Carl Stirling summed up to the judges that 'superior orders' would not give the accused a defence 'if in obedience to a command they committed acts which both violated unchallenged rules of warfare and outraged the general sentence should have been imposed,' he said. 'These men were with international law, as it then was – and still is.'

The result: all eighteen defendants were found guilty. But their sentences varied. Fourteen of the accused who actually fired a gun or participated in the shootings were sentenced to death.

Max Wielen, who had helped to select the victims, and had passed on to the Gestapo twenty-seven of the thirty-six escaping officers recaptured in his area, got life imprisonment.

Two men who had been unwilling members of the Gestapo and were only drivers, were sentenced to ten years imprisonment.

Subsequently, Lieutenant-General Sir Richard McCreery, Commander-in-Chief, British Army of the Rhine, commuted one of the death sentences to life imprisonment. The man concerned was called Heinrich Boschert. There seems to have been a genuine doubt whether he was just a driver or also acting as a guard.

Eventually, at Hamelin Prison, Hamburg, on 26 February 1948, thirteen men were hanged for the murder of the Sagan Fifty. They were the only ones directly responsible to be hanged – besides Keitel and Kaltenbrunner.

In October 1948 three more Gestapo men were put on trial in the Curio Haus. One was acquitted. Two were sentenced to death – but one had his sentence commuted to life imprisonment, and the other was not even confirmed by the BAOR Commander-in-Chief because there was a possibility of mistaken identity.

Max Wielen was released from jail in October 1952, after serving only five years of a so-called 'life' sentence. It is extremely unlikely that any of those sentenced with him are still in jail.

'Wings' Day has told me that, although he thinks it was right to put as many culprits as could be found on trial, he does not believe they should have been hanged. 'A pretty heavy prison sentence should have been imposed,' he said. 'These men were under their SS oath of loyalty to the Führer, and it was a very strong oath.'

Wing Commander Stanford Tuck disagrees. 'Of course, they should have been hanged! Anyone who shoots a man like that, knowing him to be an escaping prisoner-of-war and without having had any trial whatsoever, deserves the ultimate penalty. He commits murder – and should pay for it!'

Was 'exemplary justice' done? Some will say that the penalties fell far short of the crime. But the Hamburg trial has a message still relevant for armies today. A message addressed not only to generals but to NCOs and privates. It is that each must be the master of his own conscience. He cannot put his conscience in another's keeping by saying 'I obeyed orders.'

20 *Comrie Camp*
The War Criminals who Escaped the Headlines

The empty hut was intimidating. The floor was grey concrete; double-tier bunks, without covering, stood along the 120-foot-long walls. It was a bleak, chill place.

I was in Perthshire, Scotland, standing in one of the large Nissen huts at the Army's Cultybraggan Camp. In the distance rose the Aberuchill Hills, first outposts of the Highlands. Less than a mile to the south huddled the small town of Comrie.

'There is only a small skeleton staff in the camp. Nowadays this place is only used for training,' said an official. 'It is not in operation all the year round.'

But during the Second World War the camp was very much in full-time operation. It was packed – with German prisoners. 'There were six thousand prisoners there at any one time,' a local resident, Sandy Lauder, told me. It was a maximum security camp. 'Out of the way, you see. Remote. It would be difficult to escape from.

'They say two Germans got away once. They cut their way through the barbed wire – two fences of it. But they only got five miles. And they were so exhausted they were glad to be caught!'

It was here at Comrie in this deserted hut, on a cold December night in the last year of the war, that there had been enacted a strange, grim scene. German prisoners-of-war had set up their own secret court martial, and had sat in judgment on one of their comrades.

The man on trial was Prisoner of War No. 788778 Feldwebel (Sergeant-Major) Wolfgang Rosterg. His fate – and the subsequent fate of those who tried him – provides a unique episode in the history of military justice.

Rosterg was a tall, thick-set man in his mid-thirties. He came from Lübeck, a manufacturing town in Northern Germany.

He was not a volunteer, but a conscript.

He was a German, called up into the German Army. That was all. He was not a Nazi. He was too old to have been press-ganged into the Hitler Youth. He had chosen not to join the National Socialist Party. He had travelled outside Germany in pre-war years. He spoke five languages fluently and came from a prosperous middle-class family. And he was disenchanted with fighting Hitler's war.

In September 1944, as the Allied Armies swept across North France, he committed the unforgivable sin for a serving German soldier. Convinced that Germany had lost all hope of winning the war, he deserted to the enemy. He gave himself up to an advancing British platoon. As later events proved, he was no coward; he simply had had enough of senseless slaughter.

Shipped to Britain, Rosterg spent several weeks at a POW camp near Devizes in Wiltshire. The war was going badly for Nazi Germany. The German frontier at Aachen had been crossed. For the first time since Napoleon, foreign soldiers were fighting on West German soil.

The Devizes camp swelled with newcomers. Arrogant, proud, young men. Fanatical Nazis who felt themselves shamed by their capture.

Rosterg was not one of their number. He quickly became camp interpreter. He sided with the British authorities. He refused to be drawn into talk of escape. Openly, he stated his anti-Hitler views.

I have spoken to a man like Rosterg. An ex-German prisoner-of-war, now in his early fifties, who settled down in this country after the war, married a Scots girl, and has never returned to Germany. Like Rosterg, he fought in the German Army merely because he was a German: he never joined the National Socialist Party. Unlike Rosterg, he prudently kept his views to himself.

Sitting back in his comfortable, modern living room he gave me a fascinating insight into what it was like to be a non-Nazi in a German prisoner-of-war camp in Britain during the final stages of the Second World War:

'There were more Nazis than democrats. You had Nazis who were nice chaps – you had Nazis who were swine. You had to be careful about what you said in the hut about Hitler. If you said anything against Hitler, they might grab you and kill you – plenty of that happened. They would try to get you in the dark.'

In the Devizes Camp in late 1944 there were many fanatical Nazis. Foremost among them was twenty-year-old Erich Koenig. Son of a Vienna University professor he had risen in seven months of active service to the highest non-commissioned rank in the German Army. He worshipped Hitler as a god.

Early in December 1944 Koenig inspired and programmed what could have proved the greatest escape coup of all time – a mass breakout from the Devizes camp during Christmas week. The plan was to overcome the guards, relaxed, and at less than full strength, capture the arms store at an Army barracks next door, cut the telephone wires, release all the prisoners – and launch a surprise assault on a nearby armoured division tank depot.

The scheme – crazy, wild, impassioned – was then to advance on London!

'No escape story of the Second World War was more daring in concept, more fantastic, more ambitious, more hopelessly fanatical than that of the prisoners of Devizes,' has written the late Colonel A. P. Scotland, chief British interrogator of German prisoners.

But someone talked.

The camp authorities heard of the plot. Christmas leave was cancelled. A few days before Christmas an armed military detail entered the huts – and twenty-eight German prisoners-of-war, Erich Koenig at their head, were marched out and driven away in trucks. Koenig's face was white with fury and frustration.

Twenty-seven of the twenty-eight men were Koenig's fellow ringleaders in the unsuccessful escape plot. The twenty-eighth was Wolfgang Rosterg. Why him? Why throw this well-known non-Nazi and camp official into the same group as the thwarted escapers, livid with rage?

To this day, no satisfactory explanation has been given. 'The implication is that he was the man who had betrayed the Devizes escape plot and now was being shipped off with the ringleaders so that he could continue to keep them under observation,' an ex-Army officer involved in the case has told me.

But that hardly makes sense. If he was the man who disclosed the Devizes plot to the authorities, the first people to realize that would have been the twenty-seven young men sitting with him in the Army trucks lurching towards London. He was hardly likely to be an effective stool-pigeon thereafter. At the very least, he would be the last person they would talk in front of.

And if he was not the Devizes traitor, what sheer unimaginative cruelty it would have been to send this unarmed man – notoriously unsympathetic to Hitler's cause – in the same party as the twenty-seven young Hitler-fanatics!

'Why did they do it?' the ex-German prisoner I have already quoted has asked me. 'Either way, they were sending that poor man to his death. It was unfair.'

Rosterg was *not* the man who gave away the Devizes plot secret. Colonel Scotland, who carried out the interrogation of the twenty-eight draftees from Devizes when they arrived in London, has stated tersely in his memoirs: 'Wolfgang Rosterg was innocent of the suspected betrayal.'

The truth is that no one deliberately betrayed the escape plan. There was no conscious treachery. Careless talk gave away the plan. According to Colonel Scotland: 'A careless word concerning the arms store, overheard by one of the German-speaking Camp officers, was in fact the first blunder.' As Mr Oliver Philpot, the famous British wartime RAF officer who escaped from Stalag Luft III with Eric Williams and the late Michael Codnor in the celebrated 'Wooden Horse' exploit has told me: 'It was far more a real danger that careless talk would give away your plan than that the chap in the next bed was a traitor.'

But that is a British view. Sane and reasonable. Rosterg's fellow companions on the draft from Devizes were not in the mood for sanity or reason.

Colonel Scotland's superiors decided that the Devizes ringleaders – and Rosterg – would be shipped at once to the maximum security camp at Comrie.

The detachment arrived late in the afternoon of 22 December 1944. The men were split up into twos and threes, and assigned to different huts. Rosterg – and Koenig – were put in Hut 4, Compound B, which still stands today.

How Rosterg behaved, within minutes of entering that hut,

makes me convinced that he was not a British agent, working for Military Intelligence – but a very brave man, determined to show where his sympathies lay.

Remember that Comrie was a maximum security camp. That, by very definition, the majority of its inhabitants would be hard-liners and militant Nazis: otherwise, they would be in some other more comfortable camp.

Yet almost at once Rosterg asked for a copy of *Lager-post* – the official German prisoner-of-war newspaper, published under British auspices and anathema to any dedicated Nazi. 'No one reads it here,' a Comrie prisoner told him. 'It is full of enemy propaganda!'

'Well, I'll read it!' Rosterg replied. 'And I'll read the English papers too, if I get a chance.'

Koenig pushed forward: 'You don't believe in National Socialism then?' he asked. 'No. I don't believe in that nonsense any more. I've been about the world too much!' was Rosterg's courageous – but reckless – reply.

'All right! We'll see about this fellow!' someone said quietly. It could have been Koenig. It could have been one of the other prisoners. Rosterg had set himself apart from them all.

Some time after midnight, as the camp searchlight swept intermittently over the darkened huts, there was a noise beside Rosterg's bunk. He stirred. 'Who is there?' he asked. He sat up to see Koenig, kneeling beside him – emptying the contents of his kit bag on to the floor.

A diary, a written list of names, other documents fell out – some in English. 'What do these things mean?' Koenig asked. 'Answer, you dog!'

And the last violent hours of Wolfgang Rosterg's life began.

There is no point in spelling out in detail the brutality and degradation of Rosterg's 'trial'. Other prisoners crept in from nearside huts. Koenig and his Devizes comrades constituted themselves Rosterg's judges.

Two 'court orderlies' stood beside the accused man – and beat him over the head with iron bars when he refused to answer, or gave an answer his accusers did not wish to hear.

Stubbornly, he denied that he was a traitor, that he had betrayed the escape plot, or that the English language contents of his kit-bag meant anything other than that he liked practising his English.

Hatred swelled in the crowded hut. The assembled prisoners nearly a hundred of them – raised their voices in the Nazi marching song, the Horst Wessel anthem to drown Rosterg's screams.

The camp was guarded by Polish soldiers under the command of British officers. Though puzzled by the sound of singing, they did not intervene.

With a rope round his neck, Rosterg was dragged to the senior German prisoner's hut. He was told to hang himself. He refused. He was hauled out half-conscious into the clearing outside the hut, the rope still around his neck. 'You are an SS man.' Koenig told Kurt Zuelsdorff, a twenty-year-old Panzer grenadier. 'I make you responsible on your honour as a soldier. You know what you have to do.'

And so, according to their lights, did other German soldiers, conscious of their 'honour' in that terrifying wintry scene just before dawn.

The next day Rosterg's body was found in a latrine block forty yards from the hut where the 'trial' had been held. He was hanging by a rope which had been thrown over a pipe. He had been treated so savagely that he was unrecognizable. It was his injuries which had caused his death.

German military justice – summary and horrifying – had done its work. Now British military justice took over. Its pace was much slower, more deliberate.

First, the civil authorities were brought in. Some weeks earlier, a prisoner had committed suicide at Comrie Camp. Now, when the camp adjutant walked into the local Registrar's office formally to register Rosterg's death, the assistant registrar greeted him with the mock query: 'Not another suicide?' 'No,' was the grim reply. 'This time it's murder!'

That evening, in accordance with usual Scots legal practice, two doctors carried out a post mortem in the presence of senior local police officers. Their report went to the Procurator Fiscal, the law officer who decides whether to prosecute in cases of sudden or suspicious death.

Then the military authorities stepped back into the picture. Prisoners at the camp were interviewed. Rosterg's background at Devizes was investigated. Hundreds of statements were taken. A full-scale murder inquiry was set in motion.

The war went on. Hitler's armies continued to retreat. The

half-crazed Führer shot himself in his Berlin bunker. Field-Marshal Montgomery accepted the German unconditional surrender at Luneburg Heath. Exultant British prisoners of war streamed out of the camps in Germany. War criminals and traitors were arrested and charged with crimes against humanity, and with treason.

Eventually, over six months after Rosterg's body had been found, and when most Germans held in Britain were looking forward to returning to their families, eight German prisoners of war were charged before a military court with his murder. The court – with a red-tabbed colonel as its president – sat in a large oak-panelled drawing-room at No. 8 Kensington Palace Gardens, London.

A sleek modern apartment block now stands on the site. Then, it was the famous 'London Cage', a Georgian mansion used as headquarters for prisoner-of-war interrogation, and an important transit camp for prisoners from all over the country.

The eight accused, standing stiffly to attention in new uniforms supplied by the British authorities especially for the trial, were: Erich Koenig, Kurt Zuelsdorff, Staff Sergeant Joachim Goltz – and five other young NCOs. All of them had been in the transfer party from Devizes. No prisoner already at Comrie was charged with Rosterg's murder.

The way in which these men were defended, and the integrity shown by the two British Army officers who undertook that task reflect nothing but honour upon the legal system of our country.

The man who represented Erich Koenig – pin-pointed by the Prosecuting Officer as 'the brains behind the whole of what was done' – was Captain Roger Willis. A peace-time barrister and Territorial Army officer, he had been called up early in the war, was captured by the enemy in North Africa – and at the time that Rosterg was being put to death at Comrie, he was himself still a prisoner of war in German hands.

Released from captivity in April 1945, this was his first court appearance since returning to England. He defended three other prisoners in addition to Koenig.

Now, Captain Willis is His Honour Judge Willis, a distinguished circuit judge.

The other defence lawyer was Major Russell Evans, now practising as a solicitor in his native Wales. He represented four men, one of them Staff-Sergeant Joachim Goltz, who not merely admitted but boasted it was he who had put the rope round Rosterg's neck.

The court martial lasted eleven days. Two of Judge Willis's clients maintained that a mistake had been made and that they were not among the prisoners taking an active part in manhandling Rosterg. They were acquitted. But not one of the other six tried to evade guilt.

Zuelsdorff, for instance, told the court: 'I had suffered from betrayal by Rosterg – either by him or his friends. I was very excited and disgusted with this man. I thought he was a traitor and deserved death. I was prepared myself to carry out that sentence and kill him.'

Rolf Herzig, a twenty-four-year-old sergeant and ex-Hitler Youth leader – one of the men defended by Major Evans, said: 'Rosterg was a traitor. At times like that, one remembers the English proverb, "Right or wrong, my country first".'

Goltz, when asked why they hanged a man whom they admitted they knew was already dead, replied: 'Because I was of the opinion that a traitor should be found hanging.'

'This traitor to his fatherland had to be found hanging by the British authorities,' said twenty-one-year-old seaman Josef Mertens, another of the accused.

All six were convicted of murder.

Before the court adjourned, Captain Willis rose in his place. Choosing his words with infinite care, he said: 'There is one other matter in the minds of the accused. They have told me – and although it is a matter I cannot prove, I have reason to believe it true – that in 1943 an attempt to escape was made and planned by British RAF officers in a prison camp near Breslau.

'That attempt was in fact abortive because the plan was given away to the German prison camp authorities by a British officer. He was then hanged by the British officers in the camp, and the German authorities did not take any steps to punish the people who were responsible for it.

'That is a matter which weighs very strongly in the minds of the accused at this moment. They do not appreciate even now why they are being treated differently from British prisoners in Germany.'

At a time when immediate post-war, anti-German feeling

was running highest, that was a bold statement to make in open court. It was promptly denied by the Air Ministry. But Captain Willis did not make the statement lightly. He did it because the men he was defending wanted him to – and because his duty as defence counsel demanded that he put everything before the court that might aid in mitigation of guilt.

'I remember it caused quite a stir,' Major Evans has told me.

The 'stir' was not sufficient to serve its purpose. Five of the six convicted German prisoners were hanged. They died together in the largest multiple hanging for over a century at Pentonville jail, London, on the morning of 6 October 1945. Their last request – denied by the authorities – was that they should be shot 'like soldiers'.

The sixth prisoner, Sergeant Rolf Herzig, was not executed. Instead he got penal servitude for life. Why was he treated differently? The reason has never been made public before. Major Russell Evans, recalled this incident from the past:

'Defence inquiries had produced two witnesses who were able to prove that Herzig was not present at the scene of the crime and that in his case it was a mistaken identification by certain prosecution witnesses. He was strongly advised in his interests that these two witnesses be called.' But Herzig was convinced – possibly mistakenly – that denying his own alleged role would lead to questioning in which he would incriminate others. Though, in fact, the others had not tried to deny their guilt.

'His instructions were quite emphatic that the witnesses be not called,' said Major Evans.

But after the court martial was over, Major Evans was able to persuade Herzig to sign a petition, which the major supported with affidavits from the two witnesses.

'The petition was directed towards the grant of a pardon and not against sentence,' says Major Evans. 'Somewhat illogically, however, it had the effect of reducing the death sentence to one of imprisonment for life.'

Logically, indeed, it should have entailed his complete acquittal and immediate release. But Major Evans continues: 'About a year later I was able to take the case up again with the then Solicitor-General through my MP, and Herzig was discreetly released and has been a free man since.'

Major Evans's overall review of the case: 'I am reasonably

satisfied that the court came to a proper finding of fact.

'I was, however, appalled and remain appalled that the sentence of death by hanging was, in fact, carried out.'

It is possible both to agree – and disagree – with this conclusion.

One final question mark remains: Is there any truth in the allegation made in open court by Captain Willis? Did the incident in the British prison camp in Breslau in 1943 really happen? Did RAF officers commit their own Comrie-style murder?

I have done my best to find out. But it is almost impossible to prove a negative: that it did not happen. I am content to report what Oliver Philpot, the British escaper, told me sitting in his London office:

'It could have happened. It could quite likely have happened. It's perfectly possible – but one just doesn't know.

'The fury generated by a tunnel being given away is pretty high. You've worked on it for months, perhaps more. Plus you know that you, or one of your friends, could be shot as you come out of it. Anyone putting his friends into that danger is pretty well beyond the pale.'

28

DATE DUE

~~Due 14 Days From Latest Date~~

		OCT 17 1993
JUL 8 1974	APR 1 4 1975	
JUL 2 4 1974	MAY 2 3 1975	
AUG 3 1974	JUL 9 1975	
SEP 3 1974	AUG 2 6 1975	
OCT 2 1974	NOV 1 4 1978	**WITHDRAWN**
JAN 3 1975	NOV 2 9 1984	
JAN 2 0 1975	MAY 1 0 1986	
FEB 2 2 1975	DEC 1 1986	
MAR 8 1975	MAY 2 8 1988	

F°TE
.9B75

**Redwood
Library and Athenaeum
NEWPORT, R. I.**

LIBRARY BUREAU CAT. NO. 1166.3